SIGNS OF LIFE

rock art of the upper Rio Grande

Dennis Slifer

Ancient City Press
Santa Fe, New Mexico

Book design by Kathleen Sparkes, White Hart Design, Albuquerque, NM
Cover illustration and design by Faith DeLong

International Standard Book Number
1-58096-004-9 clothbound
1-58096-005-7 paperback

I am grateful to the following authors, poets, and publishers for granting permission to use excerpts from their work: Kathleen Church for "Morning on Tshirege" by Peggy Pond Church; Gordon Grant and the Maturango Museum for "The Shaman at Ending"; Bill Weahkee and 5 Sandoval Indian Pueblos, Inc. for "Petroglyph Area Is Sacred Place for New Mexico Pueblos"; Benito Cordova for his Spanish translation from his Ph.D. dissertation; Random House, Inc., and the estate of Robinson Jeffers for "Hands"; and New Directions Publishing Corporation for Octavio Paz's "Configurations."

Slifer, Dennis.
  Signs of life : rock art of the Upper Rio Grande / by Dennis Slifer
      _____ p. _____ cm.
  Includes bibliographical references and index.
  ISBN 1–58096–004–9 (alk. paper). —
  ISBN 1–58096–005–7 (pbk.: alk. paper)
        1. Indians of North America—Rio Grande Valley—Antiquities.
  2. Indian art—Rio Grande Valley.   3. Rock paintings—Rio Grande Valley.
  4. Petroglyphs—Rio Grande Valley.   5. Rio Grande Valley—Antiquities.
  I. Title
  E78.R56S58   1998
  709'.01'13097896—dc21   98-6968
                                                              CIP

10   9   8   7   6   5   4   3   2   1

CONTENTS

Preface   ix

Acknowledgments   xvi

Chapter 1 The Land and the People   1

The Upper Rio Grande Watershed   6

      Paleo-Indians   9

      Archaic Period   10

      Mogollon Culture   13

      Anasazi-Pueblo Culture   13

      Apaches, Navajos and Utes   18

Chapter 2 The Rock Art   23

What Is Rock Art?   23

Rock Art Styles   31

      Archaic Rock Art Styles   33

      Mogollon Rock Art Styles   37

      Anasazi/Pueblo Rock Art Styles   40

      Rio Grande Rock Art Style   43

      Navajo Rock Art   47

      Apache Rock Art   49

      Ute Rock Art   49

Conservation and Access to Sites   51

Chapter 3 Northern Sites   55

Rio Grande Headwaters and
the San Luis Valley, Colorado   56

Rio Grande Gorge, New Mexico
State Line to Pilar   64

Española Valley, Black Mesa,
and Rio Chama   78

Jemez Mountains, Pajarito Plateau,
and White Rock Canyon   88

CONTENTS

Santa Fe River Canyon   93

Galisteo Basin and Vicinity   102

Middle Rio Grande, Cochiti to Rio Puerco,
   Jemez River, and West Mesa   118

Tompiro District, Abo Arroyo   138

Rio Puerco Watershed and
   North Plains Basin   142

Piro District, Rio Puerco to San Marcial   159

Chapter 4 Southern Sites   171

   Black Range   174

   Sierra Caballos   176

   Tonuco Mountains   179

   Sierra de las Uvas   179

   Doña Ana Mountains   182

   Mesilla Valley and Franklin Mountains   184

   Hueco Tanks State Historical Park   185

   Alamo Canyon   189

   Lobo Valley   193

   Mimbres Basin   194

   Salt Basin   198

   Tularosa Basin   201

   Three Rivers   203

   Rio Bonito and Arroyo del Macho   207

Chapter 5 Sites with Public Access   215

   Colorado   215

     Carnero Creek   215

     Dry Creek   216

CONTENTS

New Mexico	218
Bandelier National Monument	218
Chaco Culture National Historic Park	220
El Malpais National Monument and El Malpais National Conservation Area	222
El Morro National Monument	223
Glorieta Mesa	225
La Cienega Area of Critical Environmental Concern	225
Petroglyph National Monument	227
Puyé Cliff Dwellings	231
Rio Bonito Petroglyph National Recreation Trail	233
Salinas National Monument	233
Three Rivers Petroglyph National Recreation Area	234
Tomé Hill	237
White Rock Canyon	239
Texas	242
Hueco Tanks State Historical Park	242
Lobo Valley	248
Notes	251
Bibliography	261
Index	266

…They had left drawn on the rocks their suns, their serpents,
and scattered among the dust the broken potsherds
with their symbols of cloud, of rain, of the eagle flying.
And so without words I knew that man is mortal
and doomed both to live and to die, but what he worships
lives on forever.

Today with my own world crumbling toward ruin
I know this still, and I greet the child who will stand here
Upon Tshirege and watch the morning blossom
and feel under her questioning hand the living grasses
weaving substance of sunlight and the dust of a fallen city.[1]

—*Peggy Pond Church*
"Morning on Tshirege"

PREFACE

The idea for the structure and scope of this book came from my connection with the land, both in my professional and private life. I live within the watershed of the Rio Grande near the ancient capital city of Santa Fe. As an important contemporary art center and an area known for its abundant creative and spiritual energy, this place seems to have a venerable tradition of creativity as manifested by the many nearby galleries of prehistoric rock art. Often in spectacular settings deemed sacred or powerful, these sites feature striking ancient images painted and carved on stone. From my house the nearest prehistoric pueblo ruin is only a mile away, and within a radius of twenty miles there are dozens of ruins and rock art sites. From here, in several directions I can see promontories on which are located ancient shrines and vision quest sites. Obscure and unknown to most contemporary people, these stone rings, scattered petroglyphs, and red handprints under sheltering ledges reveal places once known as power spots to peoples more in tune with their surroundings than most individuals are today. I have focused on learning the lessons of such places, as they are a unique aspect of living here. I try to perceive this landscape in terms of the flow of time and water—the two elements that conspire to shape it and determine its character.

Whenever it does rain in this desert, water runs off my roof into ephemeral arroyos that are the headwaters to the sandy swale of Pueblo Cañon—the nearest drainage feature identified on maps of the area, named for a Pueblo ruin. Pueblo Cañon then joins Gallina Arroyo, which joins San Marcos Arroyo, which joins Galisteo Creek. Galisteo Creek drains the scenic and historic Galisteo Basin, with its many ruins and rock art sites, and then flows twenty miles west to its confluence with the Rio Grande near Santo Domingo Pueblo. Thus, water from the drainage area between my house and the Rio Grande runs near many prehistoric features, eventually joining the Rio Grande on its long journey south to the Gulf of Mexico.

Like the ancients, I am also focused on water. In my work as a scientist and regulator protecting the water resources of the state of New

Mexico, I must think in terms of watersheds. Where the ancients prayed for abundant moisture and fertility, I seek ways to abate water pollution and heal ravaged lands symptomatic of our century's rampage on natural resources. Descendants of the ancient peoples are still living here in the Rio Grande Valley and are still asking for blessings on this land. Without knowing much about each others' cultures or efforts, we are in effect working together to protect the natural world from the rapid onslaught of technological society.

Considering my profession and where I live, it seemed natural to select the concept of a watershed as a unifying context of this book. One of the principal ideas conveyed by rock art is a sense of place in the landscape. Rock art sites, be they sacred or mundane, are integrated into the landscape by the creative action of people who knew intimately their surroundings and their relationship to the natural world. The holistic perspective of seeing the land in terms of watersheds may approximate the way the ancients viewed the physical world—thus providing an additional reason for discussing the rock art in such a context.

Geopolitical borders, those artificial grids of straight lines imposed on our maps, are not conducive to describing the same landscapes known to the creators of southwestern rock art. Such peoples knew no private property; no state or federal lands; no city or county jurisdictions; no highways; and no vapor trails in the sky. However, they were keenly aware of territory, since they walked everywhere; they knew which way the water ran because it was a life-sustaining element. Uphill and downhill were important distinctions; springs, streams, and storm water runoff patterns were vitally important to their survival and well-being. They knew everything there was to know about this landscape that sustained them, especially about the location and behavior of water—the most precious resource in this arid land. Because water courses were their lifelines for survival and travel across this land, not surprisingly, moisture and fertility were major components of their religion and therefore common themes in rock art.

Today, we can drive up and down the Rio Grande corridor, crossing the great river and its tributaries so quickly we barely notice them. We also live in a time when fewer individuals observe or respond to the natural environment than ever before. A generation of landscape illiterates, few of us can read our surroundings for an indication of its health or wealth. The land looks a lot different now than it did 500 or

1,000 years ago—cities, highways, billboards, casinos, mobile homes, shopping malls, landfills, open-pit mines are all obvious changes. Less obvious to most observers is that the dried-up, sediment-choked, weed-infested stream channels of many tributaries of the Rio Grande were formerly perennially flowing streams that supported fish and lush riparian vegetation. Now, there are fewer springs, more gullies and deep arroyos, and less grass cover than in prehistoric times. Consequently, in describing the rock art of the area encompassed by the watershed of the upper Rio Grande, I have discussed the distribution and setting of the rock art in a natural geomorphic context. As I comment on rock art sites throughout the watershed from my perspective as an environmentalist, I also briefly assess the environmental conditions of those areas that have suffered significant change since prehistoric times.

In addition to defining a region by its water drainage and ecosystems, the term "watershed" also can be seen as a metaphor for a changing worldview. In these critical times of expanding populations, resource depletion, habitat loss, and atmospheric changes, being able to perceive our surroundings more like the ancients did—with respect, humility, and a feeling of connectedness—will benefit both us and the land. It is my hope that people will experience the rock art as a window on the past to perceive something of the ancient artists' physical and spiritual worlds, and use that insight to better understand our place in the landscape of today. As mysterious symbols from socioreligious beliefs of past cultures, rock art may lift the veil on the spirit world, help us appreciate human nature, and give us a better perspective of our present condition.

Along with thinking about watersheds, I spend much time in the past—researching rock art and ancient cultures. Seeking out rock art sites becomes a sort of pilgrimage for me, even if on a subconscious level. I believe that the enigmatic symbols appeal to our universal need to be connected to a place, a tribe, and a spirit life. Although we cannot know for certain what the rock art means, this limitation of understanding does not seem to undermine our ability to appreciate it. In fact, rock art is perhaps more enjoyable because of the aura of mystery surrounding it. It is, after all, a visual and symbolic code, created by preliterate people who possessed a rich creative and spiritual life. It speaks to us across the centuries and millennia about the human condition, without need for translation into words. Thus, this book is as much a celebration as an analysis of rock art and the land that contains it.

Included in the book are descriptions of more than a hundred rock art sites in the upper Rio Grande region, beginning near the headwaters of the Rio Grande in Colorado and progressing downstream through New Mexico to south of El Paso, Texas. Although more than 300 illustrations are included here, it is beyond the scope of this book to give a comprehensive inventory of all the sites, a survey that would require many volumes to contain the thousands of images.

In this book, the term "upper Rio Grande" refers to the territory drained by the river from its headwaters in Colorado to south of El Paso, Texas, as well as the interior basins adjacent to the Rio Grande Valley. Because of their importance, a few rock art sites slightly outside these boundaries have been included, such as Chaco Canyon National Historic Park and Three Rivers Petroglyph National Recreation Area. Although it is a somewhat arbitrary determination, some precedent exists from the terminology used by early Spanish explorers and settlers who followed the river on their long journeys north along El Camino Real from Mexico into the frontier. They separated the valley of New Mexico into two districts as seen from Santa Fe: the territory of the Rio Arriba (upriver, north of Santa Fe) and that of the Rio Abajo (downriver, south of Santa Fe).

For this book, images have been selected that not only represent the various rock art style(s) of a site but also those that are visually and aesthetically interesting. Whenever possible, I have chosen images that have not been previously published. In recent years a plethora of books about rock art of the Southwest have been published, and some images are becoming clichéd. One of the unique features of this book is that some relatively unknown sites are presented—the result of more than a decade of fieldwork in the region. These fresh images will be appreciated by both the scientific community and the general public familiar with existing rock art literature.

In addition to including images from obscure sites, I also present previously unpublished images from well-known sites by using drawings to depict rock art images that are so weathered or faded that they do not photograph well. At many sites, such images are often the rule rather than the exception. Since most books on rock art have selectively presented only those images that photograph well, the public is sometimes shown a relatively skewed sample and deprived from experiencing some of the many images which, although faint and difficult to discern, are equally interesting in symbolic content. The drawings in this book were produced as accurately as possible using a combination of field sketches, notes, and photographs. With the exception of very large or small figures, I have chosen not to include devices that indicate scale in the photographs or drawings, as it detracts from aesthetic enjoyment of the images. Likewise, specific location information is excluded from the illustrations and the text in order to protect these resources and the privacy of landowners.

Chapter 1 provides background information about the land and the people associated with the rock art. Chapter 2 discusses the various characteristics and styles of rock art in the area. Chapters 3 and 4 describe specific sites in the northern and southern parts of the upper Rio Grande region. The dividing point chosen for separating the northern and southern sites corresponds to the prehistoric cultural boundary between the Anasazi/Pueblo territory in the north and the Mogollon territory in the south. Finally, Chapter 5 focuses on sites with public access for individuals who wish to experience rock art in the field.

ACKNOWLEDGEMENTS

I owe a debt of gratitude to many people for helping me with this project. Foremost to my wife Dena for tolerating my obsession with rock art and my frequent excursions from home.

The following individuals have helped in innumerable ways; if I have omitted anyone, please forgive my error. Paul Williams, BLM archaeologist in Taos, freely shared information and spent some pleasant days in the field showing me sites in northern New Mexico. Similarly, Ken Frye, Rio Grande National Forest, was a wealth of information about rock art in the San Luis Valley, and guided me to a number of sites, despite recurring spring blizzards. Chris Larsen, fellow rock art fanatic from Timberon, was great company in the field and an invaluable guide to finding the hidden treasures at Hueco Tanks and other sites in the south.

There were many helpful archaeologists with various state and federal agencies: Tony Lutonsky (BLM, Albuquerque); Glenna Dean (New Mexico State Historic Preservation Office); Judy Reed and Gigi York (Pecos National Monument); Tim Seaman and Dedie Snow (New Mexico Archaeological Records Management); John Beardsley (BLM, Canon City, Colorado); and Vince Spero (Rio Grande National Forest).

Others who contributed are: Tom Waddell (Armendaris Ranch manager); Sheila Brewer (El Malpais National Monument); Nancy Daniel (Bosque del Apache National Wildlife Refuge); Ted Stans (Sevilleta National Wildlife Refuge); Diane Souder (Petroglyph National Monument); and Laura Holt (skilled librarian at the New Mexico Laboratory of Anthropology).

Colleagues at work who informed me about rock art sites were Jim Mullany, Larry Smolka, and Bob King. Others who helped were Bart Durham of Santa Fe; Rich Thibedeaux of Pilar, New Mexico; Katherine Wells of Lyden, New Mexico; Don Fingado of Truth or Consequences, New Mexico, who showed me sites in the Sierra Caballos; Jim Duffield of Santa Fe, who shared site information from many areas; and Polly and Curt Schaafsma of Santa Fe, who are an endless source of knowledge. I am also grateful to Susan Stacey, Brian Buettner, and John

Keith for helping me find some sites in the Jemez Mountains. In the Van Horn, Texas, area I was graciously aided by Noble Smith, Vivian Grubb, and Hock Haines. I would also like to thank my cats Zia and Sprout for knowing they should not land on the keyboard when leaping into my lap while I was writing this.

Lastly, I am most grateful to the thousands of ancient people who created the rock art, making my life and the lives of others more meaningful.

The river always purified.
It seemed to bring some
thoughts from far above,
who knew from where,
and carry others far down
stream, who knew whither.
Using the river, a person
could dream awake,
like a child.[2]

—**Paul Horgan,**
Great River

1

The Land
and the People

The People came to the river. Ever since there have been people on this continent, some of them have been hunting, farming, living, and dying along the valley of the great river. The river itself seems timeless in its long journey from mountains to sea, and assumes meaning only in terms of the people who came here beginning thousands of years ago. The People, as all tribal groups call themselves, have occupied the Southwest for at least a dozen millennia, from the Paleo-Indian hunters of the Ice Age, to Archaic hunter/gatherers, to the Mogollon and Anasazi farmers, to nomadic Athabascan tribes from the Plains, to today's Pueblos.

The history of southwestern peoples and landscapes is one of change. Humans have been here longer than the deserts have. The earliest people lived in a wetter, cooler climate than exists here now, with later peoples gradually adapting to more arid conditions. A common thread through this colorful tapestry of cultures in the Rio Grande Valley is that the native people have left traces of their existence, signs of life, through their rock art, testifying to their presence and marking their sacred places through numerous striking depictions. These ancient images on stone offer intriguing glimpses of prehistoric cultures, religion, and creativity;

they reflect a deep connection between spirit, power, and place in the landscape. The dramatic, diverse southwestern landscape is particularly rich in prehistoric significance and rock art sites. In the sheer number of sites, as well as the beauty or imagery, rock art of the Southwest is without equal in North America. Within the Southwest, the valley of the great river, the "river of life" which we know as the Rio Grande, offers the greatest array and continuity of rock art styles and traditions, from Archaic to modern times.

Certainly to understand the geography and history of the Southwest, it is necessary to study its rivers, especially the Rio Grande. The region discussed in this book, essentially the core of New Mexico, is defined by the Rio Grande, which has shaped the physical landscape and determined the course of history here. Without it, New Mexico as we know it would not exist, and the rich prehistoric and cultural legacy of the area, including its rock art, would be vastly different. Eight of the area's existing pueblos, which are situated along the Rio Grande, would probably not be here. It was the river and the life dependent on it that brought the ancestors of the Pueblos here and allowed them to thrive in this harsh land, even during times of drought. The Spanish settlers who followed recognized this reality, as evidenced by their phrase *"agua es vida"* (water is life).

When the first Europeans came to the area in the early sixteenth century, they encountered up to seventy native settlements in the valley of the Rio Grande,[3] with a population of approximately 30,000. Water from the Rio Grande and tributaries was being used to grow crops on as much as 25,000 acres of irrigated fields scattered around New Mexico. The power and importance of the river to these pueblos is described as follows in Paul Horgan's *Great River*:

*Such a pueblo typically sat on an eminence above
the river, and near to it. The river was a power
which like the light of the sky was never wholly
lost. It came from the north beyond knowing, and
it went to the south nobody knew where. It was
always new and yet always the same. It let water
be taken in ditches to the lowest fields. Trees grew
along its banks—willows, cottonwoods, young and
old, always renewing themselves. The water was
brown, as brown as a body, and both lived on earth
as brown. The river was part of the day's prayer.[4]*

Thus, the Rio Grande and its tributaries were
the lifeblood of the arid region encompassing most
of New Mexico. The geography of the region, particularly the river corridors, affected prehistoric
travel and settlement patterns.[5] Consequently, the
distribution of rock art is also determined to a great
extent by these patterns. Many rock art sites in the
region are concentrated on escarpments or boulders
adjacent to the river and at the confluences of tributaries. And it is not surprising that there is widespread occurrence of rock art symbols representing
rain, clouds, lightning, moisture-loving creatures,
and various deities in charge of springs, fertility, and
rain (Figure 1).

While prehistoric inhabitants of the Rio Grande
area only knew the region they could roam in their
lifetimes, today, with modern maps, aerial photographs, and satellite imagery, we can comprehend
the huge area of land (335,000 square miles) that
encompasses the Rio Grande Basin—more than
24,000 square miles in New Mexico alone (Figure
2). The Rio Grande Valley is a land of contrasts and
extremes. Contrary to early Spanish belief, the
source of the Rio Grande is not the North Pole but
Spring Creek and South Fork in the Sierras of

Figure 1. *Symbols representing rain, moisture, and fertility concepts from various rock art styles in the upper Rio Grande area. **a.** Rain symbols, Archaic, Rio Grande Gorge near Questa, New Mexico; **b.** Cloud terrace with rain, rainbow, and lightning, Jornada Style, Lincoln County, New Mexico; **c.** Dragonfly with cloud terraces and rainbows, Jornada Style, Lincoln County, New Mexico; **d.** Man holding ceremonial staff with cloud terrace and rain, Jornada Style, Three Rivers, New Mexico; **e.** Corn plant with cloud terrace, rain, lightning, and bird, Jornada Style, Three Rivers, New Mexico; **f.** Cloud terrace with lightning arrows, Rio Grande Style, Black Mesa, Rio Arriba County, New Mexico; **g.** Turtle petroglyph, Jornada Style, Cooke's Peak, New Mexico; **h.** Horned serpent with flute player, Rio Grande Style, Black Mesa, New Mexico; **i.** Jornada rain deity Tlaloc, Lincoln County, New Mexico; **j.** Tadpoles, near water holes, Jornada Style, Cooke's Peak, New Mexico; **k.** Jornada Style fish, Three Rivers, New Mexico.*

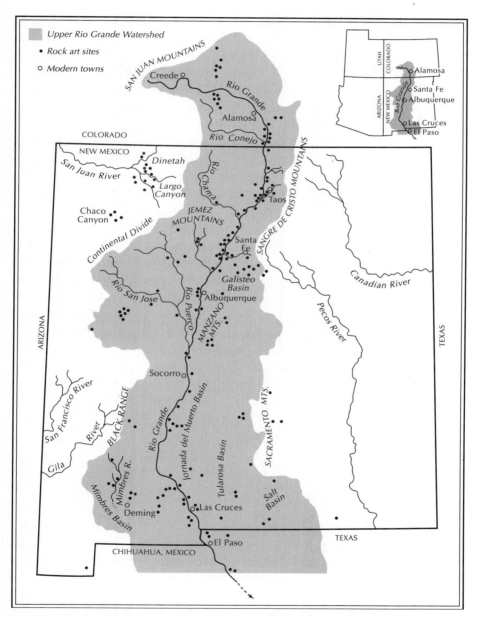

Figure 2. *Map of New Mexico showing the area of the upper Rio Grande watershed, major drainages, topographic features, and rock art sites discussed in this book.*

southern Colorado. With its headwaters at the Continental Divide in the alpine wilderness of Colorado's San Juan Mountains, and its mouth in the humid tropics at the Gulf of Mexico, the Rio Grande is the second longest river in the United States. It drains a quarter million square miles of the southern Rockies, the Southwest, and Mexico; yet at certain times of the year it is possible to walk across it in particular locations. It has a history of wild flooding, especially during spring runoff when the snow melts rapidly. The only river used more extensively for irrigation of crops is the Ganges.

Although it is impossible to know what all the prehistoric natives who lived along its banks called the Rio Grande, the languages of three of the major Rio Grande Pueblo groups (Tewa, Towa, and Keresan) contain the words *T'sina*, *Kanyapakwa*, and *P'osoge*, respectively, all meaning approximately "great river."[6] Spanish explorers referred to this river as Rio Guadalquivir, Nuestra Señora (Our Lady), Rio del Norte or Rio Bravo del Norte (Wild River of the North), Rio de las Palmas (River of Palms), and the Rio Turbio (Muddy River) before common usage settled on Rio Grande (The Great River).

THE UPPER RIO GRANDE WATERSHED

The upper Rio Grande—the territory drained by the river from its headwaters in Colorado to south of El Paso, Texas, (Figure 2)[7]—constitutes less than one-fourth of the total 1,900-mile length of the Rio Grande, and splits New Mexico for over 400 miles. More importantly, this portion of the Rio Grande contains the greatest concentration of rock art, for it was here that most of the prehistoric peoples lived.[8] South of present-day El Paso, the Rio Grande was a river to cross, not to live along—a harsher, drier, rockier land than the upper Rio Grande. Only marginal settlements of pit houses, few real towns, have been found there. The Pueblo people of the upper Rio Grande were the only ones to whom the river gave continuous sustenance. Having always been a magnet for settlement, today the Rio Grande Basin is home to ten million people, and the population is expected to grow rapidly.

In north-central New Mexico, the Rocky Mountains rise in a maze of parallel ridges from the Chihuahuan Desert to the south. The Rockies of New Mexico converge on Colorado as two forks, with space between the two forks for the Rio Grande Valley. The western fork is a mountainous range consisting of the Jemez and Tusas Mountains, which are a southern extension of the great San Juan Mountains of Colorado. The Jemez Mountains embrace one of the world's largest extinct volcanic craters, the Valle Grande caldera, measuring over sixteen miles in diameter. Its explosive eruptions forged much of the present landscape of the upper Rio Grande. Ash deposits hundreds of feet deep form cliffs of tuff, where the Anasazis built cave shelters and ceremonial chambers. To the east of the Rio Grande, the other fork of the Rockies is the great Sangre de Cristo (Blood of Christ) Range, which extends from Santa Fe to Salida, Colorado. New Mexico's highest peaks, including 13,151-foot Wheeler Peak, are in this range, as are many peaks over 14,000 feet in Colorado. This rampart forms the eastern boundary of much of the upper Rio Grande watershed.

From its high alpine origins, the Rio Grande makes a gradual transition from a cold, clear stream running rapidly in deep gorges carved through lava flows to a sluggish desert river meandering through broad valleys in the Chihuahuan Desert. South of El Paso the river becomes the international boundary between the United States and Mexico. Lower desert vegetation consists primarily of creosote bush, mesquite, and ocotillo, with steppes or grasslands at slightly higher elevations. The northern portion of the upper Rio Grande, beginning at elevations of approximately 7,000 feet in the vicinity of Santa Fe, is typical of the Upper Sonoran Zone and is characterized by piñon, juniper, chamisa, and sagebrush. Mesas and high plateaus dominate the landscape here, with the towering 12,000-foot peaks of the Sangre de Cristo Mountains looming on the east and the rugged, volcanic Jemez Mountains on the west.

In its course through New Mexico, the Rio Grande follows a north-south trace created by a deep, thirty-million-year-old rift in the earth's crust. The Rio Grande Rift Valley is bounded by two parallel fault zones, approximately thirty miles wide near Albuquerque and up to 100 miles wide in southern New Mexico. In places the rift is over 26,000 feet deep, having been filled with alluvial sediments by the river over millions of years.

The more than 10,000 years of human occupation preserved in the Rio Grande Rift is related to the geological processes that created it. The rift concentrated runoff and created an important perennial water source, as well as other valuable resources such as obsidian for stone tools, cliff walls for shelter, and a greater variety of plants and animals.[9] It is fitting that this dramatic geologic setting has long been home to such diverse prehistoric life, culminating in today's celebrated multicultural milieu.

Like the river, the flow of time is a strong and unifying process whose current has carried many different cultures through this land. To fully understand the Southwest, including its people, it is necessary to study its rivers, especially in the Rio Grande Valley, where native cultures have ebbed and flowed for thousands of years in a rich sequence unequaled in North America. Prehistoric travelers usually followed the river and its tributaries. Hunters knew game animals stayed near the streams, and farmers depended on irrigation water taken from the channels. Much ritual, religion, and art of prehistoric people was based on strong connections to water. The stream corridor supported lush, shaded riparian environments, while the desert basins away from the river were some of the harshest places on the continent. It is not surprising that a land of such extreme contrasts forged enduring and adaptable societies.

Despite its harshness, before contact with Europeans the land sustained many people and animals in the sacred web of life. At that time the spirit world was integrated with the physical, and the land was marked with sacred places and signs in many languages. In addition to living in a world where the sacred and the mundane were not separated, the natives also differed from us in their perception of time, which was seen as cyclic rather than linear. Testimony to such perception is the fact that Native American stories are more concerned about where something happened than when. All things were cyclical—the seasons, life and death, ritual and spiritual events.

𝍧 *Paleo-Indians*

People have occupied the Southwest for at least 12,000 years. Many archaeologists postulate that the first Native Americans crossed a land bridge between Asia and Alaska that was exposed intermittently during the Pleistocene ice ages between 8,000 and

23,000 years ago. By contrast, many Indians believe their people have always been here in their sacred places or that their ancestors came here from the underground, or spirit world. According to the land bridge theory, during successive waves of immigration all of North and South America was eventually populated. In the Southwest, these first Paleo-Indians are known from their distinctive fluted stone lance heads (Clovis and Folsom points), which have been found with the remains of the big game animals they stalked, such as mammoth, giant bison, camels, sloth, antelope, and tapirs. Nearly all of these Ice Age megafauna became extinct by about 8500 B.C., probably due to a combination of successful hunting strategies by the Paleo-Indians and changes in climate.

In the Southwest no rock art is known to be associated with Paleo-Indians, but some can be attributed to the Archaic people who followed. The Archaic Period (typically known as the Western Archaic or Desert Archaic in the Southwest) began with the final drying cycle of the cool, wet glacial climate preceding it, and with the commencement of the desert climate that prevails today. As the climate became more arid, of necessity people became more dependent on the fewer existing perennial streams and springs, and habitation as well as rock art distribution may reflect this.

禾 *Archaic Period*

The Archaic Period spans from about 5500 B.C. to A.D. 100. Evidence of the Archaic way of life has been documented from most parts of the Southwest, where slight regional variations have been described.[10] During this time, people in the Southwest were hunter/gatherers and typically nomadic, at least seasonally, as a function of food supply. In contrast to the large game hunting of the Paleo-Indians, there was more emphasis on gathering wild plants and killing small animals such as rabbits. Populations remained small and unconcentrated. From artifacts found in dry caves in the Southwest, we know that these people were skilled in basketry, textiles, and woodworking. Housing was impermanent, and natural shelters such as caves and rock overhangs were often used. The earliest known rock art in the region is attributed to this culture. Many impressive rock paintings and engravings of this era are found in caves and on cliffs, much of which suggests shamanic religious activities. At sites within the northern portion of the upper Rio Grande, Archaic rock art is primarily abstract in style, while in the southern portion there is a combination of both abstract and representational styles. The nature and distribution of Archaic and other rock art styles are discussed in Chapter 2.

By 1000 B.C. the lifestyle of southwestern hunter/gatherers began to change as they learned to cultivate corn (maize), beans, and squash, which were introduced to the area by trading contacts with ancient societies in Mexico. Gradually becoming more sedentary with dependence on crops and irrigation, the next distinctive cultures of the region developed by 300 B.C., with the advent of village living and the use of pottery.[11] At first, small communities were scattered across expansive territories; then after A.D. 750 small villages began to grow into towns and even cities (pueblos) with distinctive stone or adobe architecture.

In the territory encompassed by the upper Rio Grande, two contemporaneous principal cultures evolved—the Mogollon in the south and the Anasazi in the north (Figure 3).

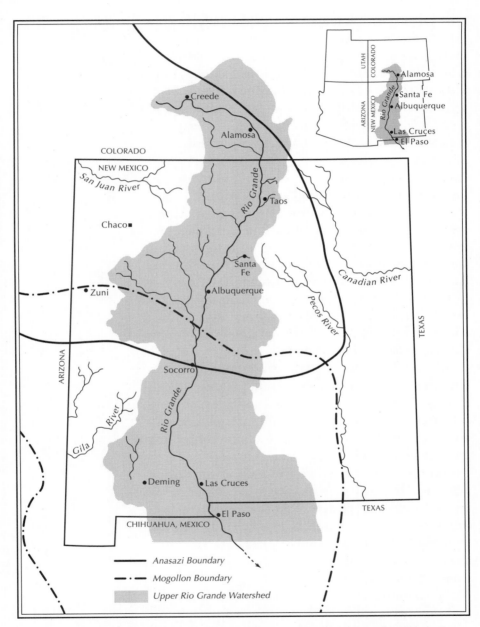

Figure 3. Map of the upper Rio Grande area and boundaries of prehistoric culture areas. (After Schaafsma, 1980.)

禾 *Mogollon Culture*

Mesoamerican civilization strongly influenced the development of Mogollon culture in the south, including rock art symbols.[12] In turn, some of the ideologies of Mogollon rock art were apparently adopted by the Anasazi peoples in the north (in particular the masks associated with the kachina cult, discussed later in this chapter). The Mogollon people lived in a time of complex cultural developments and inhabited a highly diverse territory. The Western, or Mountain, Mogollon territory encompassed the rugged, wooded highlands of southwest New Mexico and southeast Arizona, including the drainages of the Gila, San Francisco, and Mimbres Rivers. The Eastern, or Desert, Mogollon territory extended east to the arid basin and range country of the Chihuahuan Desert as far as the Guadalupe and Sacramento Mountains and south into Texas and Chihuahua. The Desert Mogollon territory is further divided into the Mimbres and Jornada regions.[13] The rock art of the Jornada and Mimbres regions is collectively known as the Jornada Style and was influential in the development of Pueblo rock art to the north as well as modern ceremonial art throughout much of the Southwest.[14]

After A.D. 100, the style of settlement changed from small villages of pit houses to larger above-ground pueblos with hundreds of rooms. It is thought that the Mogollon culture was gradually absorbed by merging with the dynamic, southward-expanding Anasazi culture during the fourteenth century.[15]

禾 *Anasazi-Pueblo Culture*

The people we call Anasazis (a Navajo word

meaning "Ancient Ones," or "Ancient Enemies") originated on the Colorado Plateau from Desert Archaic people about 2,000 years ago. Their culture became the largest and best known of all prehistoric southwestern cultures. They were primarily a horticultural society, growing corn, beans, and squash for their food staples. The Basketmaker Period of the Anasazis preceded the Pueblo Period, the latter commencing around A.D. 700. Spectacular cliff dwellings and multistoried masonry pueblos with underground ceremonial chambers, known as kivas, are the architectural characteristics of the classic Anasazi period. The Anasazi tradition spans a period from at least 200 B.C. to approximately A.D. 1540, when the Spanish entered the Southwest. Modern Pueblo peoples living along the Rio Grande, and at Hopi, Zuni, and Acoma, are descendants of the Anasazis.

Unlike many of their neighbors who shared common Desert Archaic origin and lifestyles, the Anasazi people exhibited a tendency to radical change throughout their history. Their culture became more complex with time, perhaps due in part to the well-documented contacts with the cultures of Mexico across the desert to the south, where maize, beans, and squash were first domesticated. These foods became the staples of village life throughout the Southwest, and Anasazi civilization was supported by them. Many other developments from Mexico, and elsewhere, shaped Anasazi culture, including pottery, irrigation techniques, the bow and arrow, cotton and loom weaving, as well as esoteric knowledge and religious ideas.[16]

Trade relationships were widespread and dynamic. Although not entirely restricted by watershed boundaries and topographic divides, travel and trade corridors were certainly influenced by these features, especially in the upper Rio Grande region.

Here the high north-south trending ranges that parallel the river in most of New Mexico tended to restrict east-west traffic to passes across the mountains or to certain canyons. Anasazi turquoise was mined in the Southwest, and in the Cerrillos Hills south of Santa Fe there is a prehistoric turquoise mine and a peak named Mount Chalchihuitl—a Nahuatl (Aztec) word meaning blue stone. Between the twelfth and fifteenth centuries, the Anasazis traded with the great city of Casas Grandes in Chihuahua. In general, the Anasazi people accepted and often modified many ideas and objects influenced by the complex and powerful societies of Mexico.

Today, there are nineteen Pueblo Indian tribes with a combined population of 50,000. The Anasazis are alive and well in the Rio Grande Valley and at Acoma, Zuni, and Hopi, although some Pueblo people prefer the Hopi term "Hisatsinom" (Ancient People) to describe their ancestors. Despite four centuries of political domination by European-derived cultures, the Pueblo people still thrive and have preserved much of their ancient heritage.

When the Spanish explorers arrived in the Southwest in the sixteenth century, they found about 100,000 Pueblo people, mostly around the southern and eastern edges of the Colorado Plateau. Some of these towns were already hundreds of years old, and some are still occupied today. The largest pueblos supported about 3,000 people. Each was an independent community but with extensive political, social, and economic ties to other pueblos.

Ritual and religion permeated all aspects of Pueblo life, although there are no words in Pueblo languages for religion. Of primary importance was maintaining harmony with nature, and much ritual was focused on bringing adequate rain, bountiful crops, good health, and fertility. The kachina cult was of great significance at most pueblos. Personified by masked dancers, kachinas are deities that represent ancestors, the unborn, and "Cloud People" who control weather and fertility. Although a subject of debate among scholars, it has been proposed by Polly and Curt Schaafsma that the development and importance of the kachina cult in Pueblo territory can be traced in their rock art, beginning in the fourteenth century.

All peoples who have adapted to living in arid regions consider water sacred and rain a blessing. Southwestern peoples often distinguished between male and female rain; male rain is the hard, aggressive rain that falls from violent summer thunderstorms accompanied by thunder and lightning, whereas female rain is the soft, gentle rain that soaks into the earth. There is much innate sexual symbolism expressed in ritual and art about the father (sky) fertilizing the mother (earth) with rain in order for the seeds to germinate and plants to grow. Corn is often perceived as the children of such a union, and nurtured accordingly (Figure 4).

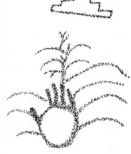

Figure 4. Petroglyph of corn plant sheltered by human hand, under a cloud terrace symbol for rain. Piro District, Rio Grande near San Marcial, New Mexico.

To the Pueblo peoples, lakes and springs were sacred—considered entrances to the world below. Gods and heroes were born out of springs, and came and went between worlds through pools. Every pueblo had sacred springs somewhere, for they had supernatural qualities—reflected perhaps in the fact that when rain fell and disappeared there was still water that always came up out of the ground.

Awanyu is a water deity depicted in Pueblo rock art (with a related form in Jornada Mogollon art). A horned or crested serpent (Figure 5), he is the guardian of springs and underground waters. At Zuni he is Kolowis, the great horned serpent, a patron of rivers and irrigation who lives in the sacred

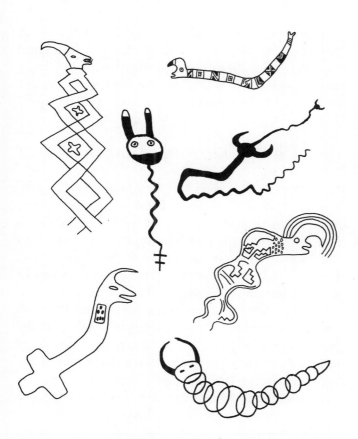

Figure 5.
Examples of
petroglyphs and
pictographs of
the horned, or
crested, serpent
(Awanyu) from
various rock art
sites in the upper
Rio Grande
region.

springs. He can withhold water or cause floods as punishment for wrongdoing or neglect of ceremonies. A story is told that when the Rio Grande dried up during a drought following the Pueblo Revolt of 1680 it did not flow again until a virgin was sacrificed to the horned water deity.[17]

The river must have been a source of wonder to native people. Elaborate worlds of ritual and worship centered around it. Following initiation and dances, men and boys went to the river for ritual cleansing. And after a birth the midwife took the afterbirth to the river and threw it in—in an act of purification. Boys caught smoking before they had qualified in the hunt were thrown into the river as punishment. Fish were not eaten because legend told they were bewitched relations who had been transformed after falling into the river from a magical bridge of feathers between two towns.[18]

᙭ *Apaches, Navajos and Utes*

Indian newcomers to the upper Rio Grande region arrived about A.D. 1500. People speaking Athabascan languages migrated south on the Great Plains from Canada and soon moved westward into the Pueblo area of central New Mexico. These Plains-oriented buffalo hunters were ancestors of the Apaches and Navajos. By 1540, they had established extensive trading contacts with the Pueblos. Originally referred to as Apaches or Querechos by Spanish chroniclers, by 1626 the Navajos were apparently seen as a separate Athabascan group living and farming on the upper Chama River.[19] The Athabascans borrowed ideology and art from the Pueblos (who in turn had borrowed from the Mogollons) and developed their own unique forms of expression.

The lifestyle of the Athabascans changed dramatically with their acquisition of the horse from the Spanish in the early 1600s. This development allowed great mobility for hunting or raiding their neighbors. Depictions of horses in their rock art can thus be quite accurately dated (Figure 6).

Today, the Navajos are the largest Indian tribe in the United States and occupy a very extensive area in the old Anasazi territory of the Colorado Plateau. Their homeland, before occupying their current reservation, was known as the Dinetah, a vast and beautiful system of canyons draining through

Gobernador and Largo Canyons into the San Juan River in northwest New Mexico (Figure 2). Although the Dinetah is located just outside the geographic boundaries chosen for this book, it is included because it contains the best examples of early Navajo rock art, as well as some Anasazi images. Further, it is possible to easily walk or ride a horse from the headwaters of the Rio Chama, a Rio Grande tributary, across the Continental Divide and into the Dinetah canyons of the San Juan watershed.

Rock art of the Apaches is less well known than that of the Navajos. Rock art believed to be of Apache origin is not concentrated in a particular region such as the Dinetah but is found at relatively few sites scattered over a large area, primarily from southern Arizona through southern New Mexico and in west Texas and northern Chihuahua. Some of these sites, as with the Dinetah rock art, occur beyond the boundaries selected for this book but are included because they are rare and because the nomadic Apaches were not confined to any particular watershed. Today, there are two Apache reservations in New Mexico—the Jicarilla and the Mescalero.

In the seventeenth century, Apaches became fierce raiders of pueblos and the early Spanish settlements along the Rio Grande, but in the 1700s they began to retreat from the Plains in the face of even fiercer nomads—the Comanches. A few examples of historic rock art believed to be of Comanche origin are found scattered throughout the eastern plains, far beyond the eastern edges of the Rio Grande watershed.[20]

The Numic-speaking Ute Indians are apparently also recent newcomers to the upper Rio Grande region, although their ancestors were probably Desert Archaic residents of the Great Basin and the northern periphery of the Southwest for thousands

a.

b.

Figure 6. Illustration of the horse in Athabascan rock art from the upper Rio Grande region: a. petroglyph, Rio Grande at Arroyo Hondo, Taos County, New Mexico; b. petroglyphs, probably Apache, Alamo Mountain, Otero County, New Mexico.

of years. Utes probably moved into the San Luis Valley and headwaters region of the Rio Grande in the late 1500s.[21] Their primary territory was the western slope of Colorado and eastern Utah, but the Mouache Band utilized the San Luis Valley seasonally for hunting and gathering.[22] They had trading contacts with the northern and eastern pueblos (Taos, Picuris, Pecos) and were known to winter in the warmer terrain of New Mexico. After acquiring the horse in the 1800s, they began raiding their Pueblo neighbors, and eventually joined with their Comanche cousins to raid Spanish settlements. Anglo settlement of Colorado and the gold rushes of the nineteenth century spelled doom for the raiding nomadic Utes, and an 1863 treaty ended their claim to the San Luis Valley. Although not yet well understood, a number of apparent Ute rock art sites exist in scattered locations around the San Luis Valley. Primarily pictograph sites, usually in red, they are often located near streams in areas that would have provided good resources for foraging.

"Among the languages of American Indians there is no word for art. For Indians everything is art... therefore it needs no name."[1]
—Jamake Highwater,
The Primal Mind

"In the creation of all art, many helpers come forward to support the vision."
—Anonymous

"All art worthy of the name is religious."
—Henri Matisse

2

The Rock Art

WHAT IS ROCK ART

There are basically two kinds of rock art—petroglyphs and pictographs. Petroglyphs are pecked, carved, or abraded images, whereas pictographs are painted onto rock surfaces with natural pigments, usually in caves or under protective ledges. Petroglyphs are generally found on rocks such as sandstone or basalt that have a dark surface or patina, known as rock varnish, that forms slowly as a result of weathering, as well as microbial and chemical alterations. When the rock varnish is removed by pecking or carving with another stone, the lighter-colored unweathered rock is exposed, producing a visual contrast. Sometimes smoke-blackened walls of caves or ceremonial chambers provided a similar dark background for producing images (Figure 7). Making petroglyphs was time-consuming, difficult work. Although petroglyphs have a high degree of permanency, they will eventually darken, or repatinate, as the weathering process continues on the rock surface. It can take hundreds to thousands of years for petroglyphs to completely repatinate, and the process differs depending on micro-climatic factors at various sites. The degree of repatination can be a relative means of dating different petroglyphs on the same rock since the fresher-looking images are more recent than the dark ones.

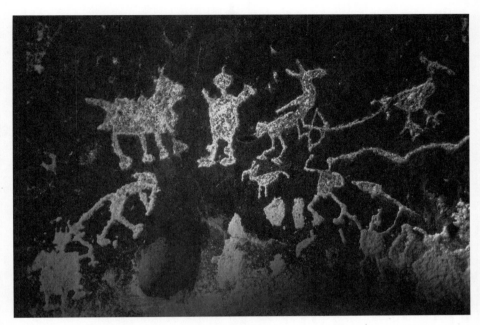

Figure 7. Petroglyphs carved on smoke-blackened walls of a ceremonial chamber excavated in tuff (volcanic ash), Sandia Cave, Los Alamos, New Mexico.

Pictographs are more vulnerable than petroglyphs, and unless they are protected from the weather will not usually last as long.[2] To produce pictographs, natural pigments such as iron oxides (hematite or limonite), white or yellow clays and soft rock, charcoal, and copper minerals were used to create a palette of red, yellow, white, black, blue, and green colors. Organic binders were utilized to mix the powdered mineral pigments; binders could be some combination of fluids such as plant juices, egg, animal fat, saliva, blood, urine, and water. Most pictographs are relatively small, although some are life-sized.

From the period of early hunter/gatherers to the time of complex agricultural societies, rock art continued to be produced in constantly evolving styles, until there came to exist a bewildering array of stylistic elements in rock art.

Whether rock art should properly be thought of as "art" has long been a subject of scholarly debate among archaeologists and art historians. American Indians had no word for art since creativity was part of daily life. While the term rock art, like other terms about ancient or mysterious subjects, is not perfect and does not suit everyone, its popular usage has pervaded our language and consciousness. At the same time, it is clear that the ancient symbols on rock can be complex and powerful metaphors—much more than mere adornment.

Regardless of what we call it, apparently petroglyphs and pictographs were left on rocks by the Indians for a variety of reasons and purposes. Reasons for creating rock art could have included marking territory and features such as trails, springs, and shrines; depicting shamanic prayers or visions; recording rituals, successful hunts, and battles; ensuring rain, bountiful harvests, and fertility; making designs for the pleasure of creating; or simply chronicling human presence in a location. In all cases it seems that a deliberate act of creation took place, as rock art is usually aesthetically pleasing regardless of intention. Moreover, it is nearly always located in special places since rock art is frequently connected with supernatural and spiritual domains.

Perhaps the best definition of rock art comes from expert Polly Schaafsma, who calls it "an artifact of ideas" and describes it as "a visual record from ancient societies that consists largely of images from the realm of the sacred, symbols of former cognitive universes. These images on stone give substance to visions, beliefs, cosmologies, gods, and other supernaturals. Petroglyphs and rock paintings served as means to communicate myths, stories, cultural values, and abstract ideas from one generation to the next."[3]

Despite the debate about terminology, there is consensus among scholars that rock art is not "writing" and is a language only in the sense that symbols are used to represent things in a nonliteral manner. Today, we can understand rock art styles to varying degrees. For example, the more recent Pueblo rock art is more readily interpreted through ethnographic accounts because the beliefs of the artists who created it have been preserved by their descendants. By contrast, millennia-old rock art of Archaic peoples is relatively inscrutable because there is no other record of their beliefs. Ultimately, we cannot know the meaning of most rock art, but it will always engage us because it represents mysterious, intangible realms. Moreover, rock art challenges us to integrate our own physical and spiritual worlds. While observation and logic are employed to define various rock art styles and to suggest meaning, it is important to recognize that wonder is just as significant as analysis—perhaps more so if the full benefit of experiencing rock art is acknowledged. The creators of rock art most likely did not engage in our artificial distinction between physical and nonphysical realities, and such unified perception is present in their rock art as a cohering force that holds together the different elements in a panel, connects the rock art to the landscape, and puts the viewer in closer touch with both the physical and spiritual worlds—reflecting personal and universal power, as well as almost every other aspect of human behavior.

One of the more intriguing explanations for some types of nonrepresentational rock art (often described as abstract or geometric) is the neurological model that suggests some rock art is entoptic ("within the eye") phenomena. According to this

concept, certain geometric visual imagery is project-
ed by the human optic nervous system and precipi-
tated by an altered state of consciousness. Altered
states of consciousness can be induced by psychoac-
tive drugs (peyote, Datura, mescal, and so forth),
drumming, chanting, dancing, sensory deprivation
(as in a vision quest), hyperventilation, or intense
concentration.[4] Through such activities, many of
which are employed in shamanic practice, individuals tend to perceive a relatively common set of fun-
damental forms such as grids, dots, parallel and
zigzag lines, nested curves, and thin meandering
lines. Adherents of neuropsychology hypothesize
that some rock art motifs that exhibit such geometric patterns may be products of shamanic practices
or other forms of altered states of consciousness.
Such motifs may be the records of visions, perhaps
giving us a glimpse inside the consciousness of
shamans. This model cannot, however, give us accurate information about the cultural role played by
the creators of such perceptual phenomena.[5] Thus,
questions such as the following arise: Was some
rock art made by an experienced shaman, by a
shaman's apprentice, or by a shaman's patient as part
of a curing ceremony? What rock art was produced
by a group of artists and what was created by a single individual? How much acceptability was there
for individual, idiosyncratic expression within culturally defined norms of expression? Which aspects
of a particular style were instinctual and which were
consciously employed? Intriguing questions like
these only make us more fascinated by rock art and
its aura of mystery.

We know that Anasazi/Pueblo rock art, and
probably most other rock art, was often made near
places in the landscape imbued with mythic significance or at shrines where rituals took place.[6]

Figure 8. Some rock art is associated with cracks or openings in the rock. At this petroglyph site, arms and open hands seem to reach out and wave from cracks in the basalt boulder. Northern Tewa Province, Black Mesa, Rio Arriba County, New Mexico.

Although many sites are near villages, some are in very remote areas. Prominent high points and confluences of streams or canyons are often favored places. Because caves and rock shelters were thought to be entrances to the underworld, they are often sites of rock art. Even though rock art often occurs at places of ritual significance, the location and function of rock art can be as varied as the landscape itself.

Since many rock art sites are places deemed sacred or to have power, it is interesting to consider the nature of that power. Some sites seem to be located specifically around prominent cracks or openings in the rock (Figure 8), some of which may be places that have been struck by lightning. In addi-

Figure 9. Petroglyph images of a pair of legs seem to portray a person (shaman or spirit-being?) diving into the earth through an opening between boulders. Jornada Style, Three Rivers, Otero County, New Mexico.

tion, magnetic anomalies of basalt rocks have sometimes been linked to petroglyph panels,[7] and openings in the rock have been described as locations where supernaturals or shamans' spirits can enter the underworld or emerge to this one (Figure 9). It was believed that the sacred realm could be entered when cracks opened in the rocks, revealing tunnels to the spirit world. Animals that could move in and out of the cracks, such as lizards and snakes, were considered messengers between this world and the supernatural. These creatures are very common elements in rock art of the Southwest.

Rock openings sometimes resemble vaginas and were thus seen as powerful sources of fertility energy, analogous to the womb of the earth itself. In some cultures puberty and fertility rituals were conducted at such sites, which could entail the creation of rock art around these sacred places, and ritual rebirth by crawling through womb-like tunnels in the rock.

Moreover, another intriguing possibility is that rock art focused on prominent features of the rock and could thus reflect aspects of Native American cosmology in a graphic way similar to the image of the *axis mundi*. In ancient cosmology, the *axis mundi* (axle of the world) pictured the world spinning on a shaft that penetrated the earth at its center/navel. Each nation placed this hub at the center of its own territory. It is conceivable that some rock art which is focused on prominent vertical cracks (or other special landscape features) reflects aspects of Native American cosmology. Native concepts of a vertically layered cosmos, of which the earth is but one layer in a series between the sky and underworld, tend to support such interpretation.

In addition to significant locations, some rock art sites seem to have special acoustical properties.[8] Rock overhangs, alcoves, caves, and canyon walls can have dramatic resonance and echo-producing effects, which would accentuate the effects of drums, chants, flutes, or other ritual sounds. Consequently, some rock art may have been created at specific sites to enhance rituals, and certain images may have been used repeatedly as a way of addressing the earth or contacting earth spirits. Moreover, certain rocks with deeply worn grooves or pits (cupules) were probably ritual sites where contact with supernatural forces was facilitated by the act of rubbing or striking the rock. For example, images related to fertility sometimes have deep pits in the genital areas, and images related to hunting may show evidence of ritual repecking on certain animals. In addition, some large rock slabs may possess special acoustical properties that make them ring like a bell or gong when struck with another rock. Such sites could have been marked with petroglyphs and used repeatedly to contact the spirits.

Further, hunting magic or ritual is suggested by the placement of some rock art near prominent game trails at narrow passes, canyons, or at jump sites where animals could have been driven over cliffs. Scenes with game animals pierced by arrows or spears or atlatl darts have traditionally been interpreted in this way (Figure 10).[9]

Finally, in recent years, substantial research in the field of archaeoastronomy has focused on rock art sites that may have been created to function as solar observatories or calendrical markers of some kind.[10] For horticultural people concerned with planting and harvesting times in a land of quirky growing seasons, accurate knowledge of solstices and equinoxes would have been invaluable. One of the first examples of this kind of site to receive popular attention was the "sun dagger" petroglyph that seems to mark the solstice at Fajada Butte in Chaco Canyon.[11] Since then other sites continue to be examined for similar functions.

Figure 10. An example of possible hunting magic in rock art—a desert bighorn sheep with arrows stuck in it, Jornada Style, Three Rivers, Otero County, New Mexico.

ROCK ART STYLES

To understand its origin, meaning, and age, rock art has been classified into styles. The art of any culture group is bound by the confines of a style.[12] In regard to rock art, the main components are element inventory and figure types. The general aesthetics and technical production are also part of what constitutes a style. Once they are determined, the distribution in space and time of a rock art style

can be used within cultural and archaeological contexts to infer limited meaning to the rock art and its
development. The original work of classifying rock
art styles in the Southwest was done by Polly
Schaafsma, and information in the following sections is based largely on her publications or comes
from personal communications.

An overview of the prehistoric culture groups
known from the upper Rio Grande region was presented in Chapter 1. Currently accepted ideas of
rock art styles within this region are correlated to
those culture groups. In the northern part of the
upper Rio Grande, the rock art is primarily Rio
Grande Style and is Anasazi/Pueblo in origin, along
with some Archaic, Athabascan, and Ute sites. There
is a greater diversity of styles in the south, in what
constitutes the northern edge of the Chihuahuan
Desert. These rock art sites are products of Archaic
hunter/gatherers, the Mimbres and Jornada Mogollon cultures, Apaches, or represent transitional ideographies between the Mogollon and the Anasazi/
Pueblo groups to the north. The approximate distribution of the rock art styles in the upper Rio Grande
region is shown in Plate 1. Since there is considerable overlap of styles, and areas where distinctions
are blurred due to cultural diffusion and interaction,
detailed examples of specific styles are given in the
following chapters, which discuss rock art sites in
geographical order from north to south, beginning
at the Rio Grande headwaters.

Southwestern rock art styles can be divided into
two basic categories, representational and abstract.
Representational rock art depicts life-forms
(humans, animals, plants, supernatural beings) but is
more often highly stylized than naturalistic. Abstract
elements, be they geometric or random free-form
shapes (rectilinear or curvilinear), are not recogniz-

ably related to the real world. Generally speaking, abstract rock art in the upper Rio Grande region tends to be older and was produced by hunter/gatherers, whereas most representational rock art is newer and was produced by horticultural societies. Some rock art that is transitional between Archaic and horticultural, such as early Basketmaker, has shamanic elements.

爪 Archaic Rock Art Styles

The earliest known rock art in the region is attributed to hunter/gatherers of the Western Archaic Period. Archaic rock art styles date back as far as 2000 B.C. In the upper Rio Grande region, three styles are ascribed to the Archaic Period: Desert Abstract, Chihuahuan Polychrome, and Diablo Dam Petroglyph Styles.[13]

Rock art of the Desert Abstract Style is found throughout much of the Southwest, although its boundaries are not currently known. This style consists of zigzags, circles, triangles, wavy lines, sun disks, rakes, and snake-like designs. They typically occur on boulders or outcroppings, usually filling most of the rock faces on which they are placed. This style occurs at a number of large petroglyph sites in southern New Mexico, west Texas, and northern Chihuahua. Many are found near springs, such as at Alamo Mountain in Otero County, New Mexico. A volcanic dike near Carrizozo, New Mexico, is literally covered with petroglyphs of this style (Figure 11).

Little is known of the distribution of Archaic Desert Abstract Style petroglyphs in the northern Rio Grande Valley. It has been recorded at a few sites in northern New Mexico along the San Jose

Figure 11. Archaic rock art, Desert Abstract Style, near Carrizozo, New Mexico.

River, at Arroyo Hondo and Pilar near Taos, in the Galisteo Basin south of Santa Fe, and along the West Mesa at Albuquerque, where there is public access. Designs here are similar to those of southern Archaic sites and tend to be heavily patinated, suggesting great antiquity. Pitted boulders (cupules) are also found in these areas and are thought to be of Archaic age. In some cases, superimposed over the Desert Abstract Style petroglyphs are less-patinated Anasazi/Pueblo designs in the north and Jornada Mogollon motifs in the south. In 1993, a very interesting and unusual site of Archaic abstract petroglyphs came to light on Glorieta Mesa near Pecos, New Mexico.[14] Here, at two sites several miles apart, are scores of abstract petroglyphs on horizontal bedrock surfaces covered by up to two feet of soil (Figure 12). Discovered due to partial exposure from

Figure 12. Four-thousand-year-old Archaic petroglyphs on horizontal surface under several feet of soil, Glorieta Mesa, San Miguel County, New Mexico.

natural soil erosion, subsequent archaeological excavation and dating have determined minimum dates for these petroglyphs to be about 4000 B.C. Dating by C-14 of charcoal hearths found in the overlying soil and of the rock varnish both yielded comparable ages.[15] (See Chapter 5 for more on this site with public access.)

In the southern portion of the upper Rio Grande region, design elements of the Archaic Desert Abstract Style are similar to the northern sites, but there is often much greater superimposition and use of simple representational elements, like stick-figure anthropomorphs, tracks, or handprints. Rock features such as holes, bumps, and edges are often incorporated into the designs. In the south, there seems to be a continuity between late Archaic and early Jornada Mogollon Styles.[16]

The function of these Archaic petroglyphs is not well understood. As mentioned previously, some petroglyph sites occur near springs and may thus be related to concerns with moisture. In the Great Basin of Nevada and western Utah, rock art of this style is linked to hunting magic.[17] It seems apparent that petroglyph making was an important part of the rituals employed at these Archaic sites, and could have incorporated ideas about territorial rights or water, or pertain to appeasement of supernaturals.

Figure 13. Archaic petroglyphs in the Diablo Dam Style, Fort Hancock, Texas.

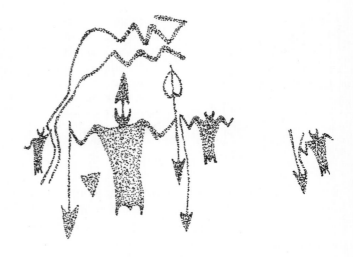

The Chihuahuan Polychrome Style of Archaic rock art is a painted style (pictographs) occurring primarily in caves and rock shelters in the southern portion of the region, in the Chihuahuan Desert of southern New Mexico, west Texas, and northern Chihuahua (Plate 1). This style is characterized by multicolored designs of short parallel lines and zigzags, circles, and dots similar to the designs of the Desert Abstract Style petroglyphs, and perhaps a variation in that tradition. In southern New Mexico there are a number of these sites, two notable examples being Picture Cave in the Alamo Hueco Mountains and Painted Grotto in the Guadalupe Mountains.

A third Archaic style, present in the southern portion of the upper Rio Grande region, is the Diablo Dam Petroglyph Style. This representational style occurs near the Rio Grande at Fort Hancock, Texas (Plate 1). There is an emphasis on long spears, projectile points, and broad-shouldered anthropomorphs (Figure 13). The appearance of large, boldly presented anthropomorphs, some of which are horned, suggests supernatural or shamanic power.[18] The emphasis on spears and points is unusual and may also have supernatural meaning. A representational Archaic painted style found in the Candelaria Peaks of northern Chihuahua may be a variation of this style.[19]

𖧪 *Mogollon Rock Art Styles*

The two major horticultural traditions that followed the Western Archaic in the upper Rio Grande region were the Mogollon in southern New Mexico and the Anasazi in northern New Mexico, both of which began around A.D. 1 and lasted at least 1,500 years.

Just as Mogollon culture is very diverse, so is the complex rock art from this region. There are two Mogollon-related rock art styles in the southern portion of the upper Rio Grande region—Mogollon Red Style and the more ubiquitous and influential Jornada Style.

Occurring temporally between Archaic rock art styles and the Jornada Style of the Desert Mogollon culture in the mountain region of southwestern New Mexico, are a number of pictograph sites of the Mogollon Red Style, which are associated with the Mountain Mogollon culture (Plate 1). These are small paintings executed in red pigments consisting of life-forms and abstract elements (Figure 14). These sites occur mainly in the headwaters of the Gila, San Francisco, and Mimbres Rivers, in the Black Range, and in the boot heel area of southwestern New Mexico. Just as the Mountain Mogollon and the Desert Mogollon cultures are distinct geographically, so the rock art of these provinces shows evidence of different ideologies.[20]

Figure 14. Pictographs of bird tracks and stick figures in the Mogollon Red Style (the terrace-shaped figure is a Jornada element), Chloride Creek, Black Range, Sierra County, New Mexico.

Figure 15. Tlaloc, a Jornada Style rain deity derived from Mesoamerica. Pictograph in cave at Hueco Tanks State Historical Park, El Paso County, Texas.

Both the Mimbres and Jornada regions of the Desert Mogollon Culture shared a common art tradition that led to development of the important Jornada Style after A.D. 1050. As stated earlier, there is evidence, based on patination and superimposition, of continuity between the Archaic Desert Abstract Style, the Mogollon Red Style, and the classic Jornada Style.[21] The Jornada Style is datable from its appearance on decorated Mimbres ceramics. This style is a major one in the Mogollon area, and is found throughout the Chihuahuan Desert region of southern New Mexico. It reflects a significant cultural shift due to contact with the high cultures of Mesoamerica, including the Casas Grandes area, and it influenced the rock art tradition of the Anasazi/ Pueblo region to the north. The Jornada Style is

known for its rich inventory of visually stunning figures, including masks and faces, mythical beings, animals, blanket designs, horned serpents, fish, insects,
and cloud terraces. The largest and most complex
sites are in the Rio Grande Valley and the Tularosa
Basin to the east, while others occur in the Mimbres
drainage. Notable petroglyph sites are at Three
Rivers (with public access), Arroyo del Macho, and
south of Cooke's Peak. Some outstanding examples
of Jornada Style paintings are found at Hueco Tanks
Historical Park east of El Paso, Texas, where there is
limited public access. (See Chapter 4 for a description of these sites.)

A stylized anthropomorphic figure that may be
related to Tlaloc, a rain deity ("He who makes things
grow") from ancient Mexico, is found at nearly every
Jornada Style site. The Jornada "Tlaloc" is a trape-
zoidal-shaped figure with huge goggle-like eyes; the
torso is typically decorated with elaborate geometric
designs or cloud motifs (Figure 15). Another figure
found in Jornada Style rock art is the horned, or
feathered, serpent, also derived from a Mexican deity
(perhaps Quetzalcoatl) associated with water and
moisture. A figure analogous to this potent deity is
commonly seen in Pueblo rock art of the Rio
Grande Style in the north, where it is best known as
Awanyu. However, Jornada Style horned serpents
have a single forward-pointing horn, whereas horned
serpents in Pueblo rock art are depicted with one or
two horns (Figure 5).

The many elaborate masks portrayed in Jornada
Style rock art are important because it is believed
they were adopted into the rock art of the Rio
Grande Style and reflect the development of the im-
portant Pueblo kachina cult of the fourteenth century
(Figure 16). The Jornada Style persisted in southern
New Mexico until approximately A.D. 1400.[22] The

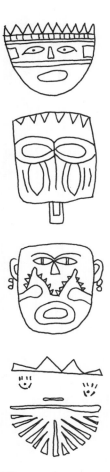

*Figure 16.
Examples of
Jornada Style
masks,
pictographs,
Hueco Tanks
State Historical
Park, El Paso
County, Texas.
(After Kirkland
and Newcomb
1967.)*

function of Jornada Style sites is undoubtedly complex, but the near universal appearance of elements associated with moisture, like Tlaloc, crested serpents, and cloud imagery, suggests that the rock art was placed, in part, to ensure adequate rain and good harvests in this harsh desert land. Other figures found at Jornada Style sites that are associated with water are fish, tadpoles, turtles, and dragonflies (Figure 1). Jornada Style depictions of animals and humans are the most imaginative, stylized, and creative of all southwestern rock art.

🐾 *Anasazi/Pueblo Rock Art Styles*

The dominant rock art style of the Anasazi/ Pueblo people in the northern Rio Grande Valley is a product of the early Anasazi ideologies combined with ideas borrowed from the Jornada Style region to the south. Not only has a continuity in art been recognized between Mesoamerica, Mogollon, and Anasazi cultures, but a continuity in religion has also been perceived between the religions of central Mexico and that of the Pueblos of the upper Rio Grande region. There are reasons to believe that the Tlaloc cult and masks of the Jornada Style were related to the kachina cult of the Pueblos, and that Quetzalcoatl has parallels to the horned or plumed water serpent (Awanyu) of the Rio Grande Pueblos.[23]

Rock art of the early Anasazi people within the upper Rio Grande can be identified according to the cultural stages of the Pecos Classification, from Basketmaker II and III through Pueblo I, II, and III. After the Pueblo III Period, major changes in the Anasazi world produced a new rock art tradition known as the Rio Grande Style. The elements of Rio Grande Style rock art are still maintained in ceremonial art by modern Pueblo people. Also, the Rio Grande Style had a major influence on the development of later rock art styles of the Athabascan people, especially the Navajos.

Most Basketmaker II rock art occurs on the Colorado Plateau, notably in the San Juan drainage, and is hence beyond the scope of this discussion. However, during this time in the upper Rio Grande region the artistic tradition consisted primarily of Desert Abstract Style petroglyphs, usually on talus boulders.[24] This art implies that the people living in the northern Rio Grande Valley and its tributaries during the Basketmaker II period were participating in a different ideological system than their Anasazi counterparts on the Colorado Plateau. However, rock art of later periods (Basketmaker III through Pueblo III) is more similar across a huge area from Nevada to the Rio Grande. A few distinct styles have been described for the Anasazi rock art of this transition time leading up to the distinctive Rio Grande Style about A.D. 1300, but they are primarily in the San Juan drainage. In the area of the upper Rio Grande, this period of Anasazi rock art is not well understood.[25] In the northern Rio Grande region, there are petroglyphs of quadrupeds, stick figures, lizards, flute players, tracks, birds, and textile and pottery motifs—all of which are similar to the early Anasazi rock art of the Colorado Plateau, and which are thought to date between A.D. 1000 and A.D. 1300.[26] Such early Anasazi rock art is found at small sites along the Rio Grande Valley from the vicinity of Socorro to north of Taos and into the San Luis Valley, and contains a mix of elements from Colorado Plateau Anasazi designs, Mogollon designs, and regionally distinct elements. Some notable pre-Pueblo IV Anasazi petroglyph sites occur at the West Mesa near Albuquerque, along

*Figure 17.
Early Anasazi
(pre-Pueblo IV)
petroglyphs,
Santa Fe River
Canyon, Santa Fe
County, New
Mexico.*

the Santa Fe River (Figure 17), on the Pajarito Plateau, in White Rock Canyon near Los Alamos, and near Taos. Among these sites, there is public access to the sites at Petroglyph National Monument, White Rock Canyon, Bandelier National Monument, and Puyé Cliff Dwellings (see Chapter 5). After A.D. 1100, there is a marked increase in the quantity of Anasazi rock art in the northern Rio Grande region, and it has a greater similarity to the Anasazi rock art in other areas. During this time (Pueblo III), there was considerable population growth and expansion in the Anasazi world, which probably resulted in greater communication of ideas.

Figure 18. Example of Rio Grande Style anthropomorph, Galisteo Basin, Santa Fe County, New Mexico.

乑 Rio Grande Rock Art Style

After A.D. 1300 (Pueblo IV), the Rio Grande Valley was the center of the Pueblo world, and populations increased significantly. In addition, a dramatic new rock art style was developed—the Rio Grande Style. The majority of all rock art in the northern Rio Grande Valley was produced in this style during the Pueblo IV Period, from A.D. 1300 to approximately A.D. 1700. Rio Grande Style rock art sites vary from large sites with thousands of petroglyphs to small isolated locations with only a few elements. They are found near habitations and at prominent natural features located miles from any settlements, sometimes in nearly inaccessible locations.

This style is quite different from the early Anasazi rock art that preceded it. Kachina-like masks are common, anthropomorphs are large and often stylized (Figure 18), and shield bearers and hump-backed flute players are prevalent and highly varied. Many types of animals are represented, with birds and snakes being the most common. Cloud terraces, crosses, stars, corn plants, and handprints are also found. Individual expression seems apparent in the complex and highly varied designs, yet the elements are part of a system that ascribed supernatural significance and ritual meaning to nearly every symbol.

Within the framework of the Rio Grande Style, regional variations are recognized (from south to north): Piro/Tompiro, Southern Tiwa, Southern Tewa (Tano), Keresan, Western Towa, Northern Tewa, and Northern Tiwa (Figure 19). For the most thorough and authoritative description of Rio Grande Style rock art and its regional variations, see Polly Schaafsma, *Rock Art in New Mexico*.[27]

Some examples of Rio Grande Style are presented in subsequent chapters as the various rock art sites are described. Several major differences of regional variations are that the southern portion of the Rio Grande Style region contains prominent kachina and other Jornada-derived elements, as may be expected since these districts are contiguous with the

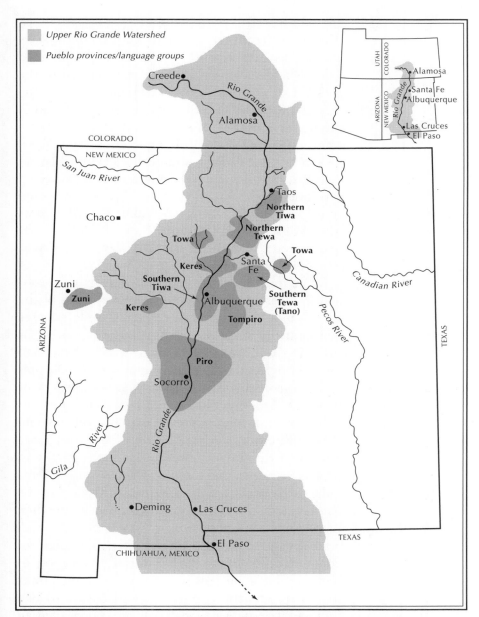

Figure 19. Map showing Pueblo Provinces/language groups in the upper Rio Grande and regions of Rio Grande Style rock art variations. (Adapted from Mednick 1996.)

Jornada territory; these elements appear with decreasing frequency in the rock art of the various Pueblo districts moving northward and ending in Taos, where kachina imagery is very limited in the rock art of the Northern Tiwa region. Some outstanding Rio Grande Style rock art sites are found in the Abo area near Mountainair, in the Galisteo Basin south of Santa Fe, along Albuquerque's West Mesa, in White Rock Canyon and on the Pajarito Plateau near Los Alamos, and in the Santa Fe River Canyon. Of these sites, Salinas National Monument at Abo ruins, Petroglyph National Monument at Albuquerque, White Rock Canyon, Bandelier National Monument, and the Puyé Cliff Dwellings near Española have public access (see Chapter 5).

The role of rock art in the Pueblo world is probably comparable to its role in other cultures of the Rio Grande region, but due to the Pueblo people's continuity of tradition, there is more potential for inferring the meaning of many elements at Rio Grande Style sites. The sheer number of such sites seems to communicate something about territory or presence. The prevalent sacred contexts of most of the rock art further express Pueblo worldview and the significance of ritual. Some of these sites are associated with sacred shrines, clan gatherings, war, protective power, and hunting. One of the few symbolic carryovers from earlier Anasazi rock art to the Rio Grande Style is the figure of Kokopelli, the flute player, as a fertility symbol.[28] After A.D. 1300, rock art became much more important as a medium of communication in the Pueblo world. It was a way of merging the latent power of a place with the power of human creativity. The detailed nature of Rio Grande Style indicates that rock art represented an important medium, one that deserved significant investment of time and energy.

𝕽 *Navajo Rock Art*

Rock art styles of Navajo origin are in reality a product of acculturation and intermarriage between Athabascan peoples and Pueblo groups (Jemez, Cochiti, Tewa) who fled the Rio Grande area after the Pueblo Revolt of 1680 to escape Spanish reprisal and to join the Navajos in the Dinetah area of north-western New Mexico. The Navajos adopted many aspects of Pueblo religion and ritual during what is known as the Gobernador Phase (approximately A.D. 1696 to A.D. 1775), and it is from this period that the first Navajo rock art is known.[29]

The Gobernador Representational Style, which has similarities to Pueblo art of the time, occurs in the upper San Juan and the Gobernador and Largo Canyon drainages of northwest New Mexico (Plate 1), as well as in Chaco Canyon and a few locations in the Rio Puerco watershed. Depictions of cere-monial figures and Navajo deities (Yei's), shield bearers, cloud terraces, birds, and corn plants are often seen in seventeenth-century Navajo rock art (Figure 20). Both petroglyphs and pictographs are found in this style, and often beautifully executed. Canyon junctions were favored locations, and Navajo rock art probably functioned as shrines.[30]

A unique feature of Navajo rock art is the star paintings (planetaria) found on the ceilings of rock overhangs at dozens of widely scattered sites throughout northwestern New Mexico and north-eastern Arizona. The paintings are small stars de-picted as crosses several inches across, in red, black, gray, or white. At some sites other elements are also present, such as small birds, dragonflies, animals, and circles. Many are placed in seemingly inaccessi-ble locations—as high as fifty feet above the cave floor in some cases. To paint such sites, the Indians

*Figure 20.
Navajo rock
art in the
Gobernador
Representational
Style, Largo
Canyon, San
Juan County,
New Mexico.*

must have gone to great lengths, employing such aids as ropes, poles, or scaffolding. They are undoubtedly ceremonial, sacred sites.[31]

With the close of the Gobernador Phase, Navajo rock art became more secular. Rather than featuring ceremonial and supernatural themes, the undifferentiated style of later Navajo rock art focuses on scenes of everyday life executed in a more natural fashion, including incised or scratched petroglyphs as well as pictographs and charcoal drawings. Canyon de Chelly in Arizona contains some of the finest late Navajo rock art, examples of which represent actual historic events. In late Navajo rock art, the horse is much more prevalent and creatively depicted than in Gobernador Phase rock art. The sandpaintings for which the Navajos are well known evolved out of the earlier rock art ceremonial motifs of the Gobernador Phase.

冧 Apache Rock Art

With the acquisition of the horse in the 1600s, the Apache lifestyle evolved from one based on bison hunting, foraging, and gardening to one based on raiding. Through a combination of raiding and trading with their Pueblo neighbors, the Apaches acquired some of the Pueblos' ideas about religion and its expression in ceremonial art. Relatively little is known about Apache rock art, which is widely scattered over a large area (Plate 1). Polly Schaafsma states that "...the work at these sites represents a rather miscellaneous collection of rock paintings and petroglyphs obviously relatively recent in origin, but often so limited or undiagnostic in context and style that...one cannot always be certain who made them."[32] The horse and rider are common elements, as are bison, shields, snakes, lizards, masks, small animals, and abstract designs. Anthropomorphic figures depicted with sunburst head motifs, horned headdresses, and carrying staffs probably are associated with shamanic practices (Figure 21).[33] In the southern Rio Grande region, some significant sites are at Hueco Tanks, Texas (which has public access), and in the Guadalupe Mountains and Alamo Mountain, New Mexico.

Figure 21. Apache petroglyph of shaman with sunburst head, Black Mesa, Socorro County, New Mexico.

冧 Ute Rock Art

Ute rock art has been studied mainly in western Colorado and eastern Utah—the area that was their principal territory at the time of historic contact.[34] Although a few sites of apparent Ute rock art occur in the San Luis Valley (which was occupied by the Mouache Band), little research has been focused on this area. Of the more than 36,000 prehistoric sites recorded in Colorado, only 438 (1.2 percent) are designated Ute, yet these people were the most recent and the largest native group known to have existed in Colorado.[35] About ten of the documented Ute archaeological sites are in the San Luis Valley. There is little archaeological data about Ute rock art, a situation that can be partly explained by their nomadic lifestyle. At the time of historic contact, Utes were making rock art of a distinctive style, as well as imitating some earlier rock art.[36] They may have incorporated symbolism and styles of various cultures due to contact with other tribes.

Although little is known about Ute rock art in the San Luis Valley, it may be possible to make some useful assumptions about it from what is known about their rock art in western Colorado and eastern Utah. Two styles have been proposed, based on research in that area: Early Historic Ute (1640–1830) and Late Historic Ute (1830–1880).[37] Both styles can sometimes be identified by their historic elements such as horses, tipis, and guns. Petroglyphs and pictographs both occur, and sites are in diverse settings. The alpine cave sites in the San Juan Mountains of Colorado are particularly interesting as only Ute rock art is found in these higher elevations.[38] Their art typically incorporates other styles.

Early Historic Ute rock art subject matter includes anthropomorphs (both on foot and mounted), shield figures, horses, bears and bear shamans, female fertility symbols, birds, weapons, and abstract linear designs. Themes of this style include battles and raids, individual power, and hunting. Biographical or narrative content is implied in some panels.[39]

Late Historic Ute rock art exhibits some continuity with the earlier style, but life-forms have more

Figure 22.
Ute petroglyph of a
horse and rider,
Shivano Valley,
Montrose, Colorado.

detail, realism, and naturalism. Although the subject matter is similar to that of the earlier style, there is less abstraction. In some ways it is like contemporaneous Plains Indian rock art, as in both styles panels tend to be crowded, and themes include aggression, male prestige, horses, and ceremonies.[40] An example of Ute rock art from the Shivano Valley near Montrose, Colorado, shows a nine-legged horse with rider—perhaps an attempt to indicate running at fast speed (Figure 22). Ute rock art is further illustrated in the discussion of the San Luis Valley in Chapter 3. Public access sites containing Ute rock art include Carnero Creek and Dry Creek in Colorado's San Luis Valley (see Chapter 5).

CONSERVATION AND ACCESS TO SITES

Every effort should be made to preserve our rich heritage of rock art. Although deterioration caused by weathering is inevitable, unfortunately much rock art has been damaged or destroyed by thoughtless human activity. Rock art is a fragile treasure— once destroyed it cannot be replaced. It should never be touched, since the salt, moisture, and oils from skin will hasten deterioration of both petroglyphs and pictographs. Chalk or other marking

Figure 23. Our rock art heritage is being lost to vandals and thieves. At this Navajo pictograph panel, a thief flaunting federal laws on public land cut out segments of the panel. Largo Canyon near Lybrook, New Mexico.

material should not be used to highlight rock art for photography since such material may hasten or retard the natural patination process of the rock, and its application obfuscates the relative dating of overlapping images. Further, an individual applying chalk may incorrectly interpret dim or faded portions of a design, thereby giving erroneous impressions to subsequent viewers. Likewise, making rubbings of petroglyphs is damaging because the rock is unnaturally eroded, and patination, lichen growth, and other natural processes are disrupted by adhesive tapes and stress from contact.

Sadly, bullet holes and graffiti are fairly common conditions encountered at many rock art sites today. Even more disturbing is the increasing evidence of stolen rock art, where fresh scars from chisels or saws, and broken-out slabs of rock, mark the previous location of a petroglyph (Figure 23). Presumably motivated by a market for actual rock art, these criminal attempts to remove examples of our prehistoric heritage ironically often result in destruction of the sought-after treasure since in the process the rock usually fractures into small pieces.

As the popularity of rock art increases, so does the number of people visiting sites. Sometimes even the sheer number of visitors has a negative impact on sites. For instance, photographers who have built bonfires in front of panels to obtain dramatic lighting effects have harmed rock art through smoke damage or thermally induced exfoliation of the rock surface. Likewise, the burning of votive candles and incense can damage sensitive sites, especially those in caves. Moreover, soil erosion due to foot traffic around heavily visited sites can alter original conditions and damage archaeologically significant features.

Fortunately, much rock art is on public land and is therefore protected by federal and state antiquity laws. And to further protect this valuable resource information about precise locations of rock art is rarely given in publications, a tradition also followed in this book. For those who wish to visit some locations, Chapter 5 lists a number of sites with public access in the upper Rio Grande region. For additional sites, inquire at appropriate land management agencies where rock art sites occur, such as the Park Service, Bureau of Land Management, Forest Service, or state parks. Always obtain permission from owners of private property before visiting sites on their land.

If you visit a rock art site, do so with the utmost care and respect. Behave as if you were in a sacred place. Tread lightly and do not touch the rock art— ever. The conservation adage "take nothing but pictures, leave nothing but footprints" is especially true when visiting rock art sites.

O sky, we say, upstanding father,
some speech must we offer;
this tight stone shall carry our voice.
And we harrow into it
the shapes of the spirit, the tall ones
whose heads shall mirror the great sun
at his clearest hour
upon our questions.
To this end
we have placed them in the high places,
watching
confronting the wind.[1]

—*Gordon Grant*,
The Shaman at Ending

3

Northern Sites

The following sections describe more than a hundred rock art sites in the upper Rio Grande region (Figure 2), beginning near the headwaters of the Rio Grande in Colorado and progressing downstream through New Mexico to south of El Paso, Texas. Included are descriptions of rock art sites in various Rio Grande tributary watersheds, adjacent river basins across the Continental Divide (San Juan, Pecos, Little Colorado), and enclosed basins (Tularosa, Salt, Mimbres) where significant concentrations of rock art are found within a reasonable distance of the Rio Grande. A brief description of each site is accompanied by illustrations of the more significant, representative, and interesting figures found there. In this book, it is not possible to present a comprehensive inventory from all the sites, a survey that would require many volumes to contain the thousands of images. Instead, images have been selected that not only represent the rock art style(s) of a site but also those that are visually and aesthetically interesting.

RIO GRANDE HEADWATERS AND THE SAN LUIS VALLEY, COLORADO

The headwaters area of the Rio Grande, which is high-elevation alpine terrain in the San Juan Mountains of Colorado, is apparently devoid of rock art. Although Indians visited many mountaintops for ceremonies, prayers, vision quests, and hunts, very little rock art is known to occur anywhere in the Southwest at elevations much above 8,000 feet.

Near Del Norte, Colorado, the Rio Grande leaves the San Juan Mountains and meanders across the broad, flat floor of the San Luis Valley before entering a spectacular gorge just north of the New Mexico State line. The steep, high mountains surrounding the valley produce a strong rain shadow effect, so that the valley floor receives as little as five inches of precipitation annually. However, the valley is provided with sufficient water from numerous streams derived from heavy snowpacks in the San Juan and Sangre de Cristo Mountains. Most of the area's rock art is located along these streams in the foothills and mouths of canyons on the west side of the San Luis Valley, as well as along the Rio Grande.

In addition to being fertile land, the San Luis Valley is one of the coldest places in the Rocky Mountains. Because it has a short growing season and winter temperatures can reach fifty below zero, the area was too cold for prehistoric maize cultivation. For this reason, the area was probably not attractive as a place of permanent residence to prehistoric natives, who nevertheless used it as a seasonal hunting ground. Thus, even though there are many Archaic Period archaeological sites in the San Luis Valley, it is doubtful there was any widespread formative-stage lifestyle, defined by the presence of agriculture and well-established village life. Instead, the region sustained an Archaic lifestyle throughout prehistoric time, although some formative-stage people occupied certain areas periodically for seasonal hunting and gathering. There is evidence of Anasazi contact in the San Luis Valley but no evidence of horticulture. Pueblo I–IV ceramic wares have been found along the Rio Grande in the southern part of the valley and at the Great Sand Dunes.[2] Further, it is known that nomadic Ute Indians controlled the valley for several centuries before it was settled by whites.

In the transition from a fertile valley used for prehistoric hunting and foraging to an agricultural area, the San Luis Valley and headwaters area of the Rio Grande have experienced some negative environmental consequences. Due to intensive water diversions for irrigation of crops, the flow of water in the Rio Grande is sometimes depleted in the valley. And although perennial creeks and tributary streams renew the flow in northern New Mexico, in southern New Mexico it is low at times.[3]

Until recently little was known about rock art in the San Luis Valley, but surveys have now documented more than fifty sites there.[4] These sites represent a range of styles, including Archaic (Oshara Tradition in this area), Anasazi, and historic Ute. Distributed in clusters on the western and southern margins of the valley (Figure 2), the greatest concentrations of panels are in the foothills of the San Juan Mountains to the north and south of Del Norte and along the Rio Grande north of the New Mexico State line. These locations provided outcrops of suitable rock surfaces and were also near diverse ecological zones that afforded good hunting and gathering opportunities. Another factor in the choice of these sites for rock art may have been the spectacular views

Figure 24. A panel of predominantly Ute pictographs, Carnero Creek in the San Luis Valley near La Garita, Colorado.

east across the valley to the snowcapped Sangre de Cristo Range and sacred Blanca Peak.

An estimated 10 to 20 percent of the rock art sites in the San Luis Valley are thought to be Ute in origin or to have some Ute elements.[5] Most of these sites, which include both petroglyphs and pictographs, are around La Garita or south of Del Norte. One of the best-known sites in the valley is a pictograph panel consisting of more than fifty elements at the mouth of Carnero Creek (Figure 24). On the National Register of Historic Places, this site is widely held to be of Ute origin. Much of it probably is Ute, but the red paintings seem to represent other styles as well, including some elements added by Hispanic sheepherders who camped nearby as late as the 1920s. Other images here may have been prehistoric designs that were repainted by Utes.[6]

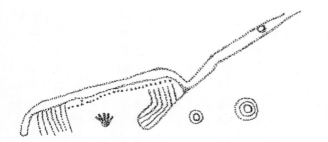

Figure 25.
Petroglyph of large, crane-like bird on the ceiling of a smoke-blackened cave on Dog Mountain, Rio Grande County, Colorado.

Among the more recent historic figures here are horses with riders, two Indians in canoes, a Celtic knot, a swastika design, five-pointed stars, and a heart with an arrow in it in the Valentine tradition. The elements thought to be older are circular sun symbol designs, rakes, snakes and other wavy lines, and a row of ducks.

In a small rock shelter across the canyon are more pictographs. At least four stick-figure flute players in black are superimposed on some faded red figures depicting a row of people holding hands. This type of stick-figure flute player without a humped back or phallus is rare and may be among the oldest flute player images in the Southwest— dating back to Basketmaker Anasazi times around A.D. 600.[7] Although the Carnero Creek pictograph site is the principal one in the valley, there are a number of others in foothill canyons to the south between Carnero Creek and Shaw Spring.

South of Del Norte on Limekiln Creek there is an interesting, enigmatic petroglyph site in a cave on Dog Mountain. Situated at an elevation of 9,000 feet, this is the highest known rock art in the San Luis Valley and in the Rio Grande watershed. Here a life-sized petroglyph of what has been interpreted as a stylized crane-like bird is pecked into the smoke-blackened ceiling of a small shelter (Figure 25). Many cranes and other migratory birds frequent the San

Luis Valley. This so-called "Big Bird" petroglyph depicts the bird as flying to the southeast, in the direction cranes fly today when winter is approaching. Perhaps this image symbolized migration to the people who made it, reminding them of the need to follow the birds south for the winter. Or perhaps it represented a shaman taking flight in the form of a crane.[8]

The style of the crane petroglyph is unusual, and its origin is unknown. Excavation of the cave floor by United States Forest Service archaeologists produced artifacts ranging from historic Ute items at the surface to late Archaic ones below.[9] Therefore, the crane petroglyph could be of Ute, Archaic, or perhaps ancestral Pueblo origin. Another possible clue was provided by a Hopi elder who visited the site and identified a checkerboard design pecked into the cave wall nearby as the pattern still worn on kilts by the Hopi Crane Clan.[10]

Several miles southeast of the crane petroglyph site is the greatest concentration of rock art in the valley, occurring in the drainages of Raton, Dry, Rock, and La Jara Creeks. All of these are petroglyph sites, which occur on patinated cliff faces of tuff, primarily in shallow canyons with perennial streams. These sites contain a mixture of rock art ranging from Archaic to historic Ute. In addition to representational styles, curvilinear abstract elements are present and rows of dots are a common motif. In fact, dot elements are common throughout the San Luis Valley and probably represent a counting or notation system. At some sites dot patterns based on the number twenty-eight have been observed, suggesting that some may have functioned to indicate the lunar cycle.[11]

A further connection with archaeoastronomy is implied by a site on the middle fork of Dry Creek that is believed to have been a type of prehistoric observatory or ceremonial location that focused on sacred Blanca Peak across the valley. (For a more complete description, see Chapter 5, "Sites with Public Access.") Petroglyphs in the vicinity consist of snake or lightning motifs, spirals, and anthropomorphs depicting male and female Utes in historic garb.

There are five known rock art sites on the south and middle forks of Dry Creek, and although most of them seem to have been sacred ritual sites, this has not prevented local vandals from desecrating them. Unfortunately, bullet holes and graffiti mar nearly every panel, even though these places are still impressive due to their astounding views and positions in the landscape.

The next drainage south contains a major petroglyph site that has attracted attention for centuries. So noteworthy was this site that early Spanish explorers called the place "Rio Piedra Pintada," or Painted Rock River, a misnomer since no paintings occur here, only petroglyphs. Today, Piedra Mountain towers over this extensive site, located along a sheltered cliff face where ancient people sought refuge for many generations. In addition to providing shelter and water, this locale was at the end of a major travel corridor across the mountains, now known as Elwood Pass. At this site, abstract designs, many of which incorporate lines of dots, are numerous and in many cases well patinated, suggesting considerable antiquity. Among the representational elements are human footprints and handprints, bear paws, bighorn sheep, and anthropomorphs in ceremonial activities, many holding staff-like objects or perhaps atlatls (Figure 26). If atlatls are indeed depicted here, their presence would date the images to Archaic or early Basketmaker times, prior to acquisition of the bow and arrow during the Basketmaker III era. A bison

Figure 26. Petroglyphs of anthropomorphs in ceremonial activities, Rio Piedra Pintada, Rio Grande County, Colorado.

Figure 27. Archaic petroglyph of bison pierced by atlatl spear, Rio Piedra Pintada, Rio Grande County, Colorado.

apparently pierced with an atlatl dart is shown in Figure 27. One of the most interesting images at this site is known locally as "The Healer" (Figure 28). This figure is depicted with very large hands, from which emanate an arching line of dots, suggesting power, magic, or shamanic healing.

Several panels of Ute origin here can be identified by the presence of horses. The best example, known as the "Ute Battle Scene," unfortunately fell from the cliff face in recent years and is now lying facedown on a large boulder beneath the cliff. This panel depicts several mounted warriors, a line of people holding hands, and a bow hunter stalking deer (Figure 29). Rather than a battle scene, it more likely portrays a series of events, a victory dance, or a celebration. Under the cliff in front of this panel, before it fell from the cliff, was found the skeleton of a Ute warrior who was wearing blue trade beads datable to the 1840s or 1850s.[12] Perhaps this petroglyph panel was created in association with his burial, or maybe he was buried there in honor of the petroglyphs or was their creator.

Only a few rock art sites are known on the east side of the San Luis Valley. It has been suggested

Figure 28. Petroglyph known as "The Healer," Rio Piedra Pintada, Rio Grande County, Colorado.

Figure 29.
Historic Ute petroglyph panel, Rio Piedra Pintada, Rio Grande County, Colorado.

that some rock alignments associated with petroglyphs near Smith Reservoir have archaeoastronomic significance. A few miles east of here is another petroglyph site on Trinchera Creek. Most of these images are abstract petroglyphs pecked on large basalt boulders, but a few representational elements such as tracks, snakes, and anthropomorphs are also present. The anthropomorph with antennae next to some plant forms (Figure 30), has been interpreted as representing the Ant People who helped the ancestral Tewas to survive when they lived underground in the Third World.[13] The Tewa origin myth tells of the ancestral people emerging from the earth through the *sipapu* (earth navel, place of emergence) near the Great Sand Dunes, which are located about twenty miles north of this petroglyph site.

The southernmost rock art sites in the San Luis Valley occur along both banks of the Rio Grande where it leaves Colorado and enters the basalt gorge that channels it for fifty miles through northern New Mexico. One such site, near the location where the Spanish explorer Don Diego de Vargas forded the Rio Grande in 1694, contains elements typical

Figure 30.
Petroglyphs on boulder, Trinchera Creek, Fort Garland, Colorado. The horned anthropomorph and plant-like shapes may be early Pueblo.

Figure 31.
Petroglyphs on
cliff adjacent to
Rio Grande,
Conejos County,
Colorado.

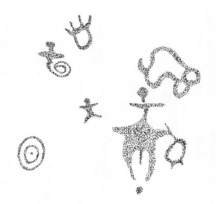

of early Anasazi Style (spirals, quadrupeds, stick figures) but is rapidly being destroyed by vandals.

Several other smaller sites are located along both banks of the river a few miles to the south of De Vargas's ford. These petroglyph panels contain Archaic elements like rakes, abstract symbols, and wavy lines, as well as early Anasazi elements such as a hunter and deer. The stylized images in Figure 31, also found at these sites, are located on low cliffs near the river in association with some small stone structures that may have functioned as shelters or blinds for hunting ducks and geese that frequent the river here. In addition, there are probably other sites hidden in the recesses and labyrinths of the Rio Grande Gorge.

RIO GRANDE GORGE, NEW MEXICO STATE LINE TO PILAR

For more than fifty miles, the Rio Grande Gorge cuts through a lava-covered plain in northern New Mexico, where dome-shaped volcanic mountains punctuate the landscape between the Sangre de Cristo Mountains on the east and the San Juan and

Tusas Mountains on the west. This section of the river was designated a Wild and Scenic River by Congress. White water rafting enthusiasts know it as the Taos Box Canyon, which at high flows contains some extremely challenging rapids. Since the river is entrenched as much as 1,000 feet deep here, access is limited to a few hiking trails from the canyon rim or down side canyons, and by one road and bridge that divides the upper and lower sections of the Taos Box. Although in prehistoric times access to the river was limited to only a few crude foot trails, the river in the gorge was nevertheless used by natives, as evidenced by a number of archaeological sites such as pit house ruins and rock art panels. Within the Rio Grande Gorge there are hundreds of square miles of rock surfaces suitable for petroglyphs; the entire gorge consists of darkly patinated basaltic lava in the form of vertical cliff faces and boulder-strewn slopes. There may be scores or hundreds of small unknown petroglyph sites scattered throughout this rough terrain. The few known sites occur at prominent locations such as confluences, old trail routes, and major springs, or in a few areas of federal land where archaeological surveys have been conducted.

Several small petroglyph sites are located at the bottom of the gorge adjacent to the Rio Grande in an area west of Questa, New Mexico. Major springs issue from the cliffs here, forming verdant oases that were no doubt sacred places as well as good hunting and foraging areas. Fertility themes are suggested by some of the images found on a large boulder at one of these sites. The rock is covered with figures presumed to be early Anasazi in origin, primarily quadrupeds (mostly game animals), snakes, vulva forms, and tracks of humans and animals, all dominated by two large anthropomorphs with exaggerated

Figure 32.
Petroglyphs on
fertility theme of
"Mother Rock,"
Rio Grande
Gorge, Taos
County, New
Mexico.

genitals or perhaps one is giving birth as shown in Figure 32. The leg of one of the figures is extended to become the tail of an animal, suggesting a possible "Mother of Game" context.[14] This site has been described as a fertility shrine or Mother Rock.[15] Such shrines often contain natural hollows suggestive of vulvas, or are incised with such symbols along with other fertility symbols. Couples desirous of children visited such sites with prayers and offerings. According to a custom of one pueblo, couples would scrape off a few grains of the rock and deposit them into ceremonial vessels or openings in the rock.[16]

Other nearby petroglyphs, also associated with springs in the gorge, are primarily images of game animals that would have been stalked by hunters in the gorge. One panel, the so-called "Big Elk Panel," shows a large, prominent animal surrounded by many smaller ones, perhaps offspring (Figure 33). It may depict an animal equivalent to the Mother of Game (perhaps the Deer Mother of Taos Pueblo).

A few miles downriver from these sites, the Red River enters the Rio Grande at a junction of spectac-

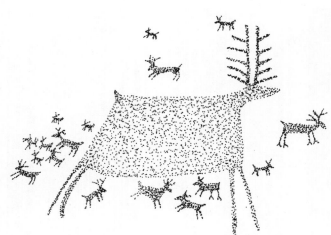

Figure 33.
The "Big Elk Panel," Rio Grande Gorge, Taos County, New Mexico.

ular, deep canyons. The Red River drains the highest country in New Mexico—the Wheeler Peak and Latir Peaks Wilderness Areas. This major tributary would seem to offer easy access to the Rio Grande, but its lower canyon is so rugged that travel is difficult and the confluence area is best reached by narrow foot trails that descend nearly 1,000 feet from the rim. This may explain the apparent absence of rock art in the Red River watershed.

Further down the gorge, approximately five miles downstream from the Red River confluence, several more petroglyph sites occur, both at the river's edge and up on the rim. A site at the mouth of a small perennial creek consists of repatinated Anasazi petroglyphs on large boulders that have been polished smooth by the flooding Rio Grande (Figure 34). Anthropomorphic figures, quadrupeds, birds, snakes, spirals, and animal tracks are present here. An interesting feature is a life-sized set of four bear paw tracks pecked into the tops of two large rocks, as if the bear was spanning them with front paws on one rock and rear paws on the other. Grandfather Bear,

Figure 34. Anasazi petroglyphs on a flood-polished boulder next to the Rio Grande, Taos County, New Mexico.

or Clumsy Foot, is greatly revered by Pueblo people, who believe he has supernatural powers—magical curing powers and the ability to counteract the power of witches.[17] Most Pueblo people do not eat bear meat, and killing the animal is taboo. If a bear is killed, a ceremony or dance is held to convert the

Figure 35. *Petroglyphs of an individual with a bear paw, Rio Grande Gorge, Taos County, New Mexico.*

bear's spirit into a friend and to free the slayer of evil influences.

The bear theme is continued at another petroglyph site three miles downstream. Here a large but headless bear is part of a panel of images located under a well-hidden rock shelter near the rim of the gorge. On the opposite side of the gorge at river's edge are a few petroglyphs of horned serpents and an anthropomorphic figure next to a bear paw (Figure 35).

Continuing downriver through the gorge, the next major tributary encountered is the Arroyo Hondo, which contains a number of significant rock art sites ranging in age from Archaic to historic. Scattered petroglyphs, mainly of Anasazi/Pueblo

Figure 36.
Petroglyphs at the
confluence of
Arroyo Hondo
and the Rio
Grande. The
horse and rider
are more recent
than the other
designs and are
probably of
Apache or Navajo
origin. Rio
Grande Gorge,
Taos County, New
Mexico.
Photograph by
Jim Duffield.

Figure 37.
Archaic
petroglyphs,
Arroyo Hondo,
Taos County,
New Mexico.

origin, are found on boulders and cliff faces near the confluence. A striking design of parallel lines next to a more recent image of a horse and rider (probably Apache or Navajo) overlooks this important confluence (Figure 36). Elsewhere in the Arroyo Hondo drainage there are a number of Archaic petroglyph sites where abstract designs are pecked on boulders (Figure 37).

A local hot spring at the edge of the Rio Grande apparently provided healing and solace to a spectrum of humanity over the years as evidenced by the nearby rock art (Figure 38). At this site a petroglyph panel features a large, horned anthropomorph with shield (a shaman?), whose right arm and hand appear to be part of a small animal clinging to his chest (the shaman's spirit helper?).

Figure 38.
Petroglyphs, Rio Grande Gorge, Taos County, New Mexico. (Redrawn from the files of the Taos BLM office.)

As the Rio Grande continues its journey south, it is still deep within an inaccessible gorge. Although the city of Taos and ancient Taos Pueblo are only eight to ten miles to the east, the Rio Grande is essentially isolated in another world until the confluence with the Rio Pueblo de Taos. This was an important prehistoric corridor from the Rio Grande to the Taos Plateau and the mountains beyond. As expected, there are significant concentrations of rock art here, both up the Rio Pueblo de Taos and downstream along the Rio Grande Gorge. Petroglyphs of Pueblo origin occur on boulders north of the confluence, where stylized anthropomorphs and many bird tracks are depicted. The female anthropomorph in Figure 39 may represent the fertility deity Mother of Game, or Deer Mother. The two disks next to her, and the rigidly stylized posture, are similar to the Mother of Game images documented in the Little Colorado River drainage of eastern Arizona.[18] South of the confluence are abstract petroglyphs that may be Archaic, as well as others of Pueblo origin in the Rio Grande Style. Among the figures at this location are bison, concentric circles, men holding birds and snakes, and masks, which are rare in Rio Grande Style rock art of the Northern Tiwa province.

The Rio Pueblo de Taos originates in the high

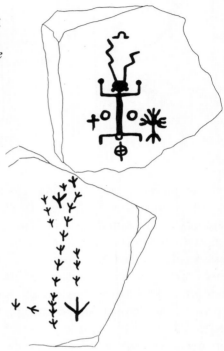

Figure 39. Anasazi
petroglyphs of bird
tracks and a possible
Mother of Game
fertility deity, Rio
Grande Gorge,
Taos County,
New Mexico.

Figure 40.
Anasazi
petroglyphs in
Lower Taos
Canyon,
Taos County,
New Mexico.

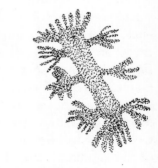

mountains behind Taos and flows perennially through the center of Taos Pueblo and eventually into the rocky Lower Taos Canyon to the Rio Grande. A number of rock art sites occur within its watershed in the vicinity of Taos. Examples are shown in Figures 40 and 41. The Arroyo Seco, a small but perennial tributary to the Lower Taos Canyon, contains several small petroglyph sites where prehistoric Pueblo rock art is mixed with historic Spanish images such as the intricate depiction of a mission church in Figure 42.

From the confluence of Rio Pueblo de Taos downstream to the village of Pilar, the Rio Grande Gorge is administered by the United States Bureau of Land Management as the Orilla Verde Recreation Area (formerly known as the Rio Grande Gorge State Park). Archaeological surveys have documented more than eighty rock art sites throughout this rugged terrain of broken volcanic rock. The river here is at an elevation of about 6,000 feet, but the canyon walls rise another 800 feet to the canyon rim. Rock art styles include Archaic, early Anasazi, Rio Grande, Athabascan, and other historic. Although no major pueblos are known to have existed in the immediate area, numerous small pit house ruins as

Figure 41.
Petroglyph panel
with flute player,
elk, and
anthropomorphs,
Rio Pueblo de
Taos, Taos
County, New
Mexico. (After a
sketch by Paul
Williams, BLM.)

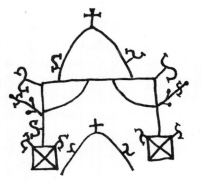

Figure 42.
Historic Spanish
petroglyph of
mission church,
Arroyo Seco, Taos
County, New
Mexico.

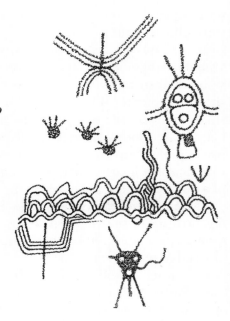

Figure 43.
A composite of Archaic and Pueblo petroglyphs, Rio Grande Gorge, Taos County, New Mexico. (Drawings by Lay Powell for the BLM.)

Figure 44.
Petroglyph of warrior with weapon, shield, and snake image on his chest, Rio Grande Gorge, Taos County, New Mexico.

well as shrines and other stone structures have been discovered. Petroglyph sites are concentrated above and below the confluence of the Rio Grande and the Rio Pueblo de Taos. Here petroglyphs of Archaic and Anasazi origin are found (Figure 43). At one site where there are two adjacent panels (one Archaic, the other Pueblo), archaeological investigations provided evidence to support the rock art style assignments.[19] The rock art here may have been primarily for ceremonial purposes since it is located on boulders along a terrace formation between vertical escarpments high above the river, with exceptional views of the surrounding canyons and mountains. On a boulder near the Rio Grande is a single imposing warrior with weapons in hand and a snake image on his body (Figure 44).

Another nearby site, probably also primarily ceremonial in nature, occurs in a spectacular setting in which a small rocky canyon ends abruptly at the top of a high cliff where there is a waterfall during wet weather. The petroglyphs here seem to be mostly Archaic; they include abstract symbols for rain, rows of dots, meandering lines, grids, bird tracks, and a few miscellaneous symbols (Plate 2). The stunning views from this location, along with some bedrock water holes, are undoubtedly reasons why the site was seen as powerful or sacred. This place would also have made a good jump site for driving game animals over the cliff, although there is currently no evidence to support such an interpretation.

A couple miles downstream from the confluence of the Rio Grande and the Rio Pueblo de Taos a major side canyon enters from the north—the Arroyo Aguaje de la Petaca. This twelve-mile-long canyon was probably another important corridor for prehistoric travel and hunting, allowing access to the plateau country to the north, as well as providing a route west into the watershed of the Rio Ojo Caliente (Hot Spring River), where many large pueblos were located. Petroglyph sites occur at the mouth of Petaca Canyon (Figure 45), scattered throughout its length, and up near the head of its drainage area. The petroglyphs on top of the large boulder shown in Figure 45 have been previously described as Hispanic Christian crosses, but they have small appendages on their bottoms, suggesting they may instead be stylized Pueblo symbols such as dragonflies or stick-figure anthropomorphs. Further, these petroglyphs seem to have an equal degree of patination, indicating they are all of similar origin. The majority of the other rock art sites in Petaca Canyon exhibit Anasazi/Pueblo Style elements.

Springs flow from the lava escarpments at several places along a major geologic fault that traverses the area, forming small riparian oases of grass, wil-

*Figure 45.
Petroglyphs on
top of a large
boulder at the
mouth of Petaca
Canyon, Rio
Grande Gorge,
Taos County,
New Mexico.*

lows, and cottonwood trees, surrounded by an almost lunar landscape of jagged lava rocks. Near most of these springs there is some rock art. Caves formed between some of the larger talus boulders often contain rock art and in some cases human remains.[20] At one such location known as "The Houses of the Holy," a series of five entrances lead to interconnected small chambers. These caves were possibly seen as entrances to the underworld, and are marked with petroglyphs such as handprints,

Figure 46.
Pueblo petroglyphs, Rio Grande Gorge near Velarde, Rio Arriba County, New Mexico.

footprints, and snakes; other elements present at these cave entrances are rows of dots, cupules, and animal tracks. Such sites were obviously sacred and served ceremonial functions.

Below Pilar, the Rio Grande Gorge becomes wider, forming a series of bench-like terraces and cliffs further away from the river. The terrain is still very rugged and covered with black basalt rock that offers almost unlimited potential for petroglyph surfaces. Unfortunately, when the highway here was originally constructed early in the century destruction of rock art occurred along the river. Then later, in the early 1990s, boulders (some as large as houses) fell from the steep slopes onto the highway next to the river, prompting the state to construct miles of ugly metal netting and pylons and further damaging a number of petroglyphs when concrete was splashed on the rocks. More petroglyphs occur on the slope and benches above the road, including a large rock covered with bird tracks and snakes, as well as other depictions of anthropomorphs, animals, handprints and footprints, dragonflies, and shields (Figure 46).

Further down the Rio Grande near the village of Rinconada are some petroglyphs located near a spring several miles east of the river. Because of the spring and the gentler topography to the east, this

Figure 47.
Petroglyph of
horse and rider,
probably
Athabascan
(Apache or
Navajo), Rio
Grande near
Rinconada, Taos
County,
New Mexico.

area is part of an old trail that once connected the Rio Grande to Picuris Pueblo and a pass across the Sangre de Cristo Mountains. Here the rock art is a combination of Pueblo and Athabascan (probably Apache) styles. On a large boulder are petroglyphs of horses with riders carrying shields and weapons and wearing hats (Figure 47), along with other anthropomorphs (one seemingly a priest wearing a frock or cape), dragonflies, and lizard-man symbols.

ESPAÑOLA VALLEY, BLACK MESA, AND RIO CHAMA

Continuing down the Rio Grande, petroglyphs occur near Embudo and on terraces above the river at the south end of La Mesita, close to where the river leaves the gorge and flows out onto the broad

Figure 48. Northern Tewa Rio Grande Style petroglyph of a ceremonial figure with the tail and head of a bird (turkey?) and carrying a shield and knife. Another rock nearby is covered with bird tracks (see Figure 49). Rio Grande at Black Mesa, Rio Arriba County, New Mexico.

Española Valley near Velarde. La Mesita was among the first rock art sites professionally described in New Mexico in a 1938 study.[21] Boulders here are inscribed with Pueblo imagery, including shields, masks, anthropomorphs, quadrupeds, handprints, turtles, dragonflies, and snakes. Shrines and other small stone structures in the area suggest that this was a ceremonial site.

As the Rio Grande continues southward across the historic Española Valley (site of San Gabriel, the first European settlement in the American interior, and the first Spanish "capital" in the territory of New Mexico, at commandeered portions of the San Juan Pueblo), it is flanked on the west by the imposing, lava-covered Black Mesa for over fourteen miles. This is one of several "Black Mesas" along the Rio Grande, most of which have rock art since their dark basalt rocks make excellent surfaces for rock art. At this Black Mesa, significant rock art sites occur along the eastern flank facing the Rio Grande and along the southern tip facing the Rio Chama and Rio Ojo Caliente. Other sites have been reported near the northeastern tip of Black Mesa but have not been documented.[22] There are signs of simple pit houses and prehistoric agricultural fields in the area of the rock art, but no large pueblo ruins are known.

The petroglyphs at these sites are typical of Rio Grande Style in the Northern Tewa province, which dominates the territory from Santa Fe to the Rio Grande Gorge and the Rio Chama Valley (Figure 19). Ceremonial figures (Figures 48 and 49), animals, cloud terraces, flute players and other fertility motifs, and horned serpents (Figure 50) are common elements. Figure 48 seems to depict a kachina dancer dressed as a bird, perhaps a turkey. Turkeys were domesticated by the Anasazis over a thousand years ago, although some researchers believe they

Figure 49.
Rio Grande Style petroglyphs of a ceremonial figure surrounded by bird (turkey?) tracks, Rio Grande at Black Mesa, Rio Arriba County, New Mexico.

Figure 50.
Rio Grande Style petroglyph of a horned serpent (Awanyu). This image is unusually large and bold in its execution. When this photo was taken in 1993, earth-moving equipment was being used in an adjacent rock quarry within 100 yards of the petroglyphs. Black Mesa, Rio Arriba County, New Mexico.

were not eaten because they were sometimes buried with mortuary offerings and corn. However, Spanish records from the 1500s mention large numbers of turkeys kept in pueblos and given to them for food, as well as Pueblo people wearing blankets and capes of turkey feathers.[23] Among the Pueblos, turkey feathers are used for prayer sticks and ceremonial costumes; and in Pueblo animal dances the woman who portrays the symbolic Mother of Game is called Turkey. At Cochiti Pueblo turkey feathers were buried on All Soul's Day so the dead could wear them in their dances, and at Zia the burial ceremony

Figure 51. *Rio Grande Style petroglyph of a horned, life-sized anthropomorph in an upside-down position, possibly indicating death or a mythological event. Black Mesa, Rio Arriba County, New Mexico.*

involves making turkey tracks beside roadrunner tracks.[24] The petroglyphs in Figure 49 may depict turkey tracks around a ceremonial figure.

One of the more impressive petroglyphs at this site is a life-sized, horned anthropomorph depicted upside down on a large boulder (Figure 51). Inverted human figures have been interpreted as representing death, or perhaps the metaphorical death of the shaman's trance state. Another possible explanation for this figure is that it portrays a supernatural or mythological event since the rays emanating from the figure's head suggest some extraordinary activity; this panel is known by the telling name "man who fell from the sky."

Kachina masks occur at Black Mesa but are less common than at Rio Grande Style sites further south. Elaborate shields and other geometric motifs

Figure 52.
Rio Grande Style petroglyph of a shield design, on southwestern flank of Black Mesa near Chamita, Rio Arriba County, New Mexico.

Figure 53.
Petroglyphs of oddly-shaped flute players, Black Mesa, Rio Arriba County, New Mexico.

Figure 54.
Petroglyph of a ceremonial figure, probably representing a Deer Dancer. Black Mesa, Rio Arriba County, New Mexico.

are also found in the Black Mesa area (Figure 52). The depictions of flute players here are especially creative, as many are rendered in the guise of animals, insects, or supernaturals (Figure 53).[25] The image in Figure 54 probably represents a participant in a ceremonial activity such as the Deer Dance, which is still performed at local pueblos. Deer Dancers wear antlers on their heads and carry sticks to simulate walking on four legs. Other anthropomorphic figures in the Black Mesa area are shown in Figure 55.

The southern tip of Black Mesa overlooks two major confluences. One is the confluence of the Rio Chama with the Rio Grande. The Rio Chama extends north for 140 miles, crossing the Colorado border and draining a watershed of more than 3,000 square miles. The other nearby confluence is that of the Rio Ojo Caliente and the Rio Chama. The Rio Ojo Caliente also flows from the north, draining the Tusas Mountains. Its fertile lower valley once supported up to seven major pueblos, most of which were in the vicinity of the hot springs that are now commercially developed as a resort. Historically, hot springs were also greatly appreciated by native peoples. Many cultures valued their healing properties and traditionally considered such places sacred and as neutral territory to be enjoyed by all, even warring groups.[26] Indians believed that hot springs were inhabited by spirits, not only because of the heat but also because of the bubbles and rippling of the surface caused by the exhalation of the spirits. Because of this great medicine, paints made with earth pigments from hot spings were imbued with supernatural power. Petroglyphs are pecked into the hard metamorphic rocks exposed along the Rio Ojo Caliente near the ruin of Hupovi Pueblo. Here there are many images of Awanyus (Figures 56 and 57), as well as anthropomorphs, circle motifs, and shields.

Figure 55.
The author's shadow plays with an anthropomorphic figure on a boulder at Black Mesa near Chamita, Rio Arriba County, New Mexico.

Along the middle Rio Chama and its tributaries between Española and Abiquiú, there are twenty-one large pueblo ruins. These Biscuit Ware Pueblos, named for their distinctive, thick pottery, are ancestral to the Tewa-speaking people of the northern Rio Grande. The largest contained between 300 and 2,000 rooms and were built as high as four stories. The population in this area was probably greater around A.D. 1400 than it is today. One of the more dramatically sited of these pueblos had the poetic name Tsipinguinge (House of the Flaking Stone Mountain), which refers to the nearby Cerro Pedernal, a distinctive peak where flint was quarried

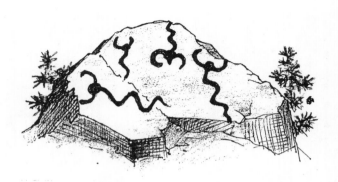

Figure 56.
*Petroglyphs of the
horned serpent
Awanyu, Hupovi
Pueblo ruin, Rio
Ojo Caliente, Rio
Arriba County,
New Mexico.
(Drawing by Lay
Powell for the
BLM.)*

for stone tools. A few minor petroglyphs can still be
discerned here in the cliff walls of easily eroded tuff
(volcanic ash).

Near the confluence of the Rio Chama and
Canones Creek, above the village of Abiquiú, lies an
outstanding petroglyph panel that was once known
as the "Abiquiú Pictures"—before this site was
destroyed by the construction of the Abiquiú Dam
along with the associated ruins of Riana Pueblo.

Figure 57.
*Composite
drawing of
petroglyphs near
Hupovi Pueblo
ruin, Rio Ojo
Caliente, Rio
Arriba County,
New Mexico.
(After drawings
by Lay Powell for
the BLM.)*

Figure 58.
A portion of the
petroglyph panel
on the Rio Chama
that was
destroyed by
construction of
the Abiquiú
Reservoir. (After
Hibben 1937.)

Unfortunately, this was not the only rock art site destroyed by dam building in New Mexico. The massive Cochiti Dam on the Rio Grande ruined thousands of petroglyphs, and the Navajo Dam on the San Juan River also flooded many outstanding sites. Numerous other sites have been similarly destroyed throughout the West.

Excavation of the Riana Pueblo site in the 1930s showed that it was destroyed by fire around A.D. 1348. The presence of charred artifacts and human skeletons, crushed by falling roof beams, indicated destruction by invading enemies.[27] Petroglyphs were located on a sandstone cliff beneath the terrace on which Riana Pueblo was situated. The drawing in Figure 58 is made from a 1936 photograph that shows many bold, solidly-pecked designs typical of Anasazi rock art, such as flute players, birds, anthropomorphs, shields, snakes, and corn plants, as well as some historic images of Christian crosses.

At many rock art sites in the upper Rio Grande region, Christian crosses have been added to the prehistoric images; these are often interpreted as Spanish/Catholic attempts to eradicate the "evil magic" of the "pagan images" that threatened the balance of order and the holy faith of New Mexico. One such effort in the Abiquiú area is documented in the following excerpt from Spanish colonial records for June 1763:

> *I went to the said district with the intention of destroying and annihilating, in as much as possible, the adoration sites (adoratorios), and places where they might have been worshiping; or places where detestable idolatry, superstitions, or vain observations might be committed presently. Having been informed that on the south side of this Pueblo, a distance of about two thousand varas, there was a large, ancient stone idol with drawings that they called the Strong Lion (el Leon Fuerte) to which …the native(s) of this territory offered…sacrifices …I reconnoitered everything and found said stone with the aforementioned drawings; and while destroying everything at the site, I found some very old human bones….*
>
> *I ordered the removal of said stone from its center, the erasure of the drawings, and the place exorcised by the Reverend Padre Minister (Friar Juan Jose Toledo). Fastening a holy cross at this place I moved on to the northern part of the Pueblo, guided by the aforementioned Joachin, where on the side of a cliff were drawn the figures which appeared on the margin of my previous dilijencia. They were erased and destroyed by me; and in the surroundings we drew crosses and the place was exorcised by the Reverend Padre Minister. And a holy cross was hoisted in the most eminent part of the site.*
>
> > **Carlos Fernandez**
> > **Juan Pablo Martic**
> > **Jso Lorenso Baldes**
> > **Julo Baldes**[28]

There is a record of another rock art site north of Abiquiú, in the area west of present-day Ghost Ranch, that was destroyed in the 1930s during road construction.[29] It was described in *New Mexico Magazine* as follows:

> *...a panel of apparently Comanche authorship was discovered showing a raid upon the Pueblos by a band of Comanches on horseback, and shooting guns. This places the date as sometime after the coming of the Spaniards, for before their advent firearms were unknown among the Indians. There are nearly a dozen Comanches in feathered war bonnets mounted on pudgy ponies, attacking a Pueblo man who is running away as fast as possible, a Pueblo woman with bow and arrow is bravely trying to defend her man.... I wonder if this might not be one of the incidents commemorated in the Pueblo Women's dance, which shows the time the women defended their pueblo when attacked by Plains Indians while their own men were busy on the hunt or in the field? This is one of the very interesting historical dances of the Pueblos. The Plains Indians were always more realistic in their picture writings than were the cliff dwellers and the Pueblos.[30]*

Apparently this fascinating battle scene was never photographed or sketched before it was destroyed. Anthropologist E. B. Renaud remarks on his futile search for it in 1938 by saying: "The historic panel and other pictures had all been the victims of the building of the new branch of the road, clipping over a certain distance [of] the cliff to make room for the highway between it and the creek. One of the most significant petroglyphs of New Mexico is gone forever, entirely destroyed by the inexorable march of progress!"[31]

JEMEZ MOUNTAINS, PAJARITO PLATEAU, AND WHITE ROCK CANYON

Returning to the Rio Grande at Española, the river is flanked on the west by the Jemez Mountains and Pajarito Plateau for the next fifty miles. This area was the territory of the Northern Tewa Pueblos from about Velarde to Cochiti, and the Keresan Pueblos from Cochiti to south of Bernalillo (Figure 19). South of Española the river passes another Black Mesa, where scattered Rio Grande Style petroglyph sites occur. Below the Otowi Bridge, where the road to Los Alamos crosses the Rio Grande, the river flows through another deep, spectacular gorge—White Rock Canyon. Named for the town of White Rock, the designation is a misnomer since the entire canyon is black as a result of the geologically recent lava flows from volcanic eruptions in the Jemez Mountains. There are many rock art sites in White Rock Canyon (more than 2,000 petroglyphs have been recorded here), as well as in the tributary canyons that enter it from the deeply dissected Pajarito Plateau to the west.[32] This area was placed on the National Register of Historic Places in 1990 with the establishment of

Figure 59.
Petroglyph of people under a blanket-like design, White Rock Canyon, Santa Fe County, New Mexico.

the White Rock Archeological District. In this canyon is the unusual and whimsical petroglyph design that seems to portray people under a blanket (Figure 59)—with five heads (three males and two females?) but only four sets of legs emerging from the blanket. A fertility theme is evident in the petroglyph panel carved into a smoke-blackened cave in a Pajarito Plateau canyon wall (Figure 60). Here a flute player, along with other beings, accompanies two individuals meant to portray either a birth or coitus scene. A stunning example of ceremonial art, in Cave Kiva near Los Alamos, shows a shield figure and horned serpent, flute player, and an arrow-swallower with an apparent assailant (Figure 61). Many other examples of cave art from the smoke-blackened and mud-plastered walls of cavates in the Pajarito area were recorded in a 1917 study.[33] Unfortunately, since these sites are extremely fragile and subject to destruction by erosion and vandalism, many examples recorded at the turn of the century no longer exist.

The sites in White Rock Canyon consist of petroglyphs pecked into basalt boulders, whereas those in the tributary canyons and on mesatops of the Pajarito Plateau are pecked or incised into the softer tuff (volcanic ash) exposed there, or in some cases, are in smoke-blackened ceremonial chambers and living quarters (cavates) that were dug into the tuff (Figures 7, 60, and 61). The Pajarito Plateau is strewn with hundreds of pueblo ruins, including many large Pueblo IV villages such as Tsankawi, Otowi, Tsirige, and Puyé (see Chapter 5, "Sites with Public Access," for more on the rock art at Tsankawi and Puyé). Many such prehistoric sites are preserved in Bandelier National Monument and Santa Fe National Forest, while others are now within the controlled boundaries of the United States

Figure 60.
Petroglyphs
carved into the
smoke-blackened
wall of a cave
room, showing a
humpbacked flute
player with a
fertility scene,
Pajarito Plateau,
Los Alamos
County,
New Mexico.

Figure 61.
(Page 90-91)
Petroglyphs
carved into
the smoke-
blackened wall of
ceremonial Cave
Kiva, Pajarito
Plateau, Los
Alamos County,
New Mexico.

Department of Energy's Los Alamos National Laboratory. The juxtaposition of so many ancient and sacred sites with the high-tech trappings of nuclear weapons research and development is ironic indeed. The once-sacred springs that flow from the canyon walls are now monitored for evidence of radioactive contamination of the aquifer beneath Los Alamos (see Chapter 5, "Sites with Public Access," for more information on rock art in White Rock Canyon).

At Bandelier National Monument near Los Alamos, there are many Rio Grande Style petroglyphs associated with ruins in Frijoles Canyon beyond the visitor center, as well as at the detached unit of the monument known as Tsankawi (see Chapter 5, "Sites with Public Access," for more information on Bandelier). Although pictograph sites are fairly rare in the White Rock Canyon and Pajarito Plateau area, deep within the backcountry wilderness of Bandelier National Monument there is a well-preserved, painted cave site where colorful pictographs adorn the wall of a large rock shelter (Figure 62). Another much smaller painted cave is found in a side canyon near the mouth of White Rock Canyon (Plate 3). Here there are square-bodied

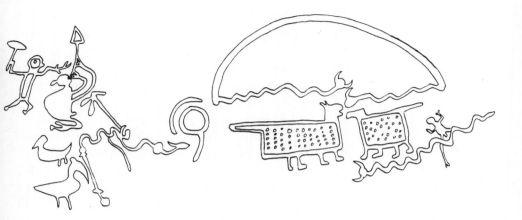

ceremonial anthropomorphs in shades of yellow, red, and white, along with snakes and other beings in red.

The free-flowing Rio Grande emerges from White Rock Canyon to be impounded by Cochiti Dam, one of the world's largest earthen dams, built by the federal government on Cochiti Pueblo lands despite sixteen years of resistance. Seepage from the miles-long earthen dam has caused 800 acres of the pueblo's once-fertile farmland below the dam to become waterlogged.[34] A further effect of this reservoir was to inundate hundreds of rock art sites under tons of mud and water. Archaeologists were given only a few weeks to make a hurried survey of these sites before the reservoir was completed in 1966.[35]

Figure 62. Partial view of the pictographs in Painted Cave, Bandelier National Monument. The pictographs, done mostly in red and white, depict a koshare (clown figure) on the left, with two kachina masks, a horned serpent, handprints, a spiral, and an anthropomorph.

Figure 63.
A composite drawing showing some of the Keresan petroglyphs that were destroyed by the Cochiti Reservoir, Sandoval County, New Mexico. (After Schaafsma 1980.)

Most of the petroglyphs were located on boulder-strewn terraces on the west side of the river along an old trail that ran from Cochiti Pueblo to Frijoles Canyon, now in Bandelier National Monument, although one site was at Cochiti Springs at the mouth of the Santa Fe River. In a subsequent protest to these lost sites, an artist photographed the reservoir from various angles and printed the New Mexico Laboratory of Anthropology survey numbers of the destroyed rock art sites on top of the watery landscapes.[36] A few examples of ruined rock art sites are shown in Figure 63. Some historical records of various activities by the Cochitis in lower White Rock Canyon help explain why there was so much rock art concentrated there.[37] Adolph Bandelier mentioned that the area was used formerly by Cochitis for communal fishing and hunting, and horses were herded in Frijoles Canyon. This part of the river was also used for ceremonial purposes. For empowerment,

warriors went at night to a location called Muskrat House. Participants in kachina ceremonies and drummers praying for power and success also retreated to specific locations in White Rock Canyon. Most of the rock art in this area is relatively recent, dating from the Pueblo IV period to historical times.

SANTA FE RIVER CANYON

The first perennial tributary to the Rio Grande below Cochiti Dam is the Santa Fe River, which enters from the east a few miles downstream. To say that today's Santa Fe River flows perennially into the Rio Grande is misleading; there is flow, but it consists entirely of treated sewage from Santa Fe's wastewater treatment plant. Above the treatment plant, the Santa Fe River no longer flows between Santa Fe and the plant except after storms—its channel only a vestige of what it must have once been. In place of a diverse riparian ecosystem filled with trees, birds, fish, and animals there is now a barren arroyo with eroding banks.[38]

By contrast, in prehistoric times the entire Santa Fe River was a healthy environment and also served as a major passageway from the Rio Grande into the mountains above present-day Santa Fe. The Spanish conquistador Don Diego de Vargas camped here in 1693, writing in his journal that the area along the river was so densely wooded that the stars were obscured.[39] When the Spanish arrived in the area, there were a number of Keresan pueblos thriving in its watershed, including one at the site of Santa Fe's present-day plaza. There are significant concentrations of Rio Grande Style petroglyphs along the lower fifteen miles of the Santa Fe River, from near its confluence with the Rio Grande (where dam

Figure 64.
*Keresan Pueblo
Rio Grande Style
petroglyph from
La Bajada
escarpment,
Santa Fe County,
New Mexico,
showing a phallic
figure with a
spiral over
the heart.*

Figure 65.
*Keresan Pueblo
Rio Grande Style
petroglyph from
La Bajada
escarpment,
Santa Fe County,
New Mexico,
showing two
anthropomorphs
sharing the
same head.*

construction destroyed some sites) to the southwestern edge of Santa Fe.

Seven miles of the Santa Fe River Canyon and 3,556 acres of public land (BLM) are administered as the La Cienega Area of Critical Environmental Concern (ACEC).[40] The area contains nationally significant cultural resources, including more than 4,000 petroglyphs and associated pueblo ruins and other prehistoric sites, dating from about A.D. 700 to the historic period.

About seven miles up the Santa Fe River from the confluence is a steep, lava-capped escarpment known as La Bajada (The Descent). For many travelers the climb up La Bajada represents the point where one leaves the Chihuahuan Desert and enters northern New Mexico—the Rio Arriba. In prehistoric times, foot travelers could walk up the Santa Fe River through the narrow canyon it has cut through La Bajada, or clamber up the escarpment through basalt boulder fields on an old Indian trail to the mesatop. During the Spanish colonial period, El Camino Real (The Royal Road) was built through the Santa Fe River Canyon, linking Santo Domingo Pueblo on the Rio Grande to the Santa Fe area. Petroglyphs are found along the old Indian trail route (Figure 64) and in the canyon along the river (Figure 65).

Figure 66.
Petroglyph of an individual with headdress holding a curved stick or ceremonial objects, Santa Fe River Canyon at La Bajada, Santa Fe County, New Mexico.

For the past forty years, travelers venturing into the mouth of the Santa Fe River Canyon at La Bajada encountered rock art in a devastated landscape that included an open-pit mine filled with radioactive water—the result of a short-lived uranium mining operation on public land here in the 1950s, which probably destroyed a number of petroglyphs.[41] Some of the petroglyphs near the old uranium mine appear to be Archaic Desert Abstract Style, but the majority are Rio Grande Style (Figure 66).

Images of birds are very common symbols in the rock art of the Santa Fe River Canyon, perhaps indicating a more suitable riparian environment once existed here to provide diverse bird habitat (Figure 67). The BLM has stated that the current riparian area in the Santa Fe River is in a nonfunctional condition. The Santa Fe River and La Cienega Creek are two of the few permanent streams in the area, both containing critical riparian habitat.[42] La Cienega translates into English as "the marsh," and the abundant water in such an arid environment attracts a great variety of wildlife, especially bird species.

Many other petroglyphs, some quite unusual, are found on boulders and cliff faces near the Santa Fe River all along the five-mile canyon. The cliff-face

Figure 67. *Composite drawing illustrating various bird design petroglyphs in the lower Santa Fe River Canyon, Santa Fe County, New Mexico.*

Figure 68. *Rio Grande Style petroglyphs on a cliff face, Santa Fe River Canyon, Santa Fe County, New Mexico.*

petroglyph panel in Figure 68 shows a prominent anthropomorph with head appendages and a sash around the waist, along with birds and snakes. A number of historic petroglyphs also occur here, including a figure riding a horse and wearing a Spanish colonial-style hat (Figure 69).

The striking design in Figure 70 represents a ritual arrangement of arrows or spears with hourglass shapes attached—often a symbol for war.[43] The animal portrayed in Figure 71 is probably the wood rat (Neotoma), which was not only a food source for some Pueblo people but also served as a metaphor for certain mother-being concepts in Keresan mythology.[44] This one, which has front feet cloven like game animals and rear feet like a rodent, seems to stand

Figure 69.
Historic petroglyph of a horse and rider with Spanish colonial-style hat, Santa Fe River Canyon, Santa Fe County, New Mexico. (Drawing courtesy of the Taos BLM Office.)

Figure 70.
Petroglyphs showing a ritual arrangement of arrows or spears with hourglass-shaped war symbols on the shafts, Santa Fe River Canyon, Santa Fe County, New Mexico.

Figure 71. *Rio Grande Style (Keresan) petroglyph depicting a wood rat or its metaphorical analogue in Keresan Pueblo mythology, Santa Fe River Canyon, Santa Fe County, New Mexico.*

Figure 72.
Rio Grande Style (Keresan) petroglyph depicting a copulation scene, Santa Fe River Canyon, Santa Fe County, New Mexico.

over or protect some smaller animals, perhaps offspring. A fertility context is evident in a nearby petroglyph on a boulder where a copulating couple is depicted (Figure 72). Fecundity and moisture themes are also expressed on the petroglyph panel next to the river, where game animals and rain images are prevalent in relation to human handprints (Figure 73).

Similarly, rain and fertility kachinas are typical of petroglyphs at a small site located in a tributary side canyon near the base of Tetilla Peak (Figure 74)—an isolated peak rising from the mesatop above the Santa Fe River Canyon. With commanding views up and down the Rio Grande Valley, Tetilla Peak was probably a powerful place to the Pueblo people, who left a few petroglyphs at its summit as evidence of their presence.

Near the upper end of the Santa Fe River

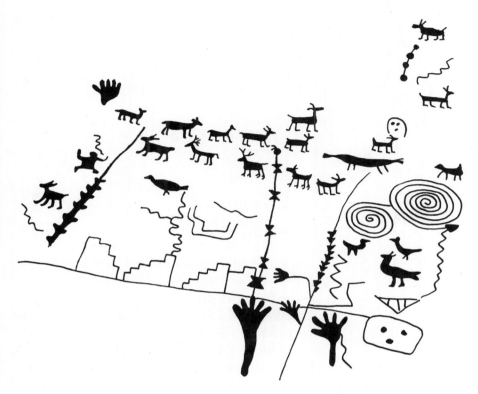

Figure 73.
*Rio Grande Style
(Keresan)
petroglyph panel
featuring game
animals and rain
symbols, Santa Fe
River Canyon,
Santa Fe County,
New Mexico.*

Canyon, at La Cienega and La Cieneguilla, some major concentrations of petroglyphs decorate the edges of escarpments formed by lava flows. Abundant meadows and springs, as well as the Santa Fe River, supported several pueblos in this area. Like those at other sites along the Santa Fe River, the petroglyphs here are primarily Rio Grande Style. In addition to the numerous bird depictions mentioned previously, another characteristic of these sites is a proliferation of flute player images. There are probably in excess of a hundred images of this important Kokopelli figure recorded here—depicted with great diversity and creativity.[45]

Figure 75.
Petroglyph of a humpbacked, phallic flute player with two females, upper Santa Fe River Canyon, Santa Fe County, New Mexico.

Fertility and the flute player's role in reproduction were undoubtedly of great importance to the people who created the rock art at these sites. In fact, the figure of Kokopelli is shown here in explicit sexual attitudes a number of times with females, who can be identified, if not by their genitalia or breasts, by the distinctive hair whorls on the sides of their head (the traditional squash blossom style worn by Pueblo maidens). Figure 75 shows a slender, humpbacked, phallic flute player standing between two females, and Figure 76 shows a recumbent flute player having sex with a female, alongside birds sitting in plants or trees. The flute player character is

Figure 74.
Petroglyphs of kachina masks with plants and rain symbols, Las Aguajes, Santa Fe County, New Mexico.

Figure 76.
Petroglyph of a humpbacked, phallic flute player with female, birds, and plants, upper Santa Fe River Canyon, Santa Fe County, New Mexico.

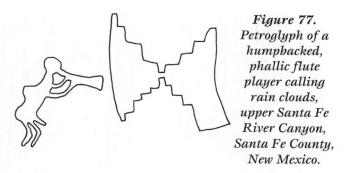

Figure 77.
Petroglyph of a humpbacked, phallic flute player calling rain clouds, upper Santa Fe River Canyon, Santa Fe County, New Mexico.

often associated with the fertility-enhancing elements of rain and moisture, as illustrated in Figure 77, where he seems to be calling rain clouds with his flute or a cloud-blower, a ceremonial pipe or tube used to blow clouds of tobacco smoke to the sky in prayers for rain. During certain times of the year, the landscape surrounding these sites echoes these themes. Every summer during the monsoon months spectacular thunderheads billow up from the highest peaks of the Jemez and Sangre de Cristo Mountains, as if called by the gods. For this reason, and others, these mountaintops have always been sacred places to local Pueblo people.

An unusual, apparently three-dimensional design is among the more eccentric elements present here (Figure 78), as is the mask or head shown in Figure 79 where both frontal and profile views are incorporated. It is a mystery why there seems to be a higher level of creativity exhibited at these sites in the upper Santa Fe River Canyon in comparison with others nearby, even though all were presumably produced by people with similar ideologies. Equally enigmatic is the unusually high density of flute player and fertility images here. Perhaps the presence of these wonderful, lively galleries of prehistoric art so close to the art mecca of Santa Fe,

Figure 78.
*Petroglyph design
of an unknown
(three-
dimensional?)
object, mountain
lion, and other
elements, upper
Santa Fe
River Canyon,
Santa Fe County,
New Mexico.*

with its myriad artists and scientists researching the
newest ideas in artificial intelligence and chaos theory, is more than a curious coincidence. Do some
locations enhance creative energy more than others?

Figure 79.
*Petroglyph of a
face or mask with
both frontal and
profile aspects,
upper Santa Fe
River Canyon,
Santa Fe County,
New Mexico.*

GALISTEO BASIN AND VICINITY

Another significant concentration of rock art
exists in the Galisteo Basin about twenty miles south
of Santa Fe. Once home to the Southern Tewa, or
Tano, people, the Galisteo Basin is drained by the
intermittent flow of Galisteo Creek, which dis-
charges to the Rio Grande a few miles south of the
mouth of the Santa Fe River.

At first glance the area seems strikingly beautiful
with its expansive, archetypally western views. The
basin was once rich in natural resources—healthy
grasslands, abundant wildlife, and numerous springs,
allowing large human populations to be sustained

Figure 80. Severe soil erosion in the Galisteo Basin, primarily the result of centuries of overgrazing, has serious impacts on natural and cultural resources. The dike containing petroglyphs at Comanche Gap can be seen in the background.

here for centuries. The equally rich cultural heritage is reflected in the spectacular rock art sites. However, this is a haunted, mostly abandoned land now, much abused by centuries of overgrazing. Today, there are deep gashes in the earth; erosional gullies more than thirty feet deep represent tremendous losses of soil (Figure 80). Some major pueblo ruins such as Pueblo Blanco are being rapidly destroyed by the accelerated rate of erosion, which is causing entire room blocks along with human remains to tumble into the arroyos.[46] Springs that once supported pueblos no longer flow. And where thousands of people used to live in freedom on the resources of communal land, the vast majority of the Galisteo Basin now consists of a few very large private ranches.

The rock art in the Galisteo Basin speaks of a very different time and environment when the area

Figure 81. These large shield-bearing warriors with weapons are prominent Tano war symbols at the Comanche Gap site, Galisteo Basin, Santa Fe County, New Mexico.

reverberated with the life-energy of thousands of Tano-speaking Indians, who built at least nine major pueblos as well as dozens of smaller ones, each with kivas, plazas, and hundreds or thousands of rooms. The modern names of these now abandoned pueblos came from the Spanish, who found at least four of the pueblos still occupied when they arrived in 1591: San Cristobal, Galisteo, San Marcos, and San Lazaro.

The population of the basin began to grow in the 1200s as the Anasazis migrated from the Four Corners area to the Rio Grande region. Small groups gradually coalesced into larger pueblos. By 1300, the primary inhabitants were Southern Tewa people (the word *Tano* means "Tewas who live nearer the sun," that is, to the south).[47] Northern Tewa people still live in the Rio Grande Valley at the pueblos of Nambe, San Ildefonso, Santa Clara, San Juan, and Tesuque, but the Southern Tewa people were nearly decimated in the seventeenth century by a combination of disease (smallpox), war, and famine. Refugees from the Galisteo Basin were absorbed by other pueblos, and some eventually migrated to the Hopi First Mesa to found the village of Hano (probably a variation on the word *Tano*), which still thrives today.

There are references in Spanish documents to the Tanos being the most warlike of the Pueblo Indians.[48] The Tanos largely resisted the Spanish and either died fighting them or moved away from the area. In the Pueblo Revolt of 1680, their warriors were the first to attack the Spanish in Santa Fe. Their aggressiveness may have been due in part to their proximity to the eastern plains, where fierce nomads—Comanches and Apaches—frequently raided. Having to constantly defend themselves, they probably took on some of their enemies' warlike traits.

Most of the rock art found in the basin is of the Rio Grande Style and occurs mainly in large complexes on dikes (long "hogback" ridges) or on sandstone boulders at the base of mesa escarpments. However, some rock art occurs in remote locations on promontories or in caves—sites no doubt considered sacred and perhaps used as shrines for ceremonies or vision quests. Elsewhere in the basin there are a few scattered sites representing much older Archaic rock art left by hunter/gatherers who lived here long before the Pueblo people arrived.

The rock art at many Galisteo Basin sites reflects the presence of a well-developed war cult or warrior society among the Tanos. The most impressive site in the basin is on a long hogback ridge at a

Figure 82.
This ferocious
warrior grimaces
menacingly from
a rock, perhaps to
startle intruders
at the Comanche
Gap site, Galisteo
Basin, Santa Fe
County,
New Mexico.

place called Comanche Gap. The dike is several miles long and covered with thousands of Rio Grande Style petroglyphs. The south-facing wall of the dike is, in Polly Schaafsma's words, "bristling with protective powers" in the form of many prominent, bold petroglyphs signifying war and strength.[49] The subject matter consists of masks, flute players, birds, animals, cloud terraces, and ceremonial figures, but war symbolism is emphasized. Large, prominently placed shields and shield bearers (Figure 81), other fierce-looking warriors (Figure 82), stars (Figure 83), and animals associated with war are abundant. This prominent land formation could have functioned as a Tano war shrine and an abode for supernaturals, one that was made more potent by the images carved on it.[50] The designs on shields are more than decorative and seem to have magical powers for war, defense, and supernatural aid.[51] The largest images are about five feet across, and since they are placed prominently at the top of the dike, they would have made a strong impression of strength to any enemies approaching the area.

The pueblos nearest Comanche Gap are Pueblo

Figure 83. *Stars and star-beings are common war symbols at the Comanche Gap site, Galisteo Basin, Santa Fe County, New Mexico.*

Blanco and Pueblo Colorado, both of which have other rock art associated with them. Pueblo Blanco is named for the white sandstone cliffs near it and Pueblo Colorado for the red rock from which it was constructed. At Pueblo Blanco the nearby petroglyphs are most notable for the large size of the images, including several big horned serpents, the longest of which stretches about twenty-five feet across a colorful sandstone outcrop (Figure 84). Another petroglyph is of a life-sized bear (Figure 85). A sample of some of the many other images at Comanche Gap is presented in the composite shown in Figure 86.

A few miles north of Comanche Gap is a major promontory overlooking the Galisteo Basin. It must have had ritual significance to the Tanos for at its summit are small circular stone structures that were probably shrines or vision quest sites, as well as

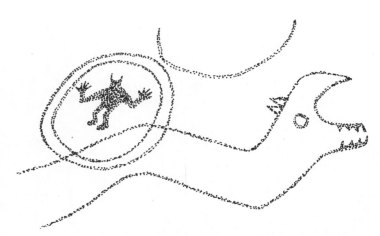

Figure 84. *A rock art site near Pueblo Blanco features several very long Awanyus (horned serpents) that stretch more than twenty-five feet across the rock face, Galisteo Basin, Santa Fe County, New Mexico.*

Figure 85. *A life-sized bear petroglyph, this one unfortunately marred by graffiti, Pueblo Blanco, Galisteo Basin, Santa Fe County, New Mexico.*

Figure 86.
*Some of the
many petroglyphs
at Comanche
Gap, Galisteo
Basin, Santa Fe
County,
New Mexico.*

some petroglyphs, including an impressive mountain lion with exaggerated claws (Figure 87). The mountain lion, or cougar, was the most powerful totem animal to hunters seeking big game such as deer, elk, or bison. The hunting chief was called Mountain Lion or Cougar Man. In many villages he protected the people against disease, and in some the Hunters' Society called upon him to treat victims of hunting accidents.[52] In petroglyphs, the mountain lion's distinguishing characteristics are a long, thin tail, small ears, and well-defined claws.

Pecked into a small, isolated butte at the foot of the promontory is a petroglyph of a man and a large

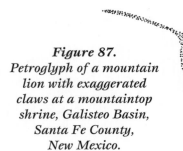

Figure 87.
Petroglyph of a mountain lion with exaggerated claws at a mountaintop shrine, Galisteo Basin, Santa Fe County, New Mexico.

Figure 88.
Petroglyph of a man and a large badger with exaggerated claws and a heart line, Galisteo Basin, Santa Fe County, New Mexico.

Figure 89.
Petroglyph panel at a remote shrine on a high hill, with bear paw, birds in a symmetrical design, and ceremonial creatures, Galisteo Basin, Santa Fe County, New Mexico.

badger, also with prominent claws (Figure 88). The badger is another animal god, valued for curing powers. Because badgers live and dig in the ground, they have special knowledge of roots and herbs. In some pueblos a woman in childbirth kept a badger paw nearby because the badger digs itself out quickly.[53] The badger in Figure 88 also has a heart line, which is a symbolic representation of the life source, or breath, of the animal.

At a site north of Galisteo Creek, also on a prominent high point, many petroglyphs, including some that are Archaic, also suggest a sacred function (Figure 89). Here there is another badger petroglyph (Figure 90), as well as a realistic depiction of human footprints (Figure 91), which generally are

Figure 90.
Petroglyph of a badger, Galisteo Basin, Santa Fe County, New Mexico.

Figure 91.
Petroglyphs of human footprints, which often represent a journey or migration, Galisteo Basin, Santa Fe County, New Mexico.

thought to represent a person's journey or the migration of a people.

In a canyon on the northeast side of the basin, handprints in pictographic stencil form record an ancient presence under a rock shelter (Figure 92). Because this small rock shelter is barely suitable for habitation, it suggests that the rock art had a ceremonial function. Handprints often served as signatures for important events such as initiations or

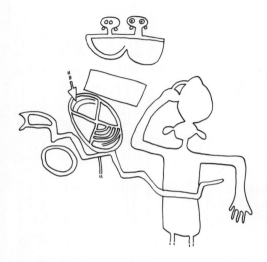

Figure 94.
Red pictograph of
a woman holding
a water jar on
her head,
at a remote
ceremonial site in
a canyon of the
Galisteo Basin,
Santa Fe County,
New Mexico.

vision quests. Leaving a handprint in a sacred place is a prayer to the spirits who live there. On the smoke-blackened interior of this same rock shelter are white pictographs of two human figures, one of which holds a bow and arrows (Figure 93).

At another remote, inaccessible cave site in a rocky canyon on the basin's west margin are still more pictographs of a ceremonial nature. Painted on the low ceiling of this cave are many hand and star stencils, a horned serpent, and a large, horned, shaman-like being—giving this cave an aura of potency and magic (Plate 4). Not far away in the same canyon under a ledge next to the stream channel is a red pictograph of a woman carrying a water jar on her head (Figure 94). Painted in red and yellow, the pictographs of a lizard and toad in Plate 5 adorn the wall of a small rock shelter that may have been a vision quest site on the northern margin of the Galisteo Basin. The fact that these sites are far from the nearest pueblo and not easy to get to is evidence that they were probably sacred places.

An isolated petroglyph near the center of the

basin shows a corn plant and an attendant being, probably a supernatural guardian of corn (Figure 95). Another depiction of a corn plant occurs at a major rock art site near one of the basin's largest pueblo ruins; this petroglyph is placed on a large rock above a natural cistern that holds water from precipitation or offerings, suggesting supplication for plentiful moisture to support the corn crop (Figure 96). This site contains hundreds of Rio

Figure 95. Petroglyph of corn with an attendant corn guardian or spirit, Galisteo Basin, Santa Fe County, New Mexico.

Figure 96. Petroglyph of a corn plant on a rock with a natural cistern that holds rainwater that probably served as a place to make offerings for plentiful rain, Galisteo Basin, Santa Fe County, New Mexico.

Grande Style images, among which are many horned serpents, warriors, and kachina masks. In the rocky outcrops surrounding this site are shrines and some older petroglyphs of early Anasazi origin such as the deer or elk with huge antlers in Figure 97.

Another long dike cuts across the center of the basin and, like the one at Comanche Gap, is covered with many petroglyphs on its south side. The photo in Figure 98 presents a sample from a large panel crowded with bold images at this site, among which is yet another badger, as well as snakes, masks, and geometric shapes.

On a small dike near Galisteo Creek are some Rio Grande Style petroglyphs, including the fertility and human sexuality scene where a phallic male is entering a detached female vulva-form (Figure 99). Not far from this site is a small cave containing numerous other such female fertility symbols carved into its ceiling.[54]

These illustrations represent only a fraction of the rock art in the Galisteo Basin, not all of which can be included in this discussion. A few notable sites also occur just beyond its eastern boundary, barely into the watershed of the Pecos River. On top of Glorieta Mesa, the escarpment that forms the eastern edge of the Galisteo Basin, two interesting Archaic petroglyph sites (Figure 100) recently came to light with over 200 petroglyphs occurring at each site (see Chapter 5, "Sites with Public Access," for more information).[55]

Only a few miles to the north lies the formerly great Pecos Pueblo (now Pecos National Historical Park). Pecos Pueblo had extensive trading contacts with the Galisteo Basin pueblos as well as with nomadic tribes on the Great Plains to the east. There are about a dozen scattered rock art sites in the vicinity, such as the rock shelter pictographs of

Figure 97. Anasazi petroglyphs of deer or elk with huge antlers, Galisteo Basin, Santa Fe County, New Mexico.

Figure 98.
A portion of a large petroglyph panel on a dike near Galisteo, Galisteo Basin, Santa Fe County, New Mexico.

Figure 99.
Petroglyph of a phallic male with female fertility symbol, Galisteo Basin, Santa Fe County, New Mexico. (After a photograph by Bart Durham.)

masks and a horned shaman or supernatural being shown in Figure 101. There would probably have been a great deal more rock art produced around the Pecos Pueblo area if more suitable outcrops existed. The predominant rocks exposed in the area are sandstone and shale of the Sangre de Cristo Formation, which tends to form rough surfaces that readily crumble and erode—poor surfaces for rock art. Even

Figure 100.
*Archaic Desert
Abstract Style
petroglyphs on
Glorieta Mesa,
San Miguel
County,
New Mexico.*

Figure 101.
*Pictographs of
masks and a
horned shaman
or spirit in a rock
shelter near
Pecos,
San Miguel
County,
New Mexico.*

so, in prehistoric times there was probably more rock
art in the area that has since then disintegrated.

At some sites near Pecos it appears that the creators of the petroglyphs tried to compensate for the
poor rock surface by pecking rows of holes instead
of continuous lines in their designs.[56] Elements
found in petroglyphs around the Pecos Pueblo area
are mostly Pueblo images such as masks, horned

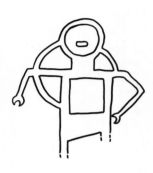

Figure 102.
*Petroglyph of an
anthropomorph
near Pecos, San
Miguel County,
New Mexico.
(After Lentz and
Varela 1971.)*

serpents, bear paws, handprints and footprints, star-beings, and anthropomorphs (Figure 102), but in general the quality is inferior to rock art of the Galisteo Basin and other nearby sites. Several unusual rock art sites that are presumed to be Pueblo in origin consist of rows of holes and deep grooves carved into the tops of large boulders. The grooves are typically located within the area of a natural depression, and may have served to collect and channel rainwater flowing off the boulders for either utilitarian or ritual purposes.[57]

MIDDLE RIO GRANDE, COCHITI TO RIO PUERCO, JEMEZ RIVER, AND WEST MESA

After leaving the Galisteo Basin and returning to the Rio Grande at the mouth of Galisteo Creek, there are minor rock art sites scattered along the river for the next ten miles, mainly on the west bank. Darkly patinated surfaces on basalt boulders and cliff faces afford many fine potential sites for petroglyphs. There are many such sites on the Rio Grande after it leaves the San Luis Valley in Colorado. An interesting example of Pueblo rock art from this area depicts an anthropomorph with a feathered headdress and a single leg with bird foot, holding aloft a horned mask (Figure 103). Kachina masks and other Rio Grande Style elements are also present at a Pueblo site located several miles up Tonque Arroyo to the east (Figure 104).

Continuing downstream, the next major tributary of the Rio Grande is the Jemez River, which enters from the west bank above Bernalillo. The Jemez River drains the central core of the Jemez Mountains, flowing south from the Valle Grande, a

Figure 103.
*Petroglyph of an
anthropomorphic
figure holding a
horned mask,
Sandoval County,
New Mexico.*

huge valley which is really part of a volcanic caldera formed by eruptions. The river flows through scenic red rock canyons past Jemez Pueblo, and continues past Zia and Santa Ana Pueblos to a dam just above the confluence with the Rio Grande. In the upper reaches of the Jemez River and its perennial tributaries, conditions during prehistoric times supported many pueblos, some quite large, on the mesatops between canyons and in some of the major valleys. The Jemez Mountains offered abundant water and wildlife, habitable topography, and fertile volcanic soil—volcanic substrate which is now ironically the bane of the Jemez area, as mining companies attempt to strip-mine pumice deposits. Fortunately, to my knowledge no rock art sites have yet been destroyed by pumice mining in the Jemez Mountains, although the principal mining company has quarried construction rock perilously close to significant petroglyphs on Black Mesa near Española (Figure 50).

The rock art sites in this area are concentrated near the mouth of the Jemez River and further upstream in its headwaters, with few between. The location around the confluence of the Jemez River and the Rio Grande is the southern limit of the

Figure 104.
Petroglyphs of
kachina masks,
Keres Province,
Tonque Arroyo,
Sandoval County,
New Mexico.

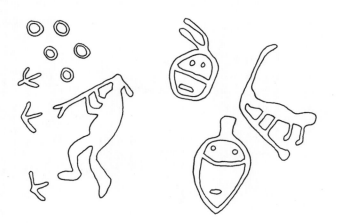

Figure 105.
Petroglyphs
involving flute
players and bird
tracks, circles,
and kachina
masks, Rio
Grande Style
(Keres Province),
near the Jemez
River, Sandoval
County,
New Mexico.

Figure 106. *Keresan Pueblo petroglyphs of a star-being with headdress and arms alongside a corn plant, near the Jemez River, Sandoval County, New Mexico.*

Keresan Pueblo region. Several large petroglyph sites are clustered here on basalt boulders at terraces close to the Rio Grande. Many remains of small rock structures occur on these terraces, including ceremonial enclosures, defense fortifications, field houses, and livestock pens. This area is at the southern ter-

Figure 107.
Petroglyphs of a bighorn sheep and hunter with bow, Keres Province, Rio Grande Style, near the Jemez River, Sandoval County, New Mexico.

minus of the Pajarito Plateau, and from here there are fine views of the Sandia Mountains to the east across the Rio Grande. Here the typical Rio Grande Style elements are present, such as flute players and masks (Figure 105). A star-being (a war symbol) with headdress and arms is pecked on a large boulder, along with a corn plant (Figure 106), overlooking the Rio Grande bosque (riparian forest). Many petroglyphs depicting game animals are solidly pecked, including deer and bighorn sheep (Figure 107). The cloven feet of these quadrupeds are sometimes shown, in addition to other bewildering attributes such as the long, curling snout and tail with spirals attached as shown in Figure 108. Unlike some other Rio Grande Style, Keresan Pueblo rock art sites to the north, at these sites fertility themes were not such an obvious preoccupation. One of the few such images depicts two couples embracing in Figure 109. There seems to have been some license to create individual, idiosyncratic images here beyond the bounds of a defined style, as seen in the strange designs of Figures 110 and 111.

Proceeding up the Jemez River, the next known sites are well into the Jemez Mountains, between Jemez Pueblo and the town of Jemez Springs. There are both petroglyphs and pictographs in this area,

Figure 108.
Petroglyph of a quadruped with cloven feet and spiral lines connected to the tail and nose, Rio Grande Style, Keres Province, near the Jemez River, Sandoval County, New Mexico.

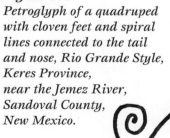

Figure 109.
Petroglyphs of two couples embracing or copulating, Rio Grande Style, Keres Province, near the Jemez River, Sandoval County, New Mexico.

Figure 110.
Petroglyphs, Rio Grande Style, Keres Province, near the Jemez River, Sandoval County, New Mexico.

Figure 111.
Petroglyph, Rio Grande Style, Keres Province, near the Jemez River, Sandoval County, New Mexico.

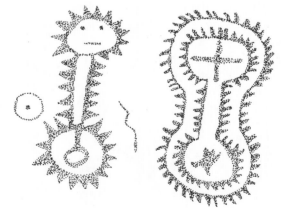

nearly always located at the base of the many beautiful tuff cliffs that ring the canyons. These rock art sites are usually associated with ruins of Pueblo III and IV Period occupation on the mesatops. Rock art sites are still being discovered in this rugged landscape of steep rocky slopes, high cliffs, and thick brush—many of which are not apparent until you are directly in front of them because the tuff does not always have a weathering patina, so petroglyphs do not have much contrast. In addition, because the tuff is soft and easily erodes, some petroglyphs here have deteriorated. Pictographs are fairly numerous in the Jemez Mountains, and are usually located in southeast-facing alcoves or rock shelters. All the major mesas in the area have some rock art on their cliffs, including San Juan, Paliza, Holiday, Cat, and Virgin Mesas. A 1991 rock art survey of San Juan and Cat Mesas documented fifty-eight sites with a total of 331 panels.[58] One conclusion from this research was that rock art in this area of the Jemez Mountains was, for the most part, not intended for public view. It was probably created by specialists or initiates, who selected locations that took advantage of the irregular topography of the area so sites were not visible from pueblos or commonly used areas. Because they are located high above the valley floor at the top of steep slopes, most rock art sites in the Jemez Mountains are not only hard to see but are often difficult and sometimes dangerous to access. Perhaps the risk involved in creating some of these images was seen as a way of imbuing them with more power or gaining favorable attention from the supernaturals.

Stylistically, much of the rock art here resembles that in the eastern section of the Jemez Mountains near Los Alamos and the Pajarito Plateau. Masks are common, and horned serpents and birds are abun-

Figure 113.
Petroglyphs of an anthropomorphic figure, flute player, snake, and cloud terrace, Holiday Mesa, Jemez Mountains, Sandoval County, New Mexico.

Figure 112.
Petroglyphs, Holiday Mesa, Jemez Mountains, Sandoval County, New Mexico.

Figure 114.
Petroglyph, Holiday Mesa, Jemez Mountains, Sandoval County, New Mexico.

Figure 115.
Petroglyphs of a humpbacked flute player in sexual union with a female, Holiday Mesa, Jemez Mountains, Sandoval County, New Mexico.

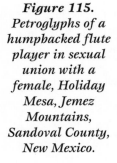

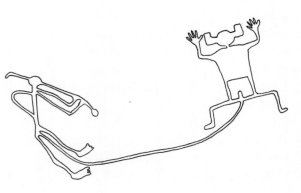

Figure 116. Petroglyph of a large ceremonial shield, Holiday Mesa, Jemez Mountains, Sandoval County, New Mexico. (Photograph courtesy of Brian Buettner and John Keith.)

dant (Figure 112), as well as the usual flute players, snakes, cloud terraces, and occasional ogre (Figure 113). Strange, fantastic beasts are also found, such as the odd three-legged animal with a bird-like beak near the ruins of Tovakwa Pueblo (Figure 114). Concerns with fertility are evident, expressed in depictions of phallic men with females, pregnant deer, and the common flute player figure, Kokopelli. The amazingly long union between the flute player and maiden in Figure 115 reaches six feet around a corner. This petroglyph seems to illustrate an amusing old story from Hopi about how Kokopelli courted and got his woman.[59]

Shield designs are also a common motif in this part of the Jemez Mountains, and can sometimes be large and visually striking (Figure 116). A number of shield petroglyphs here were once painted

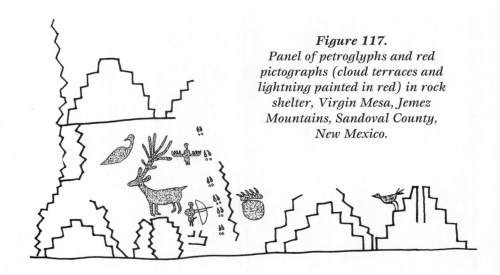

Figure 117.
Panel of petroglyphs and red pictographs (cloud terraces and lightning painted in red) in rock shelter, Virgin Mesa, Jemez Mountains, Sandoval County, New Mexico.

with red pigment, traces of which can still be seen on some of them.

One obscure little rock shelter beneath the cliff wall of Virgin Mesa contains a panel of ritual images combining petroglyphs and red pictographs. A pleasing geometric pictograph that is isolated on one side of the shelter is in good condition. Although much of the pictograph component of the main panel is faded, enough remains to produce a drawing (Figure 117). The principal motifs here are concerned with rain (the cloud terraces and lightning painted in red) and hunting (the petroglyphs of a large deer and tracks, bear paw, birds, and hump-backed hunter with bow).

Returning to the Jemez River, up several tributaries near San Ysidro (the Rio Salado to Querencia Arroyo) in the scenic Ojito Wilderness Study Area (BLM), there is a small petroglyph site. Located on horizontal bedrock at the top of a small cliff overlooking the landmark of Cabezon (an isolated volcanic plug that juts into the sky several miles to the

Figure 118.
Anasazi
petroglyphs,
Querencia
Arroyo,
Sandoval County,
New Mexico.

north) are Anasazi petroglyphs consisting of snakes, turtles, lizard-men, stars, and other elements (Figure 118). The elongated, giant footprint is a symbol seen throughout the region; it has been suggested that such large footprints may represent the footsteps of the terrifying god of fire and death, Masau. Called "bloody headed" and "skeleton man," Masau is described in myths as a blackened giant with feet the length of a man's forearm.[60] When the ancestral people emerged from the underworld to this one, they followed Masau's giant footprints in their wanderings. This image is especially symbolic at this location because it lies only 100 yards from the resting place of another giant. The fossil bones of the dinosaur known as Seismosaurus were excavated from a sandstone ledge here in the early 1990s. At a length of 120 feet, it is the largest known dinosaur species in the world, and its name was chosen to imply that this huge creature literally shook the ground with its footsteps. From the face of the cliff here, a small, smoke-blackened ceremonial cave looks out over a wild and forbidding landscape. It is interesting to speculate whether the ancients could have noticed some of the gigantic bones in the ground nearby and deemed this a place of power.

Back at the Rio Grande, the river now flows through the Albuquerque urban area—the largest city in the state with half a million residents. This portion of the Rio Grande Valley has experienced the most drastic environmental change since prehistoric times due to unrelenting urban sprawl and industrialization. Because irrigation diversions withdraw water from this part of the river, starting below Cochiti Dam, its size decreases constantly.

Opposite Albuquerque on the West Mesa escarpment west of the river is the greatest concentration of petroglyphs along the entire Rio Grande. In 1990, Congress declared 7,000 acres of this area a national monument to protect the rock art and other resources from gradual but certain destruction by encroaching development and vandalism as Albuquerque's population expanded westward. This extensive site, known as Petroglyph National Monument, contains an estimated 15,000 to 17,000 petroglyphs and numerous sacred places and shrines, some still used by Pueblo people. The monument includes the five extinct volcanoes along Albuquerque's western horizon and the entire seventeen-mile dark cliff below. Before being declared a national monument, the richness and variety of the rock art and archaeological sites along the escarpment had led to its designation as the Las Imagines National Archaeological District, listed as significant on the National Register of Historic Places. However, despite its status as a national monument, there are still threats to the integrity of this place. Due to powerful lobbying, there is tremendous political and economic pressure to construct a new highway through the monument to facilitate further growth and alleviate gridlock from people living in numerous housing developments nearby. The great rock art gallery looks down on a fast-growing city that fills the valley below and now laps at the escarpment like a rising flood tide.

Apparently this has always been a sacred place to native peoples in the upper Rio Grande region and still is.[61] Because of the controversy over preserving the monument in a pristine state, in a recent, unprecedented move the governors of five area pueblos (Cochiti, Jemez, Sandia, Santa Ana, and Zia) published an article in an Albuquerque newspaper informing the public of Pueblo views on why the West Mesa site is sacred:

> *Our ancestors chose the petroglyph area to be a sacred site because it was born with Mother Earth's great labor and power. If you walk around the petroglyphs, you can see the unique features that our ancestors saw—five volcanoes in a straight line, their once-opened vents communicating with the world beneath and the lava which they sit on. The petroglyph area is where messages to the spirit world are communicated. It is here that our Pueblo*

ancestors "wrote" down the visions and experiences they felt. This special place is central to the great protector mountains of Sandia, Mount Taylor, Jemez, Manzano, and Santa Fe. It is the center of great spiritual powers!...We consider each of these petroglyphs to be a record of visions written here of some spiritual being, event or expressions attesting to and/or guarding a person's sacrifice or offering. ...Our ancestors identified all sacred places in a special way so that other Indians passing through would know that this was a spiritual place and should not be disturbed.... The Petroglyph National Monument should be a place of reverence and prayer and used in this manner.... We ask for your support in stopping all roads through the Petroglyph National Monument.[62]

In 1996, the Park Service's proposed management plan for Petroglyph National Monument, which became controversial, called for development of up to sixteen miles of recreational trails for bicycles and horses plus private, unmarked access points for adjoining neighborhoods, while original supporters of the monument envisioned pedestrian access only. Pueblo leaders, environmentalists, and even the monument's advisory committee contend that cyclists and horses on trails would desecrate a sacred site. A recent newspaper cartoon of a petroglyph-like image of an ancient Indian riding a mountain bike reflected the controversy swirling around the West Mesa. In the early 1990s, Pueblo leaders again emphasized the importance of managing the area according to values other than recreation, telling the government that the monument area encompassed numerous spirit trails traveled by the dead, and that the cliffs are the nerve center of Pueblo culture, religion, and tradition.[63]

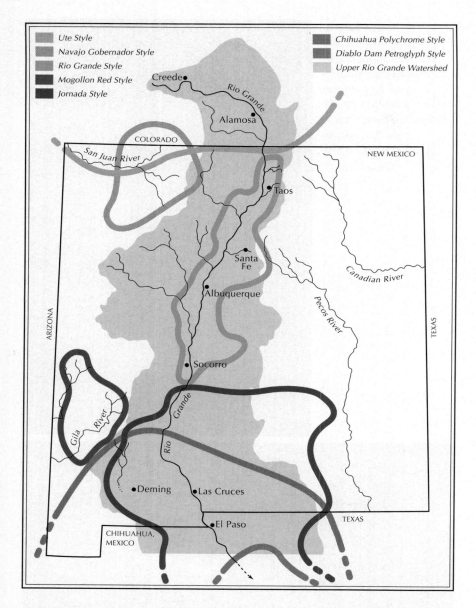

Plate 1: *Map showing distribution of selected rock art styles in the upper Rio Grande area. No boundaries are depicted for the Desert Abstract Style, which is widely scattered throughout the entire region, or for the Apache Style, which is widely scattered over the southern portion of the map area. (Adapted in part from Schaafsma 1980 and Cole 1990.)*

Plate 2: *Archaic Desert Abstract Style petro-glyphs are comple-mented by colorful lichens growing on the basalt surface, Orilla Verde Recreation Area, Taos County, New Mexico.*

Plate 3: *A colorful polychrome pictograph of a Rio Grande Style anthro-pomorph graces the ceiling of a sacred cave site overlooking the Rio Grande near the mouth of White Rock Canyon, Sandoval County, New Mexico.*

Plate 4: *Rio Grande Style pictographs on the ceiling of a remote ceremonial cave in the Galisteo Basin feature a large, horned shaman or supernatural being, a horned serpent (Awanyu), and numerous stenciled images of hands, stars, and other objects, Santa Fe County, New Mexico.*

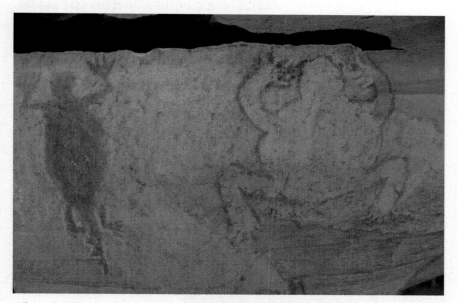

Plate 5: *These two Rio Grande Style pictographs portraying a lizard and toad or frog are painted on the wall of a small rock shelter that may have been a shrine or vision quest site overlooking the Galisteo Basin, Santa Fe County, New Mexico.*

Plate 6:
The Comanche Gap petroglyph site features striking images of anthropomorphic figures and supernaturals in the Rio Grande Style of the Southern Tewa (Tano) Province, Galisteo Basin, Santa Fe County, New Mexico.

Plate 7:
Rio Grande Style petroglyphs of hands and snakes are the dominant theme at this site along Galisteo Creek, Santa Fe County, New Mexico.

Plate 8: *Rio Grande Style petroglyph of a kneeling warrior is among many elements related to a war theme at Comanche Gap, Galisteo Basin, Santa Fe County, New Mexico.*

Plate 9: *These Rio Grande Style petroglyphs of a humpbacked, phallic flute player, kachina mask, snake, and bird are typical elements depicted on the basalt cliffs (with yellow lichens) along the Santa Fe River near La Cieneguilla, Santa Fe County, New Mexico.*

Plate 10: *The Tompiro Province near Mountainair is known for its colorful and elaborate Rio Grande Style pictographs of masks and ceremonial anthropomorphs, Torrance County, New Mexico.*

Plate 11: *An elaborate petroglyph panel with many interesting Rio Grande Style elements, including a mountain lion and tracks of lion and bear, Tompiro Province near Abo, Torrance County, New Mexico.*

Plate 12: *These Rio Grande Style masks occur in the Piro Province at the southern edge of the Rio Grande Style area in Socorro County, New Mexico.*

Plate 13: *Jornada Style masks and a bird at the Tonuca Mountains, Doña Ana County, New Mexico.*

Plate 14: *Hueco Tanks State Historical Park contains hundreds of Jornada Style pictographs of masks such as this one painted with red and green pigments, El Paso County, Texas.*

Plate 15: *The extensive Three Rivers Petroglyph Recreation Area features Jornada Style images such as the lizard, bear paws, and circle with dots motif seen on this boulder, Otero County, New Mexico.*

Today, any area of public land attracts controversy over its management, especially culturally significant places near urban areas. The Park Service staff at Petroglyph National Monument is very sensitive to these issues and tries to accommodate diverse views to the extent possible within their legal mandates. For example, they are cautious about "interpreting" the meaning of the petroglyphs and do so only when area Pueblo people or the professional archaeological community concur on an interpretation. Moreover, recently they have adopted a policy of only telling stories about the petroglyphs during the winter months, because this is the traditional season for storytelling in the pueblos—in winter the animals and spirits are "dormant" and will not hear you talking about them.[64]

An estimated 90 to 95 percent of the rock art on the West Mesa is Rio Grande Style, most of which was created in the Pueblo IV Period between A.D. 1350 and 1680. But some of the older rock art on the escarpment could be nearly 3,000 years old. In the monument area, there are also numerous archaeological sites, sixty-five on the escarpment alone, representing at least 12,000 years of human history. The monument also contains Paleo-Indian sites, some near the volcanoes but most located to the west near the shorelines of what were once Pleistocene lakes. In addition, the monument encompasses a few Archaic Period sites. The oldest petroglyphs, dating from about 1000 B.C., are found on the northern part of the escarpment and on the volcanoes. They are curvilinear abstract patterns such as circles, meandering lines, and rakes, typical of the Desert Abstract Style. The early Anasazi rock art (A.D. 700 to 900) on the West Mesa is similar to contemporary Anasazi rock art of the Four Corners region; typical images from this period consist of

Figure 119.
Rio Grande Style petroglyph of a star-being, West Mesa, Bernalillo County, New Mexico.

Figure 120.
Rio Grande Style petroglyph of a star-being, West Mesa, Bernalillo County, New Mexico. (Drawing from a National Park Service report.)

outlined crosses, sandal tracks, handprints, stick-figure men, and small, solidly pecked animals.

However, the majority of the petroglyphs at West Mesa are in the Rio Grande Style of the fourteenth century, which represents a contrast to the early Anasazi rock art. West Mesa petroglyphs are a major record of Southern Tiwa iconography, which in this location has similarities to the Keresan Pueblo rock art north near Cochiti. Although not unique to this site, the West Mesa contains numerous depictions of star-beings, many of which have headdresses and limbs (Figures 119 and 120). The petroglyph of a star-being shown in Figure 119 may be a mask with feathered headdress, diagonal facial stripes, and an arrow. Originally located on private land at the base of the escarpment, this site has recently been incorporated into the monument. The Rio Grande Style petroglyphs at West Mesa also include many interesting anthropomorphic figures, such as the depiction of a person holding what appears to be a war club in Figure 121.

The prehistoric population reached a peak here in Pueblo IV times. Many very large pueblos were built along this section of the Rio Grande during the Pueblo IV Period, some near canyon mouths of the West Mesa escarpment. Piedras Marcada ("Marked Rock") Pueblo covered seven acres and contained 1,000 rooms built in several stories around two plazas. The people farmed along the Rio Grande floodplain and also foraged and farmed in the diverse ecological zone at the base of the escarpment. Water running off the escarpment was collected, both by natural and manmade means, creating a rich habitat for many plants and animals. The common association of petroglyphs with agricultural terraces and grinding slicks (rock surfaces worn smooth by grinding seeds and herbs) indicates some of these rock art sites may have played a ritualistic role in the processing of food and medicinal plants (see Chapter 5, "Sites with Public Access," for further description of the rock art images).

At the southern edge of Albuquerque on the west side of the Rio Grande, is another Black Mesa with petroglyphs. There are hundreds of images around its rim, as well as the ruins of a Pueblo III Period habitation site (named Pure-Tuey) on its flat top. It is well situated to overlook the Rio Grande Valley and the modern Isleta Pueblo. Unfortunately, this is another area where rock art has been

Figure 121.
Rio Grande Style petroglyph of an anthropomorphic figure holding a war club, West Mesa, Bernalillo County, New Mexico. (Drawing from Schmader and Hays 1986.)

Figure 122.
Rio Grande Style
petroglyph of a
thunderbird, Black
Mesa, Bernalillo
County, New
Mexico. (After
Durham 1955.)

Figure 123.
Petroglyphs of
anthropomorphic
figures, Black
Mesa, Bernalillo
County, New
Mexico. (After
Durham 1955.)

destroyed during construction—when the path of Interstate-25 was blasted through the mesa in the 1960s. However, a few petroglyphs remain, and fortunately those that were lost had been recorded in the 1950s.[65] Rock art styles here include Archaic, early Anasazi, and Rio Grande Style. Among the inventory of elements are cloud terraces, handprints and footprints, spirals, star-beings like those at West Mesa, zigzags and other abstract designs, the ubiquitous flute player, and bird motifs (Figure 122). Anthropomorphic figures range from realistic to whimsical: among the images are what appear to be a man holding up two children or perhaps puppets (Figure 123) and a row of people suggesting a dance or maybe a journey or migration (Figure 124). Travel is also implied by the stick figures astride horses in Figure 125.

Of special interest at this site is the petroglyph that strongly resembles the L-shaped pueblo and kivas that occupied the top of the mesa (Figure 126). Another striking image is the panel depicting three people with upraised hands and looped or circular head appendages, in a field of circles (Figure 127).

About twelve miles further down the Rio Grande in the vicinity of Los Lunas is the next outcropping suitable for rock art. Two volcanic promontories on either side of the river are marked with Rio Grande Style petroglyphs. Here there are humpbacked flute players as well as masks, birds, and cloud terraces (Figures 128 and 129). Impressive designs are shields and shield bearers, one of which seems to be attacking a large horned serpent, or Awanyu (Figure 130). This scene may be an illustration of a ritual conflict between the sun and malevolent powers at winter solstice. A very similar petroglyph from the Tompiro Pueblo of Tenabo, thirty miles to the southeast, may represent the same

Figure 124. Petroglyphs of anthropomorphic figures, Black Mesa, Bernalillo County, New Mexico. (After Durham 1955).

Figure 125. Historic petroglyphs of horses and riders, Black Mesa, Bernalillo County, New Mexico. (After Durham 1955.)

Figure 126. Petroglyph resembling a map of the pueblo and kivas located nearby, Black Mesa, Bernalillo County, New Mexico. (After Durham 1955.)

Figure 127. Petroglyphs of three anthropomorphs with circle motifs, Black Mesa, Bernalillo County, New Mexico. (After Durham 1955.)

Figure 128. Petroglyphs of birds, El Cerro de los Lunas, Valencia County, New Mexico. (After Schaafsma 1968.)

Figure 129.
Petroglyphs of masks,
deer tracks, and cloud
terrace, El Cerro de los
Lunas, Valencia County,
New Mexico. (After
Schaafsma 1968.)

Figure 130.
Petroglyphs depicting
a conflict between a
shield bearer and
Awanyu, the horned
serpent, El Cerro de
los Lunas, Valencia
County, New Mexico.
(After Schaafsma
1968.)

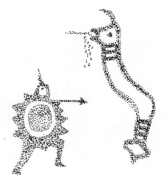

mythic struggle (see Figure 131). At Hopi, such a ceremony was recorded in 1897 by anthropologist Jesse Fewkes:

> In the prayers to the Plumed Snake, his hostility
> was quieted, and the chiefs did what they could to
> propitiate that powerful deity, who was the great
> cause of their apprehension that the beneficent sun
> (Tawa) would be overcome. Then followed the
> dramatization of the conflict of opposing powers,
> possibly representing other deities hostile to our
> beneficent father, the sun. Although the struggle
> involved, so far as the participants were concerned,
> their highest powers of endurance and bodily
> suffering, the sun shield or symbol of Tawa had
> the good fortune to resist the many assaults made
> upon it.[66]

The easternmost of these two sites at Los Lunas is known as Tomé Hill, to which there is public access. For more information, see Chapter 5.

Directly to the east of the Los Lunas sites, the Manzano Mountains form a 10,000-foot-high rampart that extends north-south for over forty miles. There are rock art sites at both ends of the range (where passes allowed east-west travel) and in some of the east-draining canyons, such as at Tajique. Southern Tiwa rock art sites consisting of petroglyphs, as well as rock paintings in small rock shelters, occur near the northern terminus of the Manzanos near Tijeras Canyon, and in canyons along the east slope of the mountains facing the Great Plains. Small paintings in red, yellow, and black pigments depict ceremonial participants, masks, and geometric designs. In one pictograph at an inconspicuous rock shelter, a large yellow sun hovers above a mountain lion with yellow body and red claws. Other pictographs, near the Pueblo IV ruin of Tajique, depict ceremonies involving what appear to be plants or staffs, along with numerous human figures—all painted in red. To create the heads of several of these human figures, fossil brachiopod shells within the limestone rock were incorporated into the design (Figure 132).

Figure 131.
Tompiro petroglyphs depicting a large feathered serpent and a shield bearer, Tenabo, Abo Arroyo, Torrance County, New Mexico.

Figure 132.
Pictographs depicting ceremonial participants (central figure's head is a fossil brachiopod in the rock surface), Tajique Canyon, Torrance County, New Mexico.

TOMPIRO DISTRICT,
ABO ARROYO

At the southern terminus of the Manzano Mountains, some interesting rock art sites occur in the vicinity of Mountainair within the drainage of Abo Arroyo, which flows west to the Rio Grande. The Abo Pass area served as an important east-west travel route connecting the Rio Grande Pueblos to the Salinas Pueblos on the edge of the Great Plains. (See Chapter 5, "Sites with Public Access," for more information on rock art at Salinas National Monument.)[67] The rock art in the Abo Arroyo drainage is at the northern extremity of the Piro region (Figure 19), in what is further subdivided into the Tompiro (Mountain Piro) area between the Rio Grande and the Great Plains. Some outstanding petroglyph sites, as well as detailed, colorful paintings in small rock

Figure 133.
Tompiro
petroglyphs of a
pair of large
feathered
serpents, Tenabo,
Abo Arroyo,
Torrance County,
New Mexico.

Figure 134.
Tompiro petroglyphs depicting a coiled snake and a star-being, Tenabo, Abo Arroyo, Torrance County, New Mexico.

shelters, occur near the Pueblo IV ruins of Abo and Tenabo in the headwater tributaries to Abo Arroyo.

Since the Piro/Tompiro regions are the south-ernmost of the Rio Grande Pueblos and adjoin the Jornada region, masks are a dominant motif in this rock art. Many fine examples of colorful poly-chrome pictographs of masks are found in canyons here (Plate 10). The pictographs of the Piro/Tompiro region are more intricate and colorful than those at other Rio Grande Style sites, with col-ors ranging from orange, yellow, and red to green, turquoise, black, and white. In addition to masks, scenes with small, detailed ceremonial figures are painted under small rock ledges.

Near the ruins of the ancient pueblo of Tenabo a pair of large horned and feathered serpents occupy a prominent location at the top of a cliff facing the ris-ing sun (Figure 133). Pecked on a boulder at the base of the slope beneath this cliff is another serpent shown with a shield bearer and a mountain lion paw (Figure 131). This scene is similar to the one described earlier at a Los Lunas petroglyph site. A more realistic depiction of a coiled snake next to a star-being is shown in Figure 134. Although not

Figure 135.
Tompiro
petroglyphs of
masks,
anthropomorphs,
and fantastic
creatures,
Tenabo, Abo
Arroyo, Torrance
County,
New Mexico.

deities of the same order as Awanyu, all snakes are considered to have supernatural qualities and are treated with reverence. Indians seldom harm even venomous snakes, believing only an evil snake that has bitten a person should be killed. Snakes are associated with water, fertility, and the ability to travel to the underworld, and in this regard frequently serve as spirit helpers to shamans.

Many petroglyph panels at Tenabo present a wide range of creatures, both realistic and fantastic

Figure 136. *Tompiro petroglyphs (traced on a photograph) of supernaturals or ceremonial participants, Tenabo, Abo Arroyo, Torrance County, New Mexico.*

(Figures 135 and 136). Mountain lions and bears, or their paw prints, are featured repeatedly in the Abo area. The panel in Plate 11 has a mountain lion with a bow over its head (perhaps indicating a Hunt Society or hunting totem), tracks of lion, bear, deer, and humans, as well as many other interesting images. At another location an isolated petroglyph of a bear exhibits typically exaggerated feet and claws, a heart line, and an arrow stuck in its rump (Figure 137). In Figure 138 a very large footprint is next to several normal-sized ones; these large foot-prints may be representations of the fearsome giant Masau, a deity who stalked the earth leaving prints as large as a man's forearm (see also Figure 118). Included in this scene are a powerful, eagle-like bird and a strange running figure with bird-like foot and head, holding a bow and arrow. Considered

Figure 137.
Petroglyph of a bear with large feet and claws, heart line, and arrow stuck in its rump, Tenabo, Abo Arroyo, Torrance County, New Mexico.

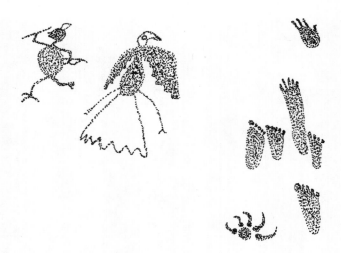

Figure 138. Panel of Tompiro petroglyphs, including an eagle, mountain lion track, running figure with bow, footprints of humans (and a possible footprint of the giant supernatural Masau), Tenabo, Abo Arroyo, Torrance County, New Mexico.

supreme among birds, the eagle was a manifestation of the power of the sun as well as a symbol of swiftness and courage—a god that could aid warriors and hunters and cure sickness. In many native cultures, the eagle was often the shaman's helper, carrying him to distant places. Since their feathers were essential for many rituals, Pueblo people captured eagles and kept them in cages on rooftops. A downy eagle feather symbolizes the breath of life, equivalent to the soul, and also represents a prayer for rain.

RIO PUERCO WATERSHED AND NORTH PLAINS BASIN

Returning to the Rio Grande, downstream about ten miles from the mouth of Abo Arroyo is the next major tributary—the Rio Puerco, which enters from the west bank. Normally just a trickle of muddy water, the Rio Puerco is at times a raging torrent of even muddier water. The Spanish friar Francisco Dominguez wrote in 1776: "It is called the Rio Puerco because its water is as dirty as the gutter of the streets...."[68] Its watershed of more than 6,200 square miles represents a large portion of New Mexico. This expansive area has an interesting history, as well as a great diversity of terrain and a significant number of rock art sites.

Today, the most obvious aspect of the Rio Puerco watershed is the deplorable soil erosion that makes it the single largest contributor of sediment to the Rio Grande. When the Rio Puerco joins the Rio Grande, it provides only 6 percent of the latter's flow but 56 percent of its silt. While there was considerable homesteading along the Rio Puerco in the nineteenth century, and the area was known as the "Breadbasket of New Mexico" for its crops of wheat, corn, beans, and pumpkins, today it is an abandoned wasteland due to overgrazing, and the region's formerly viable communities are now ghost towns. Over the 145 miles between the mouth of the Rio Puerco and the town of Cuba, the Rio Puerco sustains no inhabited town.

The Rio Puerco watershed was a mixing zone for prehistoric cultures, since it was occupied by peoples from the Anasazi Pueblo tradition to the north and the Mogollon peoples from the south. Consequently, the rock art here reflects that mixture, with overlapping and transitional stylistic qualities. In general, there are small sites scattered along the main valley of the Rio Puerco and its principal tributary, the Rio San Jose, as well as some notable concentrations of rock art in Tapia Canyon near Cabezon Peak and in the El Malpais area south of Grants.

Traveling northwest up the Rio Puerco from its mouth, the first rock art site is at Hidden Mountain, to the west of Los Lunas. Because the mountain is rather obvious in the surrounding flat terrain, its name is an enigma, as is the so-called Mystery Rock found on its flank—a small boulder covered with rather fresh-looking, curious inscriptions that have attracted attention since discovery in the 1950s. The inscriptions have been touted in numerous popular articles as being ancient script of either Phoenician, Hebrew, Cyrillic, Etruscan, Egyptian, or Moabite origin. Since there is no physical archaeological evidence in North America to substantiate any of these hypotheses, the opinion of credible experts is that the Mystery Rock is a hoax created by University of New Mexico students in the 1930s.[69]

There are, however, a number of authentic prehistoric Piro petroglyphs on outcrops at the top of Hidden Mountain, such as the solidly pecked anthropomorph with feathers on his head in Figure 139. There are also abstract designs of a nondescript nature, and ruins of a number of small stone structures (pit houses, surface rooms, and cairns) on top of the mountain. A recent-looking petroglyph of a flying saucer and "alien" are probably courtesy of some of the visitors attracted here by the aura of Mystery Rock.

Six miles up the Rio Puerco from Hidden Mountain is the confluence with the Rio San Jose, the major fork of the drainage pattern in the Rio Puerco watershed. The Rio Puerco flows from the north, originating in the forested Sierra Nacimiento on the west flank of the Jemez Mountains. To the west of this stretch of the Rio Puerco looms an extinct volcano—11,301-foot Mt. Taylor. The importance of this mountain to people who have lived near it is underscored by the fact that there are names for it in at least nine languages, including English, Spanish, Navajo, Acoma, Zuni, Tewa, Tiwa, Towa, Keresan, and Apache. Navajos call it Tsoodzil (Blue Bead Mountain); it is one of their four sacred peaks, sacred world altar of the south. Acomas call it Kaweshtima (Where the Rainmaker of the North

Figure 139.
Anthropomorph with feathered headdress, Hidden Mountain, Valencia County, New Mexico.

Lives). Spanish settlers also recognized its spiritual qualities, naming it for a saint, San Mateo. By contrast, Anglo-Americans named it for a politician (President Zachary Taylor), to honor his "sagacity, prowess, and patriotism."[70]

This country in the upper Rio Puerco region is scenic, with numerous canyons, mesas, and stark volcanic plugs dotting the landscape. More than fifty of these volcanic plugs, or necks of extinct volcanoes, ring Mt. Taylor like sentinels—a little-known geologic wonder. The largest, Cabezon, is even bigger than Devils Tower in Wyoming. Visible for many miles, it is also sacred to Pueblo and Navajo Indians. The Navajo creation story tells how the Hero Twins cut off an evil giant's head and tossed it to the east, where it became Cabezon, Spanish for "big head."

Not far from Cabezon, south of the ghost town of Guadalupe, Tapia Canyon joins the Rio Puerco from the west. This canyon was apparently an important prehistoric passageway from the Rio Puerco Valley into the high plateau country abutting Mt. Taylor to the Chaco Canyon area, forty miles northwest in the San Juan Basin. A wealth of rock art adorns the walls of Tapia Canyon, ranging in style from Basketmaker Anasazi to ancestral Pueblo and historic Navajo. At the mouth of the canyon, the small ruin of Guadalupe Pueblo stands guard over the approach at its location atop a high, narrow

Figure 140. (page 146-147)
Anasazi petroglyphs showing procession of game
animals, Tapia Canyon, Rio Puerco, Sandoval County,
New Mexico.

butte. On top of the butte, a petroglyph resembling a map has been pecked into a horizontal rock surface. Other rock art, mostly petroglyphs, extends up Tapia Canyon for several miles. At these sites, often designs with varying degrees of patination overlap, providing important clues about the rock art's age and origin. Indians visiting today are said to be impressed by the experience of power here.[71] And an impressive natural bridge spanning a side canyon heightens the sense that this is a special place.

Some petroglyph panels that were originally created by people standing at ground level are now twenty to thirty feet above the ground, testimony to the rapid erosion throughout the Rio Puerco watershed in the last few centuries. The now inaccessible panel shown in Figure 140 contains many elements but seems primarily concerned with game animals,

Figure 141.
Possible
Basketmaker
Period Anasazi
petroglyphs,
Tapia Canyon,
Rio Puerco,
Sandoval County,
New Mexico.

showing a long procession of small quadrupeds along with some larger deer or elk with antlers.

Older rock art at Tapia Canyon is represented by the boldly pecked, wide-shouldered anthropomorph with large drooping hands and feet (Figure 141). This image is similar to Basketmaker rock art of the San Juan Anthropomorphic Style that occurs to the northwest along the San Juan River; the ear appendages on the head of the figure in the lower

Figure 142.
Possible
Basketmaker
Period Anasazi
petroglyphs
(burden
baskets), Tapia
Canyon, Rio
Puerco,
Sandoval
County,
New Mexico.

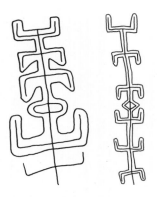

Figure 143.
Petroglyphs,
Tapia Canyon,
Rio Puerco,
Sandoval County,
New Mexico.

left, and the head composed of atlatl-like objects on the figure in the upper right are both indicative of Basketmaker origin. Other images that appear to be relatively older based on patination are the V-shaped objects with intricate internal designs and fringes (Figure 142). These objects, apparently unique to this canyon, may represent burden baskets with woven patterns and fringes. Another type of image common here is the geometric staff, or ladder-like symbol, variations of which are shown in Figure 143. These are often deeply incised or abraded, and are up to four feet high. A wide range of anthropomorphic images also occurs in Tapia Canyon. In Figure 144 the two images on the left are Navajo Gobernador Style deities, while the two figures on the right are likely of Pueblo origin.

Figure 144.
Petroglyphs of
anthropomorphic
figures of Navajo
and Pueblo
origin, Tapia
Canyon, Rio
Puerco, Sandoval
County,
New Mexico.

Figure 145.
*Petroglyphs of an
anthropomorphic
figure wearing a
hat, connected to a
horned
supernatural, Rio
San Jose, Cibola
County,
New Mexico.*

Back down the Rio Puerco to the confluence
with the Rio San Jose, there is reportedly more rock
art at Mesa Prieta. The Rio San Jose extends northwest to Grants, New Mexico, and passes through
lands of Laguna and Acoma Pueblos, paralleled by
Interstate-40. This is colorful country of red and
pink sandstone cliffs, brown and gold mesas capped
with snow-white gypsum deposits, and pitch-black
lava flows. Here there is a curious mix of picturesque
ancient pueblos perched on mesatops and industrial
havoc wreaked on the environment by government-
subsidized uranium mining during the Cold War.

On the intermittent cliffs along the south side
of the Rio San Jose, Pueblo petroglyphs are scattered (Figure 145), along with graffiti dating from
the era of motor travel on Route 66—a scenic seg-
ment of which still follows the river here. This has
been a travel route for many centuries; the Zuni-
Cibola Trail, which connected pueblos along the
Rio Grande with Zuni and Acoma Pueblos, passed
through here. Acoma people claim they have lived
atop their citadel mesa in "Sky City" since at least
A.D. 600. Mesa Encantada is one of the most scenic
landmarks in the area, and on its cliffs are pictographs in red ochre and white, such as the rain

Figure 146.
Pictograph in red
and white of a
rain deity with a
headdress of
Cloud People,
Mesa Encantada,
Cibola County,
New Mexico.
(After a
photograph by
Bart Durham.)

deity in Figure 146, who holds lightning bolts and wears an elaborate tablita-style headdress composed of numerous Cloud People, with a fringe reflecting rain.

Just east of Grants are stark, black lava flows from recent eruptions around the base of Mt. Taylor. Going south, away from the Rio San Jose, an imperceptible rise in the land is all that divides the drainage between the Rio San Jose and the North Plains Basin that contains the larger El Malpais lava flows. These hardened rivers of fire have all but filled this broad valley, covering an area forty miles long and ten miles wide.

El Malpais (The Bad Country) is the Spanish name given to these jagged lava flows, one of the most significant volcanic areas in the United States. To protect this unusual location, in 1987 Congress established the El Malpais National Monument and El Malpais National Conservation Area. The area has always been seen as extraordinary or sacred by explorers and Indians. Captain Dutton of the United States Geological Survey was one of the first white men to explore the area, and wrote in 1885 that "under our feet...is a chaos of black, rough lava of peculiarly horrid aspect." In 1908, Charles Lummis further described the region: "It is true that there are in this area a great many rivers of a sort not to be found in the east—and such strange rivers! They are black as coal, and full of strange, savage waves, and curious eddies, and enormous bubbles. The springs from which they started ran dry centuries ago.... There lies the broad, wild current, sometimes thirty feet higher than its bank, yet not overflowing them."[72]

Acoma, Zuni, and Navajo people all have creation stories that explain the rivers of fire. According to several of these, giants and monsters were slain by mythic heroes, and their blood ran over the valley and hardened into the black rock seen there now. In the Navajo version, the slain giant is the same one whose head became Cabezon, as discussed previously. For these and other reasons, the Malpais country has been sacred to all the Indians who lived near it. In 1924, Mary Austin described the powerful aura of the place: "The lava edges cut like glass and the strains and flaws of cooling look as if they had happened yesterday. There are cones too steep for climbing, and craters so deep that the Indians of that country used to drive mountain sheep into these gateless encierros to kill them at their leisure. In one of these the Apaches, who claim the Malpais immemorially, used to hide their women and their horses while the men went a-raiding.... Here are said to be the sacred places of the Apache...."[73]

A unique and ancient Indian trail, the Acoma-Zuni Trail, crosses the inhospitable lava to connect these two ancient centers. The area has a rich inventory of archaeological sites ranging from Paleo-Indian to Pueblo. A significant concentration of rock art is still being discovered and documented in the sandstone canyons where Cebollita Mesa meets the edge of the lava flows. This area has sites from both Basketmaker times and the later Pueblo periods. During the Pueblo II Period (A.D. 950 to 1175) when the Chaco Canyon civilization was taking shape, a number of outlying but related pueblos, called outliers, were connected by a series of "roads" to the Chaco centers. On the edge of the Malpais are two such outliers, the Candelaria Ruin and the Dittert Site. Pueblo III and IV Period sites are represented as well, and the rock art in the Malpais area is representative of this diverse prehistoric occupation.

The rock art at these sites represents transitional ideographies between Pueblo and Mogollon. A fine panel in Lobo Canyon (Figure 147) contains stepped

Figure 147. Petroglyph panel in Lobo Canyon, El Malpais National Conservation Area, Cibola County, New Mexico.

Figure 148.
Anthropomorphic figures in a fertility/rain context, part of the Aldridge petroglyph panel, El Malpais National Conservation Area, Cibola County, New Mexico.

Figure 149.
A bird devouring a lizard in a portion of the Aldridge petroglyph panel, El Malpais National Conservation Area, Cibola County, New Mexico.

cloud terrace designs augmented by curling lines, birds, anthropomorphs, geometric designs, and an unusual depiction possibly representing a butterfly (in the upper left). Although not a common symbol in rock art, the butterfly motif occurs in southwestern pottery, jewelry, and other ceremonial applications, such as clan symbols. It is associated with rain, fertility, and the well-being of all living things. A butterfly attached to a plume offering was used to carry prayers to the supernaturals, and also to encourage an amorous state of mind. In one ritual a drum containing butterflies made people "go crazy," meaning sexually.[74]

Another site at Cebollita Mesa is known as the Aldridge Panel, a portion of which is shown in Figure 148. Here a procession of odd anthropomorphs flank a phallic, humpbacked figure whose

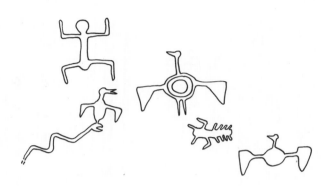

Figure 150.
Birds, an insect,
snake, and other
symbols,
Sandstone Bluffs,
El Malpais
National
Conservation
Area, Cibola
County,
New Mexico.

finger extends to connect with a cloud terrace next to the sun, suggesting a fertility context. Included in this panel is a depiction of a bird devouring a lizard (Figure 149). A few small sites are located at the edge of the lava where the flow stopped when it abutted sandstone cliffs, one of which, shown in Figure 150, consists of several birds, a snake, a lizard, an insect, and an anthropomorph.

Elsewhere in Cebolla Canyon, on a prominent cliff near the aptly named Citadel Pueblo ruin, is a fine petroglyph panel of geometric designs laid out along natural bedrock partitions and incorporating cloud terraces, triangles, and fretwork motifs (Figure 151). Within a mile is another interesting panel with square-bodied anthropomorphs, deer, lizards, snakes,

Figure 151.
Pueblo petroglyph
panel of
geometric designs,
Cebolla Canyon,
El Malpais
National
Conservation
Area, Cibola
County, New
Mexico.

and other symbols (Figure 152). This panel seems to be placed with reference to geologic features in the rock surface, with a large crack dividing the panel.

Twenty miles southwest of El Malpais the Continental Divide forms the western boundary of the North Plains Basin. On top of a steep-sided butte that straddles the divide is a small petroglyph site that apparently served a ceremonial function—considering its remoteness, commanding views, and difficult access. The rock art is associated with at least five small stone structures on top of the butte that were probably shrines or vision quest sites. A number of carefully pecked anthropomorphs with patterned bodies are among the most visually arresting images here (Figure 153). Other images include a mountain lion with stepped cloud terrace motif and a "lizard-man" (Figure 154), as well as a portrayal of a two-headed snake encountering another snake (Figure 155). The most common

Figure 153.
Petroglyphs of
pattern-bodied
anthropomorphs,
Continental
Divide at North
Plains, Catron
County,
New Mexico.

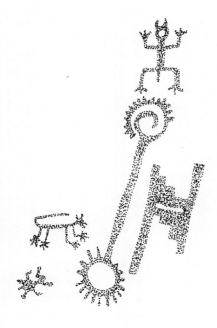

Figure 154.
*Petroglyphs of a
mountain lion,
rain and sun
symbols, and a
lizard-man
figure,
Continental
Divide at North
Plains, Catron
County,
New Mexico.*

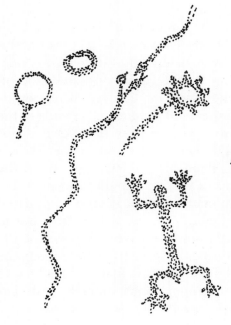

Figure 155.
*Petroglyphs of a two-
headed snake, sun
symbols, and a lizard-
man figure,
Continental Divide at
North Plains, Catron
County,
New Mexico.*

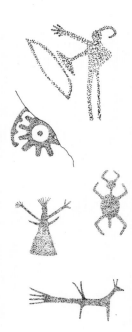

*Figure 156.
Piro Pueblo
petroglyphs, Rio
Salado drainage,
Socorro County,
New Mexico.
(Drawing of
humpbacked
figure with bow
by author, all
others from
Marshall and
Walt 1984.)*

motif at this site is the lizard-like anthropomorph, which is also found at other sites throughout the Southwest. In her study of Zuni perceptions of rock art, anthropologist Jane Young comments on these figures: "Several Zunis identified these figures as the way the Zunis looked at 'the time of the beginning' or 'in the fourth underworld...when we still had tails.' A few people even launched into telling the part of their origin myth in which the creatures, 'moss people,' are described as having tails and webbed hands and feet."[75] To other Indian people, the lizard is a power symbol. Because it so readily enters cracks and openings in rocks, the lizard was seen as a messenger for the supernatural realm of the underworld, and was commonly one of the shaman's spirit helpers. For some ritual events a lizard is rubbed over the body to give the participants power. The lizard can also be a sorcerer, perhaps because of its ability to change color or grow a new tail if it is broken off.[76]

Returning to the Rio Grande, downstream from the mouth of the Rio Puerco eight miles is the Rio Salado, on the west bank. The Rio Salado is normally dry (in fact, its bed consists of sand dunes in the lower reaches), and its drainage, which originates largely in the Datil Mountains, extends to the northwest, to the boundaries of the North Plains Basin. In this little-known area are many Piro ruins and the Alamo Band Navajo Reservation. In the Bear Mountains, a petroglyph site that probably served a ceremonial function is atop an isolated peak, near the center of the Rio Salado Basin. Sitting 300 feet below the basaltic pinnacle is the ruin of a seventy-room masonry pueblo. Among the Piro images are a humpbacked figure with a bow, as well as other anthropomorphs, animals, and geometric designs (Figure 156).

PIRO DISTRICT, RIO PUERCO TO SAN MARCIAL

Where the Rio Salado meets the Rio Grande, a large valley has been formed. A few miles downstream from the confluence the river enters the Angostura de San Acacia, a narrow gateway between two massive basaltic buttes, where it is constricted between two areas of rocky, higher ground. On the west bank is Cerro Indio, or Black Butte. A Piro pueblo ruin of over one hundred rooms marks the top of Black Butte, and numerous petroglyphs ring the edge of this important rock art site, which is located near the southern edge of the Piro Rio Grande Pueblo region. Many prehistoric sites are concentrated in this vicinity since settlements were located here because of the extensive fertile floodplain created by the restriction in the river's flow and the suitable defensive positions afforded by the rocky buttes. Silt washed down from the Rio Puerco, Rio Salado, Abo Arroyo, and numerous other tributaries fills the Rio Grande Valley here, making this one of the most important agricultural areas along the river in prehistoric times. Cerro Indio is still a strategic location at the approximate center of New Mexico, for it is the site of the New Mexico principal meridian control point from which townships and ranges within the state have been surveyed.

Depictions of masks are prolific in the rock art of the Cerro Indio site and at surrounding sites (Figures 157, 158, and Plate 12), and the craftsmanship is often outstanding in these petroglyphs. Other images found here include bold anthropomorphic designs (Figures 159 and 160), ceremonial processions (Figure 161), and supernaturals or ceremonial beings (Figure 162).

Several more Piro rock art sites exist south of the

Figure 157.
Rio Grande Style
petroglyphs of
masks and cloud
terrace, Cerro
Indio, Socorro
County,
New Mexico.

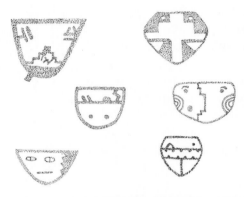

Figure 158.
Rio Grande Style
petroglyphs of
masks, Cerro Indio,
Socorro County,
New Mexico.
(Drawings from
Marshall and Walt
1984.)

Figure 159.
Rio Grande Style
anthropomorph,
Cerro Indio,
Socorro County,
New Mexico.

Figure 160.
*Rio Grande Style anthropomorphs, Cerro Indio,
Socorro County, New Mexico. (Drawings from
Marshall and Walt 1984.)*

Figure 161.
*Rio Grande Style petroglyphs of a
ceremonial procession with flute player,
Cerro Indio, Socorro County, New Mexico.*

Figure 162.
*Rio Grande Style
petroglyphs of
supernatural or
ceremonial beings, one
with bird mask and the
other with towering cloud
terrace headdress, Cerro
Indio, Socorro County,
New Mexico.*

Cerro Indio site. The petroglyph panel in Figure 163 provides the backdrop for a shrine associated with the Piedras Negras ruin, and the petroglyphs of fanciful creatures and a long-tailed bird in Figure 164 are associated with another ruin a mile to the south. These creatures are part of a large petroglyph panel facing the river that includes several large masks, footprints and handprints, geometric shapes, and many other images (Figure 165). A mile to the north are the Jornada Style petroglyphs of a mask along with lion and bear tracks (Figure 166).

In an obscure arroyo east of Socorro, a small rock shelter contains a collection of diminutive, fragile pictographs of masks and ceremonial participants who seem to be playing flutes decorated with fringe-like elements (Figure 167). These pictographs were painted in red, blue-black, white, green, and yellow, although many are badly deteriorated because the surface here is rough and crumbly. Many of them were originally painted onto a smooth surface that had been prepared by applying a mud plaster to the rock. The rough rock surfaces and the remoteness of this site suggest it was chosen for special reasons. The acoustics within the opening of this rock shelter are especially striking and may have played a role in its use for ceremonial purposes. Perhaps the flute-like depictions indicate that music was an important component of rituals that occurred here.

Approximately twenty miles to the south, adjacent to the east riverbank, the fourteenth-century Piro Pueblo of San Pasqualito is located in a defensive position on the narrow top of an isolated rocky crag at the foot of the Sierra San Pasqual. From here the valley of the Rio Abajo can be seen twisting across the desert floor to the north and south for miles. And to the south there is a view of the vast tableland of another Black Mesa, as well as the Sierra

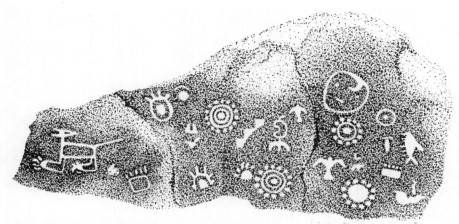

Figure 163. *Rio Grande Style petroglyph panel at a Piro Pueblo shrine, Piedras Negras Pueblo, Socorro County, New Mexico. (Drawing by Caren Walt, in Marshall and Walt 1984.)*

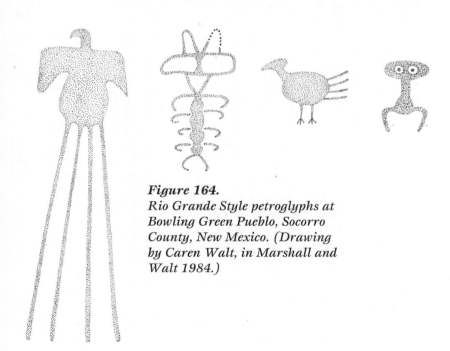

Figure 164.
Rio Grande Style petroglyphs at Bowling Green Pueblo, Socorro County, New Mexico. (Drawing by Caren Walt, in Marshall and Walt 1984.)

Figure 165. Rio Grande Style petroglyphs at Bowling Green Pueblo, Socorro County, New Mexico.

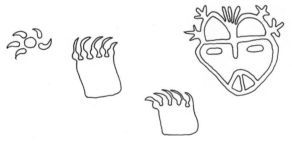

Figure 166. Rio Grande Style petroglyphs of a mask and tracks of a bear and mountain lion, near Bowling Green Pueblo, Socorro County, New Mexico.

Figure 167. Rio Grande Style pictographs of flute-playing ceremonial participants, Socorro County, New Mexico.

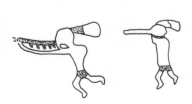

Fra Cristobal and the entrance to the dreaded Jornada del Muerto (Journey of Death). At the foot of this mesa, the Rio Grande forms vast marshlands that support teeming populations of migratory birds and waterfowl. Great vistas of sand, mesquite, and creosote bush dwarf the senses. It is at such places that it is possible to appreciate the role played by the Rio Grande in bringing perennial waters from the north onto the parched desert—water that fostered the development of diverse cultures and supported dense settlements in this otherwise barren land. There are no perennial tributaries in this part of the Rio Grande's course, yet many pueblos and villages were sustained throughout the area, along both banks at an average distance of seven miles apart.[77] Fourteenth-century Piro pueblos contained from 200 to 600 rooms, as well as plazas and kivas. A few miles southwest of San Pasqualito are the ruins of San Pasqual Pueblo in the riverine lowlands. This large site with four plazas was clearly a Piro center or capital. Despite their success in living in this harsh land for centuries, the Piros could not survive the diseases and violence that occurred with the arrival of the Spanish in the sixteenth century, and consequently no longer exist as a cultural entity here.

The San Pasqualito site contains rock art of both Rio Grande and Archaic Styles. The Rio Grande Style petroglyphs consist of masks, birds, snakes, and anthropomorphic images on the cliff face near the ruins. The Archaic petroglyphs are more typically on boulders at the base of the cliffs and include abstract designs, sun symbols, and rake-like elements perhaps indicating rain.

Ten miles farther south is yet another Black Mesa adjacent to the Rio Grande. This one, like all the others, is named for the veneer of black basalt from a lava flow that covers it. Similar to the setting

Figure 168.
*Rio Grande Style
petroglyph of a
shield bearer,
Black Mesa,
Socorro County,
New Mexico.*

Figure 168.
Rio Grande Style petroglyph of a shield bearer, Black Mesa, Socorro County, New Mexico.

Figure 169. Rio Grande Style petroglyph of a shield bearer, Black Mesa, Socorro County, New Mexico.

at Cerro Indio, here also the constriction and channeling of the river have created large, open bottomlands that were used for agriculture in prehistoric times. The petroglyphs here are primarily Piro, as well as some of Archaic, Apache, and historic Spanish and Anglo origin. They occur on boulders at the base of the mesa and on the escarpment edge at the top of the mesa. Among the Piro images are elaborate shield bearers (Figures 168 and 169), horned masks (Figure 170), and depictions of the

Figure 170. Piro Rio Grande Style petroglyph of a one-horned kachina mask, Black Mesa, Socorro County, New Mexico.

Hand, or Matia, Kachina (Figure 171). Similar depictions of this supernatural occur in the Galisteo Basin and at West Mesa.

One of the more unusual images here is a petroglyph of an apparent kachina with a bird-like beak on its mask, which is supported by a long, thin "stick" over a body that strides along with a drum, from which a bird is emerging (Figure 172). Other images here that are probably Piro include snakes (ordinary snakes—the horned serpent is conspicuously absent), handprints, cloud terraces, corn plants (see Figure 4), and bear paws.

Figure 171. Rio Grande Style petroglyphs of a Hand Kachina, Black Mesa, Socorro County, New Mexico.

Figure 172.
Rio Grande Style
petroglyph of a
bird-beaked
kachina with
drum, Black
Mesa, Socorro
County,
New Mexico.

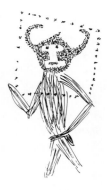

Figure 173.
Apache
petroglyph of a
shaman with a
horned headdress,
Black Mesa,
Socorro County,
New Mexico.

Petroglyphs at this site that may be of Apache origin are executed by a scratching technique rather than by pecking. In creating the shaman-like being with a sunburst head in Figure 21 and the figure with a horned mask in Figure 173, the scratching technique was used for the body and the pecking technique for the head. On an isolated boulder is a simple, scratched image of a slender, elongated man who is running or dancing while holding a long, thin object to his mouth (Figure 174). Hidden in a crack is a scene with figures only several inches high showing a sitting man (with Apache-style hair), behind whom stands a larger, phallic, pot-bellied being with a huge nose from which flow lines suggesting breath or power (Figure 175).

Figure 174.
*Apache petroglyph
created by a
scratching technique,
Black Mesa,
Socorro County,
New Mexico.*

Figure 175.
*Apache
petroglyphs
created by a
scratching
technique, Black
Mesa, Socorro
County,
New Mexico.*

Hands

Inside a cave in a narrow canyon near Tassajara
The vault of rock is painted with hands,
A multitude of hands in the twilight, a cloud of men's
    palms, no more,
No other picture. There's no one to say
Whether the brown shy quiet people who are dead intended
Religion or magic, or made their tracings
In the idleness of art; but over the division of years these
    careful
Signs-manual are now like a sealed message
Saying, "Look: we also are human; we had hands, not
    paws. All hail
You people with the cleverer hands, our supplanters
In the beautiful country; enjoy her a season, her beauty,
    and come down
And be supplanted; for you also are human."[1]

—Robinson Jeffers

4

Southern Sites

The dividing point chosen here for separating the northern and southern sites corresponds to the prehistoric cultural boundary between the Anasazi/Pueblo territory in the north and the Mogollon territory in the south (Figure 3). Consequently, the southern sites are still more than a thousand miles from the mouth of the river at the Gulf of Mexico and thus still within the area defined as the upper Rio Grande in this book (Figure 2). This part of the Rio Grande watershed, from south of Socorro to just south of El Paso, encompasses an area of approximately 5,000 square miles. It is bounded on the west by the San Mateo Mountains, the Black Range, and the Mimbres Mountains. The eastern boundary runs parallel to the Rio Grande along the spine of the Sierra Caballos, Organ, and San Andres Mountains, about five to ten miles away from the river. The river here is bordered by vast expanses of desert characterized by gently sloping plains which are broken by barren mountain ranges and isolated mountain peaks—the Basin and Range Province. Approximately 80 percent of the southern portion of the Rio Grande here is between 4,000 and 6,000 feet in elevation and belongs in the lower Sonoran life zone, characterized by creosote bush and mesquite. Lying beyond the boundaries described above are a series of arid, topographically enclosed basins; the rock art of these basins will be explored as well.

This part of the Rio Grande Valley is dominated by two large reservoirs near the city of Truth or Consequences—Elephant Butte and Caballo. These man-made reservoirs control and store the entire flow of the river. There are no perennial tributary streams flowing into the river in this stretch, and in southern New Mexico the once mighty Rio Grande is almost dead, its water sucked up in inefficient irrigation systems, diverted to support the cities of Las Cruces and El Paso. Today, this stretch is perhaps the most degraded of the entire length of the Rio Grande. Virtually all of the original cottonwood bosques have been cleared and the wetlands drained.

Unfortunately, what was once the living center of New Mexico, a healthy and varied ecosystem, is becoming nothing more than a plumbing system. By contrast, no more than 150 years ago in southern New Mexico the Rio Grande meandered across a floodplain several miles wide, seldom running dry. Aquatic creatures could take refuge in pools during times of drought. Sturgeon and other big fish lurked in the water, birds and game flourished, and grizzly bears and wolves roamed the bottomlands. But the once dense riparian forests have been replaced by a parched floodway full of weeds and trash, and all but five native fish species have been eliminated. Today, it is common for this part of the Rio Grande to dry up completely from a combination of dam storage and agricultural diversion.[2]

The area between Socorro and Elephant Butte Reservoir once supported many pueblos. The rich culture here benefited from cross-cultural exchange between the Mogollon culture to the south and west and the Anasazi culture to the north. At the time of Spanish contact, Piros inhabited twenty-two pueblos, thirteen of which fronted the Rio Grande between the mouth of the Rio Puerco and the area now covered by Elephant Butte Lake. Just prior to the coming of the Spanish there were at least forty-five settlements with a population of at least 12,000.[3]

However, the cultural history of southern New Mexico is more complex than this. Starting with the earliest occupation by Archaic hunter/gatherers, there was a continuity in Mogollon culture that persisted until A.D. 1400, followed by the Indian occupation of southern New Mexico by the Apaches in the early 1600s. Consequently, the rock art styles found in southern New Mexico reflect these different cultural groups and span a time continuum from Archaic to historic.

Continuing south, several tributaries containing rock art flow into the Rio Grande near Truth or Consequences. Prior to being renamed for the TV game show, this place was known as Hot Springs, and before that as Ojo Caliente de Palomas (Hot Springs of the Doves). It was revered as a sacred place of healing by the Apaches and also probably by the various prehistoric cultures that preceded them. Some springs were said to have specific curing properties for certain ailments, such as skin disease and aching joints. The most potent healing element was the white mud found in some springs, which had "electric power." In the past century, the area has been transformed from a riverside marshland full of sacred hot springs and doves, into a funky town next to stagnant reservoirs, with the sacred hot springs diverted for use by motels, commercial bathhouses, and executives' offices. The venerable Geronimo

Springs has been reduced to a small trickle under a gazebo on Main Street. The great Apache warrior is said to have spent some of his best days relaxing in the hot waters here with his friend Victorio, chief of the Warm Springs Apaches, before they were both captured by the United States Army.

BLACK RANGE

Near the headwaters of the tributary Cuchillo Negro Creek, named for the Apache chief Cuchillo Negro (Black Knife), are a number of small but interesting rock art sites at the base of the Black Range. On Chloride Creek are several pictograph sites under rock shelters—mostly examples of the Mogollon Red Style with a few Jornada Style terrace-like elements (Figure 14). Also nearby are some abstract polychrome paintings that may be of Apache origin.

A few miles to the southeast near Chise, several petroglyph sites are clustered near the confluence of South Fork and Cuchillo Negro Creek. One of these sites, in a small bedrock drainage, appears to be Archaic. The petroglyphs here are abstract sym-

Figure 176. Petroglyphs, Cuchillo Negro Creek, Sierra County, New Mexico.

Figure 177.
*Petroglyphs,
Cuchillo Negro
Creek, Sierra
County,
New Mexico.*

bols such as rakes, dots, rectangles, and spirals, and appear to be very old based on their repatination and degree of weathering. Nearby are several Mogollon Style panels on low cliffs. The petroglyphs in Figure 176 include anthropomorphs, birds, stylized plants, and geometric shapes. At another panel are a pair of deer (one of which has antlers) standing back-to-back, each of which stands over a bird-like symbol (Figure 177).

Figure 178.
*Apache
pictograph in red,
Ash Spring,
Sierra Caballos,
Sierra County,
New Mexico.*

SIERRA CABALLOS

From Truth or Consequences, the other tributary is Mescal Canyon, which drains the rugged country to the southeast of the city, behind the Sierra Caballos. In this desiccated land, there are two rare sources of permanent water—Ash Spring and Mescal Spring—that were of great importance to both prehistoric and Spanish travelers who left the river for the dreaded Jornada del Muerto (Journey of Death) route. At Ash Spring, a pleasant oasis except for the denuded riparian vegetation, a faded red pictograph of a mounted hunter with bow suggests the Apaches favored this place for hunting and camping (Figure 178). A few miles away in a canyon near Mescal Spring is another red pictograph of an imposing horned anthropomorph that

Figure 179.
*Apache
pictograph in red,
Mescal Canyon,
Sierra Caballos,
Sierra County,
New Mexico.*

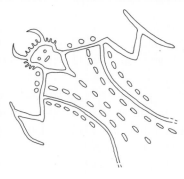

Figure 180.
*Apache
pictograph in red,
Mescal Canyon,
Sierra Caballos,
Sierra County,
New Mexico.*

probably represents an Apache shaman (Figure 179), as well as a mounted warrior in a feathered war bonnet (Figure 180).

Further down the Rio Grande another twenty miles, near Hatch, the river takes a strong turn to the east. Many rock art sites are concentrated between here and Las Cruces, along both sides of the valley. At the southern tip of the Caballo Mountains near Rincon, is a petroglyph site with a commanding view up and down the river. Here the mostly Jornada Style images are associated with a nearby smoke-blackened cave on the edge of a fifty-foot chasm, probably a ceremonial site. Petroglyphs are scattered along the bedrock channel of an ephemeral drainage, one which trapped precious runoff water in several deep, slickrock pools. Near to these water sources are at least seven images of Tlaloc, the water deity (Figure 181). Next to some bedrock mortar holes for grinding seeds and plants are other images, such as masks, lizards, snakes, cloud terraces, geometric designs, and anthropomorphs. A few older-looking images of circles, meandering lines, and rakes are probably Archaic.

To the northwest, in Palmer Park, an isolated valley in the Caballo Mountains, an elaborate petroglyph of Tlaloc is rendered in exquisite detail on a

Figure 181.
Jornada Style
petroglyph of
Tlaloc, Rincon,
Doña Ana
County,
New Mexico.

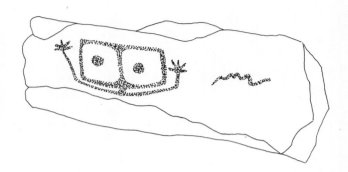

large boulder (Figure 182). Although exfoliation of the rock surface obscures some of the edges, it appears that the geometric design that forms the body is intentionally borderless, with typical large, goggle-like eyes on top to indicate the head. According to records from a 1930s reconnaissance survey of Palmer Park, the area used to have many other large boulders with rock art, all of which had "basins" on top that could hold several gallons of water. Unfortunately, these were destroyed with dynamite by unscrupulous persons seeking hidden Spanish treasure.[4] Even today the Caballos Mountains are a magnet for many treasure seekers and miners, who roam these sun-baked hills hoping to strike it rich on Spanish gold.

Figure 182.
Jornada Style
petroglyph
of Tlaloc,
Palmer Park,
Doña Ana
County,
New Mexico.

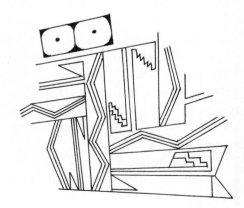

Figure 183. *Jornada Style petroglyph of a tadpole superimposed on Archaic abstract petroglyphs, Tonuco Mountains, Doña Ana County, New Mexico.*

Figure 184. *Jornada Style petroglyph of a mask incorporating an animal head, San Diego Mountain, Doña Ana County, New Mexico.*

TONUCO MOUNTAINS

The next prominent feature encountered along the Rio Grande are the Tonuco Mountains, which rise abruptly as isolated peaks standing 900 feet above the east bank of the river. At the foot of one of them, petroglyphs are found in a rugged canyon. Jornada Style images predominate, but on a number of boulders they are superimposed on dense panels of repatinated Archaic Desert Abstract Style petroglyphs. An example of this superimposition of styles is seen in Figure 183, where a large (forty-inch-tall) Jornada Style petroglyph of a tadpole overlies the older Archaic images. As is typical of many Jornada sites, ceremonial masks and activities are important themes (Figures 184, 185, 186, and Plate 13). Recently an archaeoastronomical feature was documented at this site, a further indication that rituals took place here.[5]

Figure 185. *Jornada Style petroglyphs of masks, San Diego Mountain, Doña Ana County, New Mexico.*

SIERRA DE LAS UVAS

Across the river to the west, the Sierra de las Uvas dominate the landscape. Named for the wild

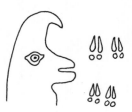

Figure 186. *Jornada Style petroglyph of a figure carrying a ritual object (horns of bighorn sheep?), San Diego Mountain, Doña Ana County, New Mexico.*

Figure 187. Jornada Style petroglyphs of a horned serpent head with deer tracks, Broad Canyon, Doña Ana County, New Mexico.

grapevines that grace some of its springs and canyon bottoms, these mountains contain petroglyph sites in canyons that drain east to the Rio Grande as well as southwest into the Mimbres Basin. At the highest point, Magdalena Peak, is an astronomy observatory and a NASA Lunar Surveillance facility. Broad Canyon is one of the Uvas' major drainages to the Rio Grande, joining the river north of Radium Springs. Several petroglyph sites are known here, in both the upper and lower portions of the canyon. Jornada Style elements such as a horned serpent (Figure 187) and a six-foot-tall Tlaloc are present. The panel in Figure 188 consists of other Jornada Style images, such as fish, snakes, human handprints and footprints, an image that may be a bird eating a salamander, and a curious quadruped that combines attributes of a bighorn sheep with the tail of a snake.

Figure 188. Jornada Style petroglyphs, Broad Canyon, Doña Ana County, New Mexico.

Figure 189. Jornada Style petroglyph of a geometric design, Broad Canyon, Doña Ana County, New Mexico.

Figure 190. *Jornada Style petroglyph of a geometric design, Broad Canyon, Doña Ana County, New Mexico.*

Elsewhere in Broad Canyon there are some elaborate geometric designs as in Figures 189 and 190. A few of the petroglyphs in Broad Canyon may be of Apache origin. The pair of horned, shaman-like figures holding snakes are drawn with the tapered torso typical of many Apache Style anthropomorphs (Figure 191). Another pair of similarly shaped

Figure 191. *Apache (?) petroglyphs of horned shaman figures with snakes, Broad Canyon, Doña Ana County, New Mexico.*

Figure 192.
*Apache (?)
petroglyphs, Sierra
de las Uvas, Doña
Ana County,
New Mexico.*

anthropomorphs with plant-like forms attached to
their arms occurs four miles to the south in a small
canyon draining into the Mimbres Basin (Figure
192). It is interesting to compare these anthropomorphs to the Apache pictograph in Figure 179
from the Sierra Caballos.

DOÑA ANA MOUNTAINS

On the east side of the Rio Grande opposite
Radium Springs and north of Las Cruces, the Doña
Ana Mountains rise dramatically. Rock art sites
occur in some of the canyons that drain to the river,
as well as in scattered locations on large boulders
lying around the base of these mountains. Lucero

Figure 193.
*Jornada Style
petroglyphs, Lucero
Arroyo, Doña Ana
County,
New Mexico.*

Arroyo, which used to be called Pictograph Canyon, drains southwest from Summerford Mountain to the Rio Grande and contains one of the largest petroglyph sites in the Doña Ana Mountains. Dozens of petroglyphs, of mostly Jornada Style, occur on both sides of the canyon. The panel in Figure 193 seems to express a hunting theme, with a game animal and hunter armed with a bow. Although several goggle-eyed Tlaloc figures are present here, the startled-looking creatures in Figure 194 are probably not representations of Tlaloc since they lack the characteristic square head and trapezoidal bodies.

At the base of Summerford Mountain, there are scattered petroglyphs and pictographs on large granite boulders. Some of the designs are purely geometric, whereas others are representational, such as the hands, feet, animal tracks, and a rabbit in Figure 195.

Figure 194.
Jornada Style petroglyphs, Lucero Arroyo, Doña Ana County, New Mexico.

Figure 195.
Jornada Style petroglyphs, Summerford Mountain, Doña Ana County, New Mexico.

Figure 196.
Jornada Style
petroglyph of
Tlaloc, near
Vado, Doña Ana
County,
New Mexico.

MESILLA VALLEY AND
FRANKLIN MOUNTAINS

Below Las Cruces other Jornada sites occur on an area of lava flows west of the river, including another Black Mesa. Here Jornada Style masks are found, as well as curvilinear designs that suggest possible Archaic ties. Across the river to the east, near Vado, abundant rock art once existed on a small hill, including the classic Tlaloc in Figure 196, but the site has been ravaged by spray paint and bullets in recent years.

North of El Paso the rugged Franklin Mountains provide some scenic relief from the urban sprawl that chokes the lowlands along the Rio Grande. A few rock art sites in caves are hidden here in deep recesses and rocky canyons. On the ceiling of one of these caves is a surprisingly well-preserved red painting of a large bighorn sheep pierced by a spear, as well as a smaller anthropomorph (Figure 197). It is miraculous that this ancient image has so far escaped vandalism, since adjacent caves are full of beer cans and other trash from the urban hordes. It is probably an Archaic Period (or early Basket-maker?) pictograph; the projectile shaft appears to be an atlatl dart (thus predating the bow and arrow), and a nearby rock shelter was found to contain evidence of Archaic habitation.

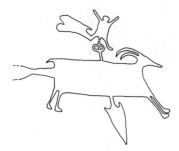

Figure 197.
Archaic Style
pictograph in red of a
bighorn sheep pierced
by an atlatl dart,
cave in the Franklin
Mountains, El Paso
County, Texas.

HUECO TANKS
STATE HISTORICAL PARK

Approximately thirty miles east of El Paso, Texas, Hueco Tanks State Historical Park contains a very significant concentration of rock art. Three massive granite outcrops hundreds of feet above the flat Chihuahuan Desert contain many natural water traps, or tanks (*huecos* in Spanish) within a convoluted topography of huge boulders, caves, and slick-rock surfaces that collect rainfall runoff and store the precious water for months. The presence of water in these natural cisterns, along with the unique plant communities made possible by this moisture, has made this a place of refuge in an otherwise inhospitable area. The many rock paintings here are an important legacy of different prehistoric cultures who found water, shelter, and food in this oasis. Over 3,000 rock paintings are hidden within the caves and crevices of the massive rocky outcrops—one of the largest concentrations of Indian pictographs in North America. An unusual feature is the large number of painted masks—more than 200 are known (Plate 14).[6]

Four distinct groups of Native Americans are known to have used the Hueco Tanks area: Paleo-Indians, Desert Archaic, Jornada Mogollon, and Mescalero Apaches. The place also has an interesting history of use by Spanish and Mexican people, as well as by other early settlers. Today, the park manages the hordes of rock climbers who throng there from around the world to climb these once sacred peaks, a spectacle that would no doubt have puzzled the ancient shamans. Although some rock art unfortunately has been damaged by climbers, more has suffered from acts of deliberate vandalism, such as spray-painted graffiti. Despite modern intrusion,

Figure 198.
Middle/Late
Archaic Style
pictographs of a
hunting scene,
Hueco Tanks, El
Paso County,
Texas. (After
Kirkland and
Newcomb 1967.)

here the paintings in their barely accessible niches provide an aura of mystery and sacredness that few other sites rival.

That Paleo-Indians (10,000 B.C.) inhabited the Hueco Tanks area is known from discovery of their distinctive Folsom points; however, no rock art is ascribed to these first nomadic big-game hunters in the area. The Desert Archaic people (6000 B.C. to A.D. 450) followed, and at least two Archaic rock art styles have been identified at Hueco Tanks.[7] The Early Archaic Style (6000 to 3000 B.C.) consists of curvilinear and rectilinear abstract designs. The subsequent Middle and Late Archaic Style (3000 B.C. to A.D. 450) is characterized by hunting scenes of game animals and humans with shaman-like qualities (Figure 198). These people hunted with the spear and atlatl, not yet possessing the bow and arrow. Both pictographs and petroglyphs in this style occur around the El Paso area, although Hueco Tanks has relatively few Archaic hunting scenes. An example from the Franklin Mountains north of El Paso was

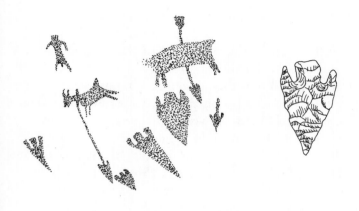

Figure 199.
Archaic Diablo Dam Style petroglyphs of an anthropomorph with "human-ized" spear points and speared game animals, com-pared with an Archaic Schumla Type point, Alamo Canyon, Hudspeth County, Texas.

previously given (Figure 197). Other nearby sites, notably Alamo Canyon near Fort Hancock, contain many petroglyphs of hunting scenes. At some sites the spearheads are drawn well enough to be identified as Archaic Schumla Type points, and the hunters' bodies are stylized to resemble these spearheads (Figure 199).

Most of the rock art at Hueco Tanks is from the Jornada Mogollon people (A.D. 450 to 1400), who lived in settled villages and practiced agriculture as well as hunting and gathering. There is evidence that there was a small village at Hueco Tanks around A.D. 1000.[8] The rock art associated with it reflects the central importance of rain and moisture (see Chapter 5, "Sites with Public Access," for more on rock art depicting this theme at Hueco Tanks).

The significance and origin of the many mask paintings here have been explored by anthropologist Kay Sutherland: "It appears that, at Hueco Tanks, Mesoamerican gods, many of whom manifested different aspects of the same elements, combined with the earlier animistic concepts of the Desert Archaic peoples to create a new religious force, manifesting itself in a religion of masked spirit beings."[9]

Figure 200.
Jornada Style pictograph of a masked dancer, Hueco Tanks, El Paso County, Texas. (After Kirkland and Newcomb 1967.)

Apparently, the masks represented ancestral spirits, similar to the kachinas of the modern Pueblo people. Consequently, the meanings of the Jornada masks must have been similar to those of Hopi, Zuni, and other pueblos in the upper Rio Grande region. The masked dancer becomes an intermediary between the spirit and human worlds, helping ensure harmony, well-being, and rain. The dancer in Figure 200 illustrates the use of masks in ritual by the Jornada at Hueco Tanks (see Chapter 5, "Sites with Public Access," for more on mask images at Hueco Tanks).

Figure 201. White pictographs of a Mescalero Apache victory dance or fertility ritual, Comanche Cave, Hueco Tanks, El Paso County, Texas.

Mescalero Apaches visited Hueco Tanks during the nineteenth century and perhaps earlier, leaving behind paintings of mounted warriors, large snakes, and ceremonies in a number of locations. The best examples are the white paintings in Comanche Cave (Figure 201). The Comanches, also Plains warriors, probably visited the area, as well as the Kiowas (see Chapter 5, "Sites with Public Access," for more details on Mescalero Apache rock art in the area).

ALAMO CANYON

About thirty miles to the southeast of Hueco Tanks the Finlay Mountains rise from the desert in the area of Fort Hancock. Alamo Canyon is one of the main drainages from here to the Rio Grande. This site has apparently been a major hunting shrine for millennia. The mouths of major canyons tend to be wildlife corridors. Today, willows and an old windmill suggest there was once a more obvious water source in this location. Many bedrock mortars and some caves suitable for habitation or ceremonial use are further signs of the prehistoric significance of the area.

As mentioned earlier, in the west Texas region there was development of a representational style of rock art in Middle/Late Archaic times that superseded the older Desert Abstract Style, indicating that changes were taking place in the symbolic system of expression among these peoples. The representational style gives us insight into the concepts of the supernatural held by these early hunter/gatherers. In the Chihuahuan Desert region along the Rio Grande between El Paso and Big Bend, there is a diverse collection of representational rock art styles from this period, including some miniature paintings of life-forms and some simple anthropomorphs resembling the Lower Pecos River Style paintings.[10] However, the most significant representational Archaic rock art in the region are the petroglyphs of hunting scenes and animals at Alamo Canyon executed in what is known as the Diablo Dam Petroglyph Style (Plate 1), which emphasizes men with long spears and distinctive projectile points. This emphasis on spears and points is rare in southwestern rock art and may indicate they had spiritual significance.[11]

The figures of the Archaic hunters have shamanic

Figure 202.
Archaic Diablo
Dam Style
petroglyphs of an
anthropomorph
with large
Schumla Type
spear points,
Alamo Canyon,
Hudspeth County,
Texas

Figure 203.
Jornada Style
petroglyph of the
head of a crested
serpent, Alamo
Canyon,
Hudspeth County,
Texas.

qualities and are shown holding spears with spear point heads and arms (Figure 202); that is, the spear points resemble stylized anthropomorphs (Figure 199). This association of hunters with spear points implies a powerful spiritual connection with hunting, and that the shaman/hunter played an important role in these animist cultures.[12] The fact that some of these figures are horned is further indication of shamanic, supernatural processes in these societies and in their rock art at this site.

Jornada Style rock art is found in the same area as the Archaic and also at several other sites a mile up the canyon. Present are such characteristically Jornada elements as Tlalocs and horned serpents (Figure 203). A large petroglyph panel known as the "Storyteller Panel" contains a fascinating array of anthropomorphs, deer and bighorn sheep, and geometric designs (Figure 204). On the sandstone boulders around this site are other petroglyphs of bighorn sheep, executed in a quite different manner (Figure 205). Some interesting anthropomorphic figures are also found here. Although the two anthropomorphs in Figures 206 and 207 are over a mile apart, their common gesture of upraised right arms suggests some related significance. The anthropomorph in Figure 206 is perhaps holding a rectangular shield with his left arm, but the right arm of the humpbacked, phallic male in Figure 207 is clearly emphasized more than the left one.

Pictographs also occur in Alamo Canyon—at a number of small rock shelters and in one cave that contains an unusual assemblage of large animals painted in white on its fire-blackened ceiling. Among them are deer, cats, an elaborate crested serpent (Figure 5), a ferocious carnivore (Figure 208), and a large bear.

Figure 204. *Jornada Style petroglyphs at the "Storyteller Panel," Alamo Canyon, Hudspeth County, Texas.*

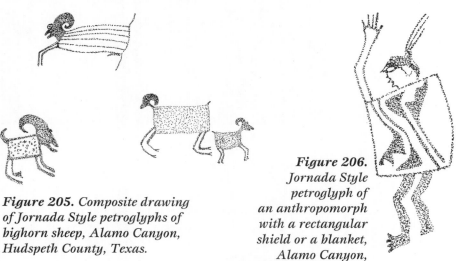

Figure 205. *Composite drawing of Jornada Style petroglyphs of bighorn sheep, Alamo Canyon, Hudspeth County, Texas.*

Figure 206. *Jornada Style petroglyph of an anthropomorph with a rectangular shield or a blanket, Alamo Canyon, Hudspeth County, Texas.*

Figure 207.
Jornada Style
petroglyph of a
humpbacked,
phallic anthro-
pomorph with
an exaggerated
right arm,
Alamo Canyon,
Hudspeth County,
Texas.

Figure 208. *Jornada*
Style pictograph of the
head of a carnivore,
painted in white on the
ceiling of a cave at Alamo
Canyon, Hudspeth
County, Texas.

LOBO VALLEY

The southernmost site discussed in this book is another sixty miles to the southeast, in the Van Horn Mountains. The Lobo Valley Petroglyph Site is on the National Register of Historic Places and is significant for the more than 200 petroglyphs dating from the Early Archaic to Late Prehistoric Periods.[13] Although other rock art sites occur in the area,[14] Lobo Valley is unique for the number and clarity of its carvings, and the long time span of the styles represented there. It is situated in a region that functioned as a natural basin and range corridor providing a north-south passageway between the Davis Mountains and the Guadalupe Mountains and Salt Basin. The area was inhabited extensively from the Paleo-Indian Period to the Late Prehistoric Period. The area, which provided excellent stone tool materials, is famous for its prehistoric quarries and extensive selection of artifacts.

The Lobo Valley petroglyphs are located in the mouth of an unnamed canyon that drains east from the Van Horn Mountains. A spring that flowed nearby in prehistoric times supported occupation at the site during various periods.

One of the finest panels at Lobo Valley is a large boulder literally covered with bold abstract designs (Figure 209). The sharp contrast of these designs is due to a slight degree of repatination, which makes it problematic to assign these particular abstract designs to the Archaic Period. Sadly, in the 1980s this boulder was used for target practice by hunters. Today, the site is owned and cared for by the Culberson County Historical Commission, which is concerned about protecting it from any further vandalism, and conducts public tours there in an effort to educate people about its value (see Chapter 5,

Figure 209. *Petroglyphs, Lobo Valley, Culberson County, Texas.*

"Sites with Public Access," for a description of the rock art).

The next sites discussed are north of Lobo Valley, in southern New Mexico just beyond the drainage divide of the Rio Grande in the enclosed basins that flank the river on both sides.

MIMBRES BASIN

The 4,400 square miles of the Mimbres River Basin lie west of the Rio Grande, between the Mexican border and the Gila Mountains. The upper reaches of the Mimbres River and a few tributaries are the only perennial water in the basin, and it is in these headwater regions that most of the prehistoric occupation took place and where most of the rock art is located.

Before European contact, this land sustained native cultures over a span of millennia, including Desert Archaic, Mogollon, and Apache. Rock art from all these peoples is present, but not in great concentrations, with the exception of several Jornada Mogollon sites. The Mimbres River is named for the Mimbres people—members of the Mogollon culture who inhabited this basin, built pueblos, created rock art, and produced the exquisite pottery designs for which they are famous. Within this region of the Mountain Mogollon, the rock art style of these agricultural peoples is still recognized as Jornada.[15] Many of the design motifs that grace Mimbres bowls and pots also appear in Jornada Style rock art— motifs that are a primary means of dating the rock art. Nearly all Mimbres ruins have been plundered and destroyed by pot hunters seeking these valuable ceramics. Fortunately, most Mimbres petroglyphs here are still intact.

In the upper reaches of the Mimbres River in Ponderosa pine forests near Lake Roberts, Pictograph Canyon contains a number of red paintings believed to be of Apache origin.[16] A meticulously painted net-like design, along with some handprints and finger stripes, is found under a small ledge, and nearby are some red paintings of lizard-man anthropomorphs, one with a three-part headdress, that resemble Apache Mountain spirit dancers (Figure 210).[17]

The distinctive 8,408-foot Cooke's Peak dominates the landscape from nearly everywhere in the lower Mimbres Basin, forming the southern end of the rugged Black Range of the Mimbres Mountains. Several interesting Jornada Style petroglyph sites lie along its southern flank in the Pony Hills area. Springs nearby facilitated prehistoric use of the area. The place also has a colorful recent history, as

Figure 210.
Apache
pictographs,
Pictograph
Canyon, Grant
County,
New Mexico.

Figure 211. Jornada Style petroglyph of a rattlesnake, Cooke's Peak area, Luna County, New Mexico.

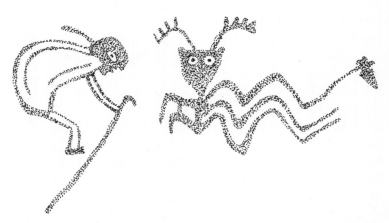

Figure 212. Composite of Jornada Style petroglyphs, Cooke's Peak area, Luna County, New Mexico.

Figure 213. *Jornada Style Petroglyphs, Apache Well, Doña Ana County, New Mexico.*

suggested by place-names like Starvation Draw, Frying Pan Canyon, and Massacre Peak.

The hundreds of images at the Cooke's Peak sites include all the characteristic Jornada elements, including Tlalocs, horned serpents, and many other creatures, such as tadpoles, turtles, and rattlesnakes (Figure 211). Also depicted are unusual anthropomorphs with mask-like faces and a humpbacked man holding a crook or staff, a figure that may be related to the Kokopelli fertility symbol (Figure 212).[18]

On a low, rocky ridge east of the Good Sight Mountains is another small Jornada site. Petroglyphs here include a crested serpent, triangles, tracks of deer and carnivores, and a finely carved, intricate geometric design on a boulder (Figure 213). Unfortunately, some of the petroglyphs at this site have been damaged and even buried by an overzealous equipment operator during construction or maintenance of a dirt road that skirts the site.

SALT BASIN

Figure 214.
Apache
petroglyph,
Alamo Mountain,
Otero County,
New Mexico.

Figure 215.
Apache
petroglyph of a
warrior with a
shield, Alamo
Mountain, Otero
County,
New Mexico.

On the east side of the Rio Grande, the expansive Salt Basin lies south of the Sacramento and Guadalupe Mountains. A land of wide-open spaces, this is a transition area between the Great Plains and the Basin and Range Province with limited surface water, so it has always been sparsely populated. There are two principal rock art sites in the basin, both located in the Cornudas Mountains near the New Mexico-Texas border. From a distance the Cornudas Mountains resemble a group of horns rising from the plains. Because of several springs there, these mountains have been inhabited for thousands of years, like Hueco Tanks. A mixture of Archaic, Jornada, and Apache rock art reflects this diverse history.

At Alamo Mountain, the westernmost peak of the Cornudas, hundreds of petroglyphs are pecked on the rocks that lie over the mountain's lower slopes, particularly in the vicinity of a spring. The Apache petroglyphs here are typified by horned images (Figure 214), narrow-waisted anthropomorphs (Figure 215), horses, and bison. Other motifs of apparent Apache origin are sets of long wavy lines and configurations based on triangles.[19]

It has been suggested that some of the Mescalero Apache images at Alamo Mountain have a stylistic affinity to certain Chiricahua Apache medicine artifacts, such as bull roarers, amulets, and medicine hats.[20] It is believed that figures common to these artifacts and certain petroglyphs at Alamo Mountain

represent the Apache God of Wind, or Controller of Water. The bull roarer is a flat piece of wood (preferably one that has been struck by lightning) attached to a long cord, and is twirled about to produce the sound of wind. It was used by Pueblo and Apache medicine men as part of power rituals connected with lightning and rain. In ethnographic accounts in the 1880s, the designs on Apache bull roarers were explained as follows: "The lines on the front...were the entrails and those on the rear side the hair [representing lightning] of their wind god."[21] In light of this information, a striking resemblance can be seen between the images on the bull roarers and the petroglyphs from Alamo Mountain (Figure 216). Both have horned figures with vertical wavy or diamond-shaped bodies, short arm-like appendages, triangular eyes, and earrings. Next to each petroglyph is a mass of wavy or zigzag lines representing the "hair" depicted on the bull roarers. The placing of wind, rain, or lightning deities on

Figure 216. Comparison of Wind God figures carved on a Chiricahua Apache bull roarer (on left) with similar figures in Mescalero Apache petroglyphs (on right) at Alamo Mountain, Otero County, New Mexico.

Figure 217.
Wind God figure
in Mescalero
Apache
petroglyphs at
Alamo Mountain,
Otero County,
New Mexico.

Figure 218.
Jornada Style
pictograph of
Tlaloc in red and
white, Cornudas
Mountain, Otero
County,
New Mexico.

rocks may have been of special ritual significance at Alamo Mountain in order to ensure that the nearby life-giving spring be kept alive by adequate rains. A photograph of one of the petroglyph depictions of the Wind God is shown in Figure 217.

At Cornudas Mountain, an isolated peak within the Cornudas Mountains, petroglyphs and pictographs are also clustered near a water source. Here a large, imposing Tlaloc is painted in red and white on an overhanging rock (Figure 218). His headdress resembles the universal rake-like symbol for rain. Other Jornada Style images here include the anthropomorph with a bemused expression wearing a bighorn sheep headdress (Figure 219).

TULAROSA BASIN

There is no obvious transition between the Salt Basin and the Tularosa Basin, which lies to the west and north. The Tularosa Basin is over one hundred miles long, lying between two huge mountain ranges—the San Andres on the west and the Sacramento on the east, with the massif of 12,000-foot Sierra Blanca. Hot, dry, and desolate, most of the basin is controlled by the United States Department of Defense for weapons and rocket experimentation, including White Sands Missile Range, Holloman Air Force Base, and Fort Bliss. It is a land of extremes that encompasses both the bright White Sands National Monument and the pitch black Malpais Lava Beds. Here rock art sites are sparse but include a few large and exceptional ones such as at Three Rivers, the primary perennial stream in the basin. Through prehistoric times this vast area was relatively tranquil, but in the past century there have been range wars between cattle barons, genocidal fighting with Apaches, and destruction of the rangeland's grasses by huge cattle herds. In the south, a frenzy of gold mining has pockmarked the hills of the Jarilla Mountains near Orogrande. A few minor petroglyph sites are scattered about the Jarilla Mountains, some of which appear to be Archaic while others are clearly Jornada.

At the foot of the White Mountain Wilderness, good springs in Willow Draw were a magnet for

Figure 219.
Jornada Style
petroglyph of an
anthropomorph
with a headdress
of bighorn sheep
horns, Cornudas
Mountain, Otero
County,
New Mexico.

prehistoric activity. A basaltic dike near the springs is covered with hundreds of rock art images for up to a half-mile (Figure 11). These petroglyphs are mostly Desert Abstract Style, and consist of irregular abstract and rectilinear geometric designs. There is, however, a great deal of confusing superimposition of images such as triangles, anthropomorphs, zoomorphs, and other elements difficult to categorize. Large areas of the dike are covered completely with repeated motifs of grids, parallel and wavy lines, rakes, circles, and stick figures. Although it is difficult to say with certainty what cultures are represented here, the rock art of this site seems to be largely Archaic, but with transitional elements that suggest some continuity from Late Archaic to Early Mogollon times, including, perhaps, some images of Apache origin.[22]

In the foothills of the Sacramento Mountains around Alamogordo, canyons contain several faded pictograph sites. At one site near Wild Boy Spring, there are anthropomorphs in white, geometric designs in red (chevrons and diamonds), and a black painting of a horse with rider who appears to hold a sword (Figure 220). These paintings are probably Mescalero Apache in origin.

Figure 220. *Pictograph in black of a mounted swordsman (probably Apache), Wild Boy Spring, Otero County, New Mexico. (From a photo by Chris Larsen.)*

THREE RIVERS

Further south, under the imposing presence of Sierra Blanca, is the outstanding Three Rivers Petroglyph National Recreation Area. This increasingly popular area is administered by the BLM for public access, and is one of the largest rock art sites in New Mexico. More than 21,000 Jornada Style petroglyphs have been recorded on this long ridge of basalt above the Three Rivers Valley. An agricultural village site on the edge of nearby Three Rivers Creek was inhabited for about 300 years by Jornada Mogollon peoples; they left an amazing pictorial record of their world on the rocks capping the ridge, which served as a good lookout, where game as well as approaching visitors or enemies could be seen.

The Three Rivers site is a showplace for the highly creative and inspired Jornada Style rock art. A large number of geometric designs are present, along with circular motifs incorporating dots and enclosed crosses (Plate 15). But this site is best known for the myriad life-forms that are depicted in an astonishing variety (see Chapter 5, "Sites with Public Access," for a more detailed description of the rock art).

In discussing the images of Three Rivers, Polly Schaafsma suggests that "the interpretation of Jornada Style life-forms goes beyond the mere identity of species. What we see here is not the work of prehistoric naturalists, but rather a group of figures carefully selected on the basis of their roles in the ideological structure."[23] She supports this supposition by comparisons with modern Pueblo symbols, which were largely derived from the Jornada. For example, images of bear paws stand for the curing powers of the bear, insects may have shamanic powers or play a role in certain myths or rituals, and eagles personify wisdom, boldness, and spiritual qualities.[24]

Figure 221.
Jornada Style petroglyph of a two-headed animal, Three Rivers, Otero County, New Mexico.

In a well-crafted petroglyph, perhaps intended to illustrate the sacred nature of twin births, is a two-headed quadruped next to another whose tail is connected to a mysterious object (Figure 221). Even insects are represented; the creature in Figure 222 is probably a moth with coiled tongue, next to the forelimb of a carnivore. More insects, including a caterpillar and an ant, are shown in the composite drawings of Figure 223. Anthropomorphic images here are equally diverse and creative. For example,

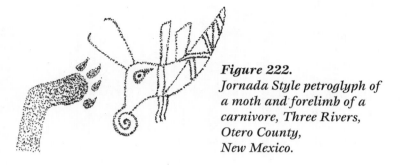

Figure 222.
Jornada Style petroglyph of a moth and forelimb of a carnivore, Three Rivers, Otero County, New Mexico.

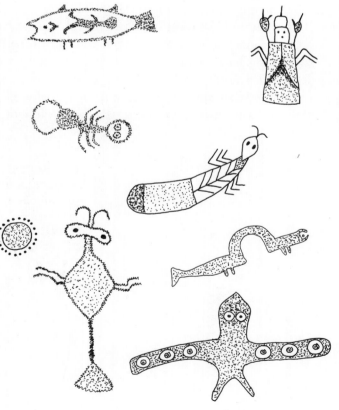

Figure 223.
Composite drawing of various Jornada Style petroglyphs of life-forms, Three Rivers, Otero County, New Mexico.

Figure 224.
Jornada Style
petroglyphs of
anthropomorphs
in ritual or
mythological
activities, Three
Rivers, Otero
County,
New Mexico.

do the images in Figure 224 depict actual people wearing masks and ceremonial garb, supernatural or mythological beings, or visions from someone's dream or trance? Is the winged figure a shaman transporting himself in flight to other realms?

Sometimes the most basic petroglyph images can seem dream-like or surreal, such as the pair of isolated, waving hands with six fingers pecked on a boulder at this site (Figure 225). In this case, however, we know that what appears to be fantastic actually has a realistic basis since archaeologists have documented

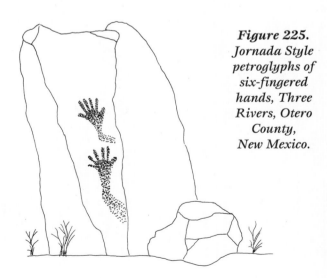

Figure 225.
Jornada Style
petroglyphs of
six-fingered
hands, Three
Rivers, Otero
County,
New Mexico.

from skeletal remains the existence of individuals having six digits in prehistoric populations.

The final rock art sites discussed in this chapter are located twenty miles east of Three Rivers near the headwaters of the Rio Bonito, which flows to the Pecos. Here, and at another site a dozen miles north in Arroyo del Macho, are several more worthy rock art sites.

RIO BONITO AND ARROYO DEL MACHO

Deserving of its name, the Rio Bonito is a pretty little stream that was obviously an attractive habitat for prehistoric people. A few miles upstream from Fort Stanton, between Carrizozo and Roswell, there are a number of small Jornada Style petroglyph sites scattered along the stream on boulders. The largest, known as Petroglyph Rock, is a large boulder in the stream decorated with images of Tlaloc-like masks and eyes, a snake, footprints, a lizard, and geometric designs (Figure 226). (See Chapter 5, "Sites with

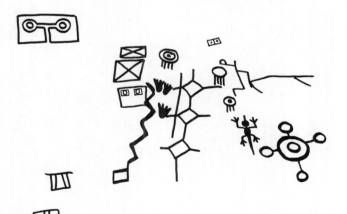

Figure 226.
Petroglyph Rock
(the Tlaloc in the
upper left is on a
nearby rock), Rio
Bonito, Lincoln
County,
New Mexico.

Public Access," for more detailed information.)

Several miles downstream is Feather Cave, a shrine that contained masses of offerings, as well as paintings of a mask, handprints, and concentric circles. This site has been interpreted as an earth-sun shrine that would have been the focus of solstice rituals. This site illustrates the sacred nature of caves, and their use for access to the supernatural by the Mogollon and other southwestern cultures.[25]

Fifteen miles to the northwest, in Arroyo del

Figure 227. Jornada Style petroglyphs, Arroyo del Macho, Lincoln County, New Mexico.

Figure 228. Jornada Style petroglyphs of masks, Arroyo del Macho, Lincoln County, New Mexico. (Drawings from Kelley 1984.)

Macho lies another Jornada Style site, rivaling the Three Rivers site in quality though smaller. Situated along a stream near a Mogollon ruin, these petroglyphs offer intriguing glimpses into the symbolic world of these people. This site also resembles the Three Rivers site in content—with images of geometric designs and cloud terraces, Tlalocs (Figure 227), masks (Figure 228), and a great variety of life-forms.

However, there are some motifs that are relatively unusual, such as the numerous images of dragonflies being held by humpbacked, sometimes phallic anthropomorphs (Figure 229). The nearby stream must have been associated with wetlands and riparian habitat that favored dragonflies, but obviously there is also an important symbolic significance being conveyed here, one which probably had a fertility context. Humpbacked, phallic figures in Jornada rock art, though not usually playing a flute, are thought to be conceptually related to the widespread fertility figure of the Anasazi/Pueblo region known as Kokopelli.[26] One of the anthropomorphs in Figure 229 appears to be playing a flute-like object.

The dragonfly motif appears elsewhere in rock art throughout the Southwest, and is also a popular

Figure 229. Jornada Style petroglyphs of dragonflies being held by humpbacked anthropomorphs, Arroyo del Macho, Lincoln County, New Mexico.

design in Indian jewelry and ceramics. Apparently the sound of the dragonfly ("tsee, tsee, tsee") resembles the word for water in some Indian languages, which may explain the belief that it is a supernatural with the power of speech and the ability to bring summer rains to revitalize springs.[27] Dakota Indians said the dragonfly warned them of danger, and killing one would bring disaster. To Zunis, killing a dragonfly was also taboo, except for ritual use; they mixed hearts of dragonflies and butterflies with certain plants to make "sun medicine," which they rubbed on their bodies for psychic purification. This medicine was only used by men, as it was thought to be an aphrodisiac for women.[28]

Another excellent example of the emphasis on fertility themes at this site is the very phallic man in Figure 230. A large dragonfly image is poised over his head and a snake over his exaggerated penis, which points purposefully at a natural vulva-like protuberance on the rock that has been enhanced by selective pecking. Perhaps the boulder on which this scene was placed served as a fertility shrine.

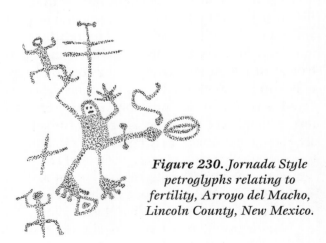

Figure 230. *Jornada Style petroglyphs relating to fertility, Arroyo del Macho, Lincoln County, New Mexico.*

Some other interesting images here are the playfully distorted anthropomorph with misplaced head and arm (Figure 231), and the finely pecked shield with feathers and image of a horned warrior (Figure 232). The encounter between a coyote and rabbit in Figure 233 may represent a mythological event, as these two animals figure prominently in the tales of most Native American cultures. The two creatures in Figure 234 are less recognizable—they appear to combine the qualities of bighorn sheep, crested serpent, and a human. Next to them the petroglyph of a human footprint enclosing the track of a carnivore is another example of the combined attributes of different species. Rain imagery is also

Figure 231. Jornada Style petroglyph of a distorted anthropomorph, Arroyo del Macho, Lincoln County, New Mexico.

Figure 232. Jornada Style petroglyph of a shield decorated with a warrior and feathers, Arroyo del Macho, Lincoln County, New Mexico.

Figure 233.
Jornada Style petroglyphs
of a coyote and rabbit,
Arroyo del Macho, Lincoln
County, New Mexico.

Figure 234. Jornada Style petroglyphs of a human footprint with a carnivore track along with two supernatural creatures, Arroyo del Macho, Lincoln County, New Mexico.

common here, as illustrated by the cloud terrace designs in Figure 235. One cloud terrace has a rainbow with lightning, and a fringe of rain. The other shows a dragonfly and a long fringe of rain, perhaps depicting the long streaks we call virga that evaporate before reaching the ground.

In keeping with the cyclic nature of things, it is fitting to end this discussion of rock art as it began—with the theme of water. In this tour of rock art within the upper Rio Grande watershed more than a hundred sites have been discussed, the majority of which contain some type of water-related imagery. Approximately 65 percent of these sites are located near an obvious water source, such as a stream, spring, or natural bedrock cistern. It is apparent from their rock art that water, fertility, and the supernatural were the primary concerns of the long succession of prehistoric inhabitants of this region.

What lessons can we learn about these subjects from the symbols? Today, we need not be concerned about human fertility since the world is overpopulated; but we do need to focus on the conservation of

Figure 235.
*Jornada Style petroglyphs
of rain symbols, Arroyo
del Macho, Lincoln County,
New Mexico.*

other life-forms to which our fate is tied. Water, especially here in the Southwest, is undoubtedly our most precious resource, and although we make some effort to protect and conserve it, too much is sacrificed to unrestricted growth. Finally, regarding concerns with the supernatural and spiritual, the fact that more people are appreciating and honoring the mystery of ancient rock art is a positive sign for humanity. Through sensitivity to the mystery of rock art, we may come to view it as a reflection of the earth's spirit and world harmony:

> *Knowing as well as sensing the devotional aspect of these inscriptions from the past is the key to the fullest appreciation of these priceless records. With the understanding comes an appreciation of the abilities of the Indian people and the ancient wise men.... These people knew the stars, the earth, the plants and animals, as well as human needs. They created a life of relative security and spiritual satisfaction with a simple guiding principle that is the nucleus of civilization—the oneness of the universe in which everything lives, and lives in harmony.[29]*

I am a history
A memory inventing itself
I am never alone
I speak with you always
You speak with me always
I move in the dark
I plant signs[1]

—Octavio Paz,
Configurations

5

Sites With Public Access

This chapter describes briefly those places with public access to rock art within the general region covered in this book (see" Conservation and Access to Sites," Chapter 2, for guidelines to follow when visiting rock art sites).

COLORADO

₮ *Carnero Creek*

An interesting panel of pictographs is located at the mouth of the Carnero Creek canyon near La Garita, off Highway 285 between Monte Vista and Saguache. There are more than fifty elements here, painted in red pigment on a rock face along the north wall of the canyon. This site is on the National Register of Historic Places, and the pictographs are believed to be primarily of Ute origin, with some designs added early in this century by Hispanic sheepherders. A portion of this panel is illustrated in Figure 24. Although this site is located on private property, the La Garita (L-Cross) Ranch generously allows interested persons to visit the pictographs. You may obtain permission, a gate key, and directions by inquiring at the La Garita Store (719-754-3755), which incidentally serves great hamburgers. Please respect this private property and the privilege of visiting it so that the opportunity will remain available.

While in the area you may also want to visit the Rio Grande County Museum and Cultural Center at 580 Oak Street in Del Norte, approximately thirteen miles southwest of La Garita. An interesting exhibit about rock art in the San Luis Valley is on display here, along with artifacts and other material pertaining to the cultural and natural history of the area. The museum is open throughout the year—summer hours are 10:00 to 5:00 Monday through Saturday, with limited hours in the fall. An admission fee is charged. For further information, contact the museum at 719-657-2847.

🐾 *Dry Creek*

Located in the San Luis Valley about eight miles southwest of Monte Vista, Colorado, the Dry Creek area contains at least five known petroglyph sites on public United States Bureau of Land Management (BLM) lands. The petroglyphs appear to span from Archaic (Oshara) time to ancestral Pueblo and historic Ute (Figure 236). The area is being managed as an interpretive site jointly by the BLM and the nearby Rio Grande National Forest. These sites are small, and all have

Figure 236.
*Petroglyphs of
uncertain origin
(ancestral
Pueblo or Ute?),
Dry Creek,
Rio Grande County,
Colorado.
(Drawing by Dave
Montgomery.)*

been vandalized to some extent, but the spectacular setting with impressive views makes visiting worthwhile. One of the sites, on the middle fork of Dry Creek, may have been used as a type of prehistoric observatory for rituals connected with the changing seasons or sacred land forms. On a high ridge with commanding views, a series of petroglyphs leads to an enclosed area surrounded by natural rock outcrops, a configuration not unlike Stonehenge. Here a notch in the encircling rock wall lines up with an unusual animal-shaped boulder (Figure 237) in the center of the enclosure (reminiscent of the Shrine of the Stone Lions in Bandelier National Monument, New Mexico) to direct the viewer's gaze out across the expanse of the valley precisely to sacred Blanca Peak. In this line of sight, there is also an unnamed but prominent conical hill, on top of which is an eight-foot-tall stone cairn. Because land managers believe that directed public visitation of the area may help stem further destruction by vandals, they are willing to promote public access to an otherwise fragile area. For information, contact the Rio Grande National Forest in Monte Vista at 719-852-5941.

*Figure 237.
An animal-
shaped boulder
that may be part
of a ritual site on
a ridge above Dry
Creek, San Luis
Valley, Rio
Grande County,
Colorado.*

NEW MEXICO

禾 *Bandelier National Monument*

Bandelier National Monument is located about twenty miles from Los Alamos on N.M. 4. The monument was created to preserve cliff dwellings and the ruins of a large pueblo (Tyuonyi) which were inhabited between A.D. 1200 and 1500. Visitors may take self-guided walks along the trails or hikes led by naturalists. The visitor center has exhibits, dioramas, films, and books on the area. At Bandelier there are many Rio Grande Style petroglyphs associated with the ruins in Frijoles Canyon beyond the visitor center, as well as at the detached unit of the monument known as Tsankawi—an unrestored pueblo ruin located a few miles north of the town of White Rock. The pictographs in Painted Cave (Figure 62) lie deep within the backcountry of Bandelier, requiring an overnight backpacking trip and a permit from the monument. Most of the monument area is part of a fifty-square-mile wilderness area traversed by seventy miles of trails (some of which are ancient) and dotted with ruins and cliff dwellings.

The majority of Bandelier's rock art is Rio Grande Style from the Pueblo IV and V Periods, and consists of the typical elements such as horned serpents, cloud terraces, flute players, various animals and birds, kachina masks, and anthropomorphic figures. The soft tuff in which the petroglyphs are carved erodes easily so many images are difficult to discern. Often petroglyphs are located high on the cliffs; these were made by people standing on the roofs of their houses, which were built against the face of the cliff. Remnants of a few pictographs are preserved in Frijoles Canyon, where designs were painted on mud plaster walls of the cave rooms that were incorporated into the cliff dwellings. Such surfaces tend to crumble and disintegrate rapidly, so that the once numerous paintings and etched designs in the plaster walls are now relatively rare. In the 1920s, Kenneth Chapman recorded hundreds of these drawings incised in remnant wall plaster of ruins in Frijoles Canyon, a sample of which is shown in Figure 238. A more detailed discussion can be found in the book *Rock Art of Bandelier National Monument* by Arthur H. and Lisa Rohn and William Ferguson.

The monument is open year-round. For more information and to inquire about hours, admission

Figure 238.
Rio Grande Style images carved into the mud-plastered walls of cave rooms in Frijoles Canyon (now Bandelier National Monument). (Drawings from Chapman 1917.)

fees, campground reservations, and backcountry permits, call the monument headquarters at 505-672-3861.

禾 *Chaco Culture National Historic Park*

Although Chaco Canyon lies just outside the area discussed in this book, it is included here because it is such a remarkable place. Located in a remote portion of the San Juan Basin between Farmington and Grants, it is reached by traveling forty miles of dirt road (from either the north or south)—roads difficult to travel in wet weather. Chaco is the premier Anasazi site, for it was the ceremonial center at the zenith of Anasazi culture. Up to 5,000 people may have lived in the canyon between A.D. 1000 and 1125. They built roads, irrigation ditches, solstice markers, and spectacular masonry pueblos. There are at least 2,000 ruins in the area—eleven major ones—as well as numerous petroglyph sites, some of which are accessible via the park trail system.

The rock art of Chaco Canyon ranges from early Anasazi (Basketmaker II pictographs) to later Anasazi (primarily petroglyphs dating from A.D. 500 to 1300) and historic-period Navajo (pecked and painted images dating from the early 1700s to the mid-twentieth century). The late Anasazi petroglyphs are the most abundant, and are found on boulders and cliff faces at habitation sites as well as in remote locations. The myriad elements present in this rock art consist of spirals, geometric designs, lizards and snakes, handprints and footprints, rectilinear or stick-form humans, and animals and their tracks. Fertility themes are a common concern in late Anasazi rock art, and are often expressed in panels with the humpbacked, phallic flute player. One panel shows dozens of flute players surrounding two females giving birth (Figure 239). The petroglyphs in Figure 240 portray a couple apparently embraced

Figure 239.
A group of phallic flute players accompanying two females giving birth, Chaco Canyon, San Juan County, New Mexico.

Figure 240.
Petroglyphs
depicting a
couple
apparently
having sex,
Chaco Canyon,
San Juan
County,
New Mexico.

in the sex act. Check with park staff to determine which rock art sites have public access. For a further description of the rock art of Chaco Canyon, see Polly Schaafsma's *Rock Art in New Mexico* or *Indian Rock Art of the Southwest*.

Both the visitor's center and campground are open year-round, and rangers conduct daily guided tours. The best seasons for visiting are spring and fall. For more information, contact the park at 505-988-6716.

禾 *El Malpais National Monument and El Malpais National Conservation Area*

El Malpais is a new national monument that incorporates large areas of BLM land into a national conservation area. Located southeast of Grants, New Mexico, the area has a fascinating volcanic terrain of lava flows, cinder cones, ice caves, and sandstone bluffs with natural arches. Inquire at the visitor center for information about or help in locating petroglyph panels, which are not on any trail and can only be accessed by cross-country hiking.

The rock art of this general area is discussed in

Chapter 3 under the Rio Puerco watershed. The petroglyph shown in Figure 241 is part of a panel of images that are typical of sites in the Cebolla Canyon area at El Malpais. It depicts a shield figure with elaborate step-fret designs, attached to a grouping of cloud terraces. The rock art of this region, being located in the zone where Mogollon and Anasazi culture areas overlapped, seems to show a blending of the stylistic elements of both groups.

For further information, contact the visitor center at 505-240-0300.

ᖆ *El Morro National Monument*

A remarkable historical monument and one of the more scenic places in New Mexico, El Morro is slightly beyond the boundaries discussed in this book, about fifteen miles west of the Continental Divide near the El Malpais National Conservation Area (west of Grants and south of Gallup, off Highway 53). Managed by the National Park Service, the monument was created in 1906 to preserve Inscription Rock—a massive sandstone bluff which, because of the pool of water it contains, attracted Indian and Spanish travelers for centuries. Stopping here for water and shelter, many travelers carved their names, dates, and messages into the sandstone walls of the cliff. The earliest historic inscription is by Don Juan de Oñate, the first governor of New Mexico under Spain, who passed by here in 1605 on an exploration trip to the Gulf of California. Early American soldiers and explorers also signed Inscription Rock in the 1800s. Figure 242 shows early Spanish inscriptions superimposed on Pueblo petroglyphs. Writer Charles Lummis called El Morro "the most precious cliff, historically, possessed

Figure 241. Petroglyph of a shield figure with cloud terrace elements, El Malpais National Conservation Area, Cibola County, New Mexico. (Drawing made from a photograph by Sheila Brewer.)

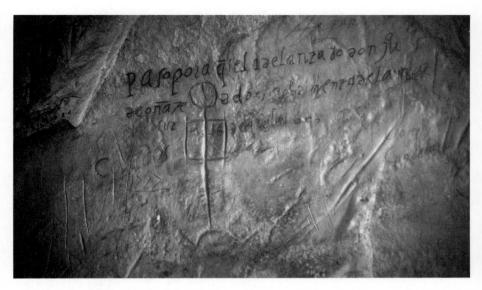

Figure 242. *Inscription by Spanish explorer Juan de Oñate (April 16, 1605) superimposed on prehistoric Pueblo petroglyphs, El Morro National Monument, Cibola County, New Mexico.*

by any nation on earth"[2]; and in 1855 United States attorney W.W.H. Davis wrote: "What a field for sober reflection this rock presents to the mind, with its inscriptions, hieroglyphs and ruined villages! It is a mute but eloquent historian of the past."[3] There are also prehistoric petroglyphs here; an 875-room Anasazi pueblo ruin on top of the mesa is named Atsinna by the nearby Zuni people, meaning "where pictures are on the rock."

A self-guiding trail leads from the visitor center to the base of the cliff, where inscriptions and petroglyphs can be seen. A trail also leads to the mesatop. The monument is open year-round. There is a small campground and picnic area, which may be closed for short periods during inclement weather. For more information, contact El Morro National Monument at 505-783-4226.

瓶 *Glorieta Mesa*

Two Archaic petroglyph sites have been unearthed on Santa Fe National Forest land on the top of Glorieta Mesa west of Pecos, New Mexico. There are over 200 petroglyphs at each site. They are relatively unusual in this area, making this a special place for rock art enthusiasts to visit. Both sites are located on horizontal bedrock exposures of the Glorieta sandstone, and have been covered with a deposit of soil up to two feet thick since their creation by nomadic hunter/gatherers millennia ago. Discovered because natural erosion was beginning to uncover them, they have subsequently been the subject of archaeological study. Dating of charcoal hearths in the overlying soil and by rock varnish techniques has established an age range of approximately 5,300 to 6,000 years for these Desert Abstract Style petroglyphs (Figures 100 and 243). Although public access to this site is limited, the Pecos Ranger District (505-757-6121) occasionally conducts small tours to these sites during Heritage Preservation Week in May.

瓶 *La Cienega Area of Critical Environmental Concern*

The BLM has designated an area of 3,556 acres eight miles southwest of Santa Fe as an Area of Critical Environmental Concern (ACEC). Within the La Cienega ACEC are three major pueblo ruins that date to different time periods spanning almost 900 years. Many rock art sites are found near these three ruins, enabling a comparison of rock art development over nearly a millennium. Over 4,000 petroglyphs are recorded along a one-mile stretch of

Figure 243. Archaic Desert Abstract Style petroglyphs, Glorieta Mesa, San Miguel County, New Mexico. (Drawings by A. J. Bock, in Abel 1994.)

basalt escarpment alone, including many fertility and Kokopelli images (see Chapter 3 for further discussion of the panels). The La Cienega pueblos were probably important in the turquoise trade because the mineral was mined prehistorically at Turquoise Hill and numerous other mines in the Cerrillos Hills about three miles to the southeast.

Although there is at this time no convenient public access to the site, the BLM hopes to acquire such access in the foreseeable future and may develop an interpretive site for the petroglyphs located in the La Cieneguilla portion of the ACEC. Among the many Rio Grande Style elements at this site are fine depictions of a variety of creatures, including mountain lions, deer, lizards, birds, and horned toads (Figure 244). The rock art at this location is discussed in Polly Schaafsma's *Rock Art in New Mexico*, in Carol Patterson-Rudolph's *Petroglyphs and Pueblo Myths of the Rio Grande*, and in Dennis Slifer and James Duffield's *Kokopelli: Flute Player Images in Rock Art*. For information about the status of this site, contact the BLM Taos Resource Area at 505-758-8851.

Figure 244.
Rio Grande Style petroglyphs at La Cienega and La Cieneguilla, Santa Fe County, New Mexico. (Drawings courtesy of Paul Williams, BLM.)

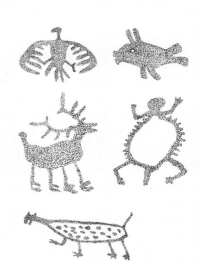

𝔐 *Petroglyph National Monument*

Petroglyph National Monument encompasses 7,000 acres on the great volcanic escarpment of the West Mesa at Albuquerque. More than 15,000 petroglyphs are protected in the monument, which was created by Congress in 1990 to preserve the rock art from destruction due to development and vandalism (see Chapter 3 for further information).

Many of the petroglyphs here express a concern with rain and fertility. The two flute players in Figure 245 seem to be celebrating male fertility (the sky deity is often portrayed in myths as fertilizing the female earth deity with rain), as they play to a ceremonial figure with a large phallus that appears to be somewhat unnatural; in certain Indian ceremonies kachina dancers wear a strapped-on gourd to simulate such an effect, and something similar may be intended here.[4]

Figure 245.
Rio Grande Style petroglyph of two flute players with phallic, ceremonial figure,
West Mesa, Bernalillo County, New Mexico.

Figure 246.
Rio Grande Style
petroglyph of a
bear shaman,
West Mesa,
Bernalillo
County,
New Mexico.

Among the Rio Grande Style petroglyphs at West Mesa, many images are repeated, such as masks, flute players, handprints and footprints, spirals, cloud terraces, lizards, birds, snakes, and horned serpents; however, some appear to be relatively unique, such as the anthropomorphic images in Figures 246 and 247. The "bear shaman" in Figure 246 has a bear paw design on its chest, claw-like feet and hands, large teeth, and a mask-like face. Similarly, the petroglyph in Figure 247 has bear paw feet, hands with claws, and a mask-like face. These figures may be expressions of the special role the bear played in healing among the Pueblo people. Because Pueblo healers invoke the aid of animal gods or spirits, especially the bear, they are known as "bears." In curing ceremonies, they wear a bear claw necklace and cover their arms and hands with the bear's forelegs, like gloves. They press the paws on their patient's hands, feet, and chest, and sometimes go outside in the dark to fight with a witch who has stolen the patient's heart.[5] One of the most unusual petroglyphs at the West Mesa occurs in Rinconada Canyon and seems to represent a being with bear-like attributes (Figure 248), primarily a large arm with clawed "hand," and an odd-shaped object attached to the creature's back. Perhaps this image represents a curing or exorcism ceremony.

Birds and bird-related symbols are common in West Mesa rock art. Eagles and hawks, powerful masters of the sky, are present throughout the area, and images of macaws and parrots also occur. These brilliantly colored birds, sometimes called Sacred Sun Birds or Sacred Rain Birds, were brought from Mexico in trade for turquoise and other objects. Because they are associated with the south, their plumage had great ceremonial value for bringing warmth, rain, and growth, and was incorporated

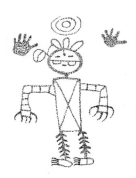

Figure 247.
Rio Grande Style
petroglyph of a
bear shaman,
West Mesa,
Bernalillo
County,
New Mexico.

Figure 248.
Petroglyph of a
being with
bear-like limbs and
unknown object
attached to its back,
West Mesa,
Bernalillo County,
New Mexico.

into sacred ritual objects.[6] Their long tails and characteristic hooked beaks are diagnostic features in Pueblo rock art (Figure 249). Other images of birds are sometimes stylized (Figure 250), or just the feathers are incorporated as a means of representing bird attributes. The petroglyph in Figure 251, from Rinconada Canyon, combines a bird body and a human head. It is possible to spend days hiking the trails through the monument and still not see all the rock art.

The monument is open year-round. For further information, contact the monument at 505-899-0205.

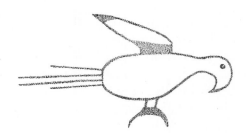

Figure 249.
Rio Grande Style petroglyph of a parrot or macaw, West Mesa, Bernalillo County, New Mexico. (Drawing from a National Park Service report.)

Figure 250.
Rio Grande Style petroglyph of a stylized bird in a ceremonial context, West Mesa, Bernalillo County, New Mexico. (Drawing from Schmader and Hays 1986.)

Figure 251.
Rio Grande
Style petroglyph
of a bird
with human
head in
ceremonial
context,
West Mesa,
Bernalillo
County,
New Mexico.

𝔎 *Puyé Cliff Dwellings*

Santa Clara Pueblo manages the ancestral pueblo ruins at Puyé Cliff Dwellings. It is located in a scenic tributary to Santa Clara Canyon about eight miles west of Española, within the 40,000-acre Santa Clara Reservation. Puyé is one of the most extensive of the ancient Pueblo cliff dwellings on the Pajarito Plateau, and the impressive views from here gave it a strategic position in the Rio Grande landscape. Among the first of Rio Grande ruins to be studied by archaeologists, the main pueblo was built between 1450 and 1475, although some of the cliff rooms date from the thirteenth century.

Typical of Pajaritan culture in its architecture and artifacts, Puyé consists of two types of dwellings: cliff dwellings and stone houses on the mesatop above. The cliff dwellings are rooms excavated from the soft volcanic ash deposits (tuff), with supplemental rooms built of stone in front of the caves in places. The cliff dwellings extend along the south face of the mesa escarpment for a mile. The mesatop pueblo consists of four large multistoried room complexes and various kivas built around a courtyard, within which ceremonial dances are held in August by residents of Santa Clara Pueblo.

Though not extensive, a selection of petroglyphs and pictographs can be seen on the cliff face in association with the cliff dwellings. The ones located high on the cliff seemingly out of reach were probably made by people standing on their rooftops when houses and porches lined the escarpment. The symbols here are typical of the Northern Tewa Rio Grande Style (primarily Pueblo IV in age) and consist of horned serpents, flute players and other anthropomorphs, various animals and birds, cloud terraces, geometric designs, shields, and masks. Like most sites on the Pajarito Plateau, where petroglyphs are carved into the soft, easily eroded tuff, these images tend to be faint and not readily discernible. There probably used to be many more petroglyphs here that have not survived exposure to the elements.

An entrance fee of $5.00 per person is charged by Santa Clara Pueblo for a self-guided tour. The ruins are sometimes closed temporarily in winter. A campground is maintained in nearby beautiful Santa Clara Canyon. For information, call Santa Clara Pueblo at 505-753-7326.

𐂃 *Rio Bonito Petroglyph National Recreation Trail*

The Rio Bonito Petroglyph National Recreation Trail was developed by the BLM's Roswell District, with volunteer help from local Boy Scouts, on BLM land along the Rio Bonito a few miles upstream from the old Fort Stanton Hospital, off Highway 380 between Carrizozo and Roswell. Winding along the stream in a very pretty area, this loop trail of 2.1 miles leads to several small petroglyph sites. The main attraction is Petroglyph Rock, a large boulder in the stream decorated with images of Tlaloc-like masks, as well as eyes, a snake, footprints, a lizard, and geometric designs (Figure 226). There is a nice campground near the trailhead. Access is by dirt road off Route 220 opposite the Sierra Blanca Regional Airport. For more information, call the Roswell BLM Office at 505-627-0272.

𐂃 *Salinas National Monument*

The Salinas National Monument headquarters is located in Mountainair, New Mexico, in the foothills of the Manzano Mountains. The monument consists of three separate units, each containing the ruins of an ancient pueblo and Spanish colonial mission churches at Gran Quivira, Abo, and Quarai. These pueblos have fascinating histories and are known for their trade in salt (hence the name Salinas) from deposits in seasonal salt lakes to the east in the Estancia Valley. Rock art occurs at a few locations in the Abo Pass area. The rock art here consists of petroglyphs and colorful pictographs in the Rio Grande Style of the Piro province. Kachina masks are a dominant theme (Plate 10), along with various animals and anthropomorphs in ceremonial activities (Plate 11). The influence of the Jornada Style from the area to the south can be seen. For further discussion of the rock art in this area, see Chapter 3, Abo Arroyo.

Although the sites are not accessible to individuals on their own, tours guided by park rangers can be arranged by calling the monument in advance at 505-847-2585. Weekday mornings are typically the best times for reserving a ranger.

𝍣 Three Rivers Petroglyph National Recreation Area

At this site, on a ridge overlooking the Tularosa Basin and Sierra Blanca twenty-eight miles south of Carrizzo off Highway 54, there are more than 21,000 Jornada Style petroglyphs, some of the most interesting in the Southwest. There are two hiking trails; one takes you up the ridge to the petroglyphs, the other to a partially excavated prehistoric village on the edge of nearby Three Rivers Creek, which was inhabited for about 300 years. The site is known for highly creative and inspired Jornada Style rock art. Although there are a large number of geometric designs, as well as circular motifs incorporating dots and enclosed crosses, the site is best known for the astonishing variety of life-forms. Although highly stylized depictions, many of the Jornada creatures found here are nonetheless identifiable, such as the mountain lion and roadrunner in Figure 252. Other creatures at Three Rivers are not recognizable and appear to be from the realm of the imagination or mythology, such as the bizarre image in Figure 253. Other images represent animals of this world, depicted in unusual ways. For example, the two sim-

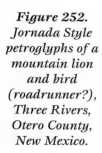

Figure 252.
Jornada Style petroglyphs of a mountain lion and bird (roadrunner?), Three Rivers, Otero County, New Mexico.

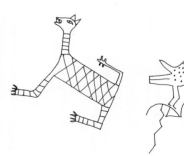

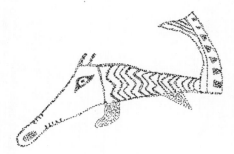

Figure 253.
Jornada Style petroglyph of an unknown creature, Three Rivers, Otero County, New Mexico.

ilar quadrupeds in Figure 254 are linked together by several connections—one stands upon the other's back, their tails are one, and a line connects legs of one to ears of the other.

Portrayals of humans at Three Rivers are as fascinating as those of animals. Many seem to be records of ritual or ceremonial activity, or perhaps mythological events. The two anthropomorphs in Figure 255 are holding a staff with the image of a canine-like quadruped. The two people in Figure 256 may be participating in a curing ritual, with the inverted individual the patient attended to by the medicine man holding a plant/herb over him. Or perhaps this scene represents a more sinister bewitching, with the shaman casting a spell over the individual. The dynamic tableau in Figure 257 appears to show an anthropomorph being attacked

Figure 254.
Jornada Style petroglyphs,
Three Rivers, Otero County,
New Mexico.

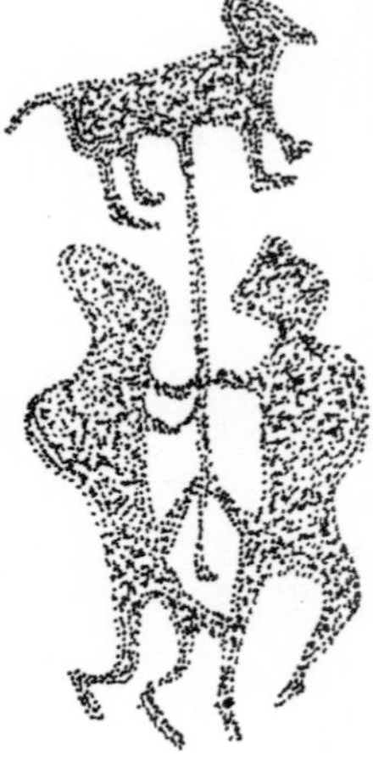

Figure 255.
Jornada Style petroglyphs of
anthropomorphs in ritual or
mythological activities,
Three Rivers, Otero County,
New Mexico.

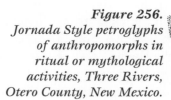

Figure 256.
Jornada Style petroglyphs
of anthropomorphs in
ritual or mythological
activities, Three Rivers,
Otero County, New Mexico.

Figure 257.
Jornada Style petroglyphs of anthropomorphs in ritual or mythological activities,
Three Rivers, Otero County, New Mexico.

by two animals—a mountain lion confronts him and a less distinct creature leaps at his back. Although this apparent anthropomorph holds an object (staff or weapon?), he also has a tail, head, appendages, and a face that does not seem quite human. This panel may represent a mythological event, with two creatures attacking another nonhuman creature. Or perhaps it represents a shaman who has altered his shape and is encountering animal spirits. Despite our attempts to interpret such images, their true meaning remains hidden and undoubtedly more complex than we envision.

Managed by the BLM, this site is open to the public year-round. There are camping and picnic facilities (a fee is charged). Since the site was vandalized in the past, the BLM now protects it by keeping a permanent caretaker or campground host there. It is well worth a visit but is very hot in summer. For further information, contact the BLM, Las Cruces District Office, at 505-525-4300.

Tomé Hill

The original small Hispanic farming village of Tomé, New Mexico, founded on the east bank of the Rio Grande below Los Lunas, had a tenuous existence in its early years due to frequent raids by Comanches and Apaches. Today, this quiet town is best known for its traditional Easter sunrise procession to the top of Tomé Hill. This isolated volcanic remnant has been the site of ceremonial activities in the prehistoric past as evidenced by the petroglyphs placed there by ancient Pueblo people.

Tomé Hill is owned by the nonprofit Valley Improvement Association, which in a joint project with Valencia County has studied the cultural resources there and developed an interpretive park and trails. The park and trails are located on the south side of the hill and are accessed via Tomé Hill Road off Highway 47. After the University of New Mexico Office of Contract Archaeology wrote a Cultural Resource Management Plan, the site was put on the National Register of Historic Places. In addition to the petroglyphs on the hill, the area is significant because a portion of the historic El Camino Real corridor is located nearby.

Figure 258. Rio Grande Style petroglyphs of humpbacked, phallic flute players, Tomé Hill, Valencia County, New Mexico. (Drawings made from photographs by Polly Schaafsma.)

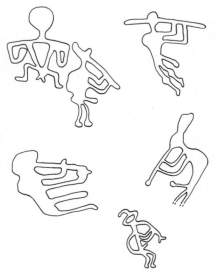

The petroglyphs, which are primarily of Southern Tiwa origin, occur on scattered basalt boulders on the slopes of the hill, and consist of images such as humpbacked flute players (Figure 258), masks, birds, cloud terraces, and other typical Rio Grande Style elements. The survey of the petroglyphs documented use of the hill from late Archaic through historic time, although heaviest use was during the Pueblo IV Period, as evidenced by the quantity of Rio Grande Style images. An archive of the site survey records can be seen at the University of New Mexico Valencia Campus Library located a few miles south of Tomé; other interpretive display information about this site can also be viewed at the Petroglyph National Monument in Albuquerque.

㡌 White Rock Canyon

White Rock Canyon Archeological District was placed on the National Register of Historic Places in 1990 in recognition of the significant rock art there. The petroglyphs in White Rock Canyon, near Los Alamos and the town of White Rock, are interesting but difficult to visit. Although there are a great many sites (more than 2,000 petroglyphs have been recorded), they are scattered and hidden on basalt boulders over a large area of rough terrain. Access into the canyon is by several hiking trails leading from the rim of the canyon at Overlook Park, on the eastern outskirts of White Rock. The trails are marked in places by dots of paint on rocks; there is a red dot trail and a blue dot trail. Be prepared for rocky hiking and a long climb out of the canyon. Another trail in White Rock Canyon that passes by some petroglyphs is accessed at Otowi Bridge on Route 502 and follows the east bank of the Rio Grande on fairly level terrain.

Figure 259.
Rio Grande Style petroglyph of a kachina mask, east bank of the Rio Grande near Otowi, Santa Fe County, New Mexico.

In White Rock Canyon most of the rock art occurs on the west side of the river, but a few petroglyph sites are found on the east; the kachina mask shown in Figure 259 adorns a trailside rock; nearby is the large boulder known as "Flute Player Rock," containing seven examples of Kokopelli.[7] The petroglyphs in Figure 260 depict two long-billed birds and a humpbacked flute player whose shape appears to mimic that of the birds. Also in White Rock Canyon is a site known as "Bird Rock," where petroglyphs of more than a dozen birds repeat the avian theme (Figure 261). An unusual horned serpent with a single eye (Cyclops-Awanyu?) occurs along with an elaborate shield bearer, seen in Figure 262. Another example of shields, along with two deer-like animals, is on a basalt boulder (Figure 263). Additional information can be found in the book *Sentinels on Stone: The Petroglyphs of Los Alamos* by Betty Lilienthal and Dorothy Hoard.

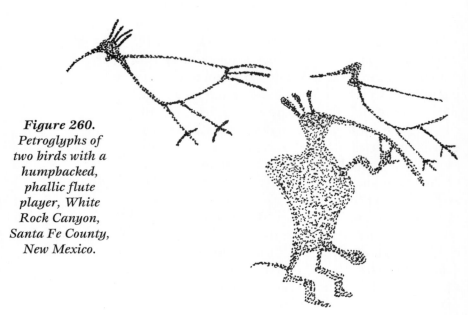

Figure 260.
Petroglyphs of two birds with a humpbacked, phallic flute player, White Rock Canyon, Santa Fe County, New Mexico.

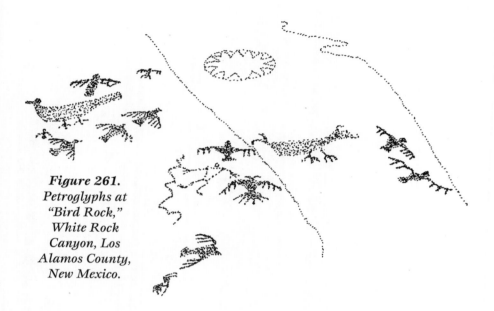

Figure 261.
Petroglyphs at "Bird Rock," White Rock Canyon, Los Alamos County, New Mexico.

Figure 262.
Petroglyphs of a horned serpent with one eye and an elaborate shield figure, White Rock Canyon, Santa Fe County, New Mexico.

Figure 263.
Petroglyphs of
a shield and
deer-like
animals,
White Rock
Canyon,
Los Alamos
County,
New Mexico.

TEXAS

𝍏 *Hueco Tanks State Historical Park*

Approximately thirty miles east of El Paso, Texas, Hueco Tanks State Historical Park contains a very significant concentration of rock art. Three massive granite outcrops standing hundreds of feet above the Chihuahuan Desert have many natural water traps and caves. The park contains 860 acres, but the convoluted topography makes it seem much larger. Over 3,000 rock paintings are hidden within the caves and crevices of the massive rocky outcrops—one of the largest concentrations of Indian pictographs in North America. An unusual feature is the large number of painted masks—more than 200 are known (Plate 14).

Most of the rock art at Hueco Tanks is from the Jornada Mogollon people, who lived in settled villages and practiced agriculture. The rock art associated with these people thus reflects the central importance of rain. Water symbolism can be seen in many paintings such as rain altars (cloud terraces), lightning, the ever-present Tlaloc figure (Figure 15), and the plumed serpent. The "step-fret" motif seen in the torso of the Tlaloc in Figure 15, and in many others here, is a common symbol associated with water and lightning. A clear association with water is obvious in the so-called "Thirsty Mask" pictograph that shows a face with tongue hanging out of its mouth (Figure 264). This red painting is placed within a crevice that contains a large, deep bedrock cistern that holds rainwater in the driest of times. The surface of the rock beneath this painting has been polished smooth by generations of Indians who climbed down into the crevice to obtain water. Higher in the same rock mass is a large cave over 100 feet long that was once used to hold up to 10,000 gallons of water by an earthen dam constructed in prehistoric times.[8] A yellow pictograph of a pottery design inside this cave is also related to water iconography since pottery vessels are used to store water. Moreover, water imagery is evident in the fishes incorporated into the mask pictograph in Figure 265.

The dancer with horned mask in Figure 266,

Figure 264. Jornada Style pictograph of a mask with a tongue hanging out (the "Thirsty Mask") in a cave with a natural water-storing cistern, Hueco Tanks, El Paso County, Texas.

Figure 265.
Jornada Style pictograph of a mask with fishes incorporated into the design, Hueco Tanks, El Paso County, Texas.

painted in white pigment, is located in a rock shelter next to a series of deep bedrock mortars. Horns are indicative of power, and this image may represent a shaman. Another white painting of an anthropomorph with shamanic qualities is found in a cave that contains a natural water hole (Figure 267). Its large eyes are indicative of Tlaloc, but the hourglass body shape and limbs suggest otherwise. Certain anthropomorphs of the Middle/Late Archaic Style in this area are similarly shaped (Figure 198), but so are some Apache anthropomorphs from various sites to the north (Figures 178 and 191, for example).

In 1939, many of the pictographs at Hueco Tanks were recorded by artist Forrest Kirkland, who made watercolor paintings of them.[9] He was the first to systematically study the masks, describing them as

Figure 266.
White pictograph of a horned dancer or shaman, Hueco Tanks, El Paso County, Texas.

Figure 267.
White pictograph of an anthropomorph/ shaman, Hueco Tanks, El Paso County, Texas.

Figure 268.
*A comparison
of Jornada
Style masks,
Hueco Tanks,
El Paso County,
Texas. (After
Kirkland and
Newcomb 1967.)*

"solid" or "outline" masks (Figure 268). The outline masks, done in red, black, gray, and white, have recognizable facial features, even expressions sometimes, and are typically located in large, open shelters along with other designs. The solid masks, done in red, black, white, brown, yellow, blue, and green, are more stylized, with blank eyes and a supernatural quality. Solid masks are found hidden in caves and barely accessible niches, suggesting they are more sacred or powerful than the outline masks.

Some of the best examples of solid masks are in a ceremonial chamber known as Cave Kiva, where eight solid masks in red and orange are arranged in a pattern along one wall (Figure 269). It has been suggested that this cave may have been associated with the planet Venus (sacred among Mesoamericans),

Figure 269. *A pair of the eight Jornada Style masks in Cave Kiva, Hueco Tanks, El Paso County, Texas.*

since the number eight is often connected with this planet's cycle.[10] Sadly, in 1993 this sacred place was defiled by a vandal, who spray-painted his name over the masks. Fortunately, however, park management was able to respond quickly and restored the pictographs before the spray paint became permanently bonded to the rock surface.

During the nineteenth century, Mescalero Apaches visited Hueco Tanks, leaving behind paintings of mounted warriors, large snakes, and ceremonies. The best examples are the white paintings in Comanche Cave. The panel of lively, fluid figures at this site is probably a depiction of a Mescalero Apache victory dance or fertility ceremony (Figure 201). It includes several large snakes, horses, dancers with musical instruments, and figures in sexual poses. These are probably realistic depictions of actual activities, even though the men's penises and the snakes are exaggerated in size (and look startlingly alike). Although many of the old Apache ceremonies were abandoned prior to this century, one that survives is an elaborate four-day puberty ceremony for girls in which masked dancers participate. Among the Chiricahua Apaches there was a loosening of restrictions on sexual behavior during victory celebrations; since the ritual life of Mescalero Apaches was very similar, this may explain some of the sensual pictographs in Comanche Cave.[11] The bold design in Figure 270 is painted next to the panel of Apache dancers. It seems to combine sun symbolism with fertility symbolism; the arrow entering a box may represent male/female union (compare to the copulating couple in the lower right of Figure 201). The paintings in Comanche Cave were probably made between 1820 and 1840 when the Mescalero Apaches raided extensively in the area.[12] Someone painted the date "1849" over some of these pictographs, establishing a minimum age. Another individual painted the quaint message "watter hear" to mark the location of a natural cistern in Comanche Cave.

Figure 270.
Mescalero Apache pictograph of sun/fertility symbols, Comanche Cave, Hueco Tanks, El Paso County, Texas.

Although the rock art at Hueco Tanks is difficult to find, since most of it is hidden in caves and rocky niches, looking for it is half the fun. Since this park has become extremely popular in recent years as a rock-climbing mecca, at certain times of the year (spring break for colleges) it can be crowded, making it almost impossible to get a spot in the small campground. In 1997, it cost $3.00 a day to enter the park. Park rangers provide guided tours to some of the rock art sites twice daily on weekends. For a more extensive description of the area, see Chapter 4, as well as the following books: Kay Sutherland, *Rock Paintings at Hueco Tanks State Historical Park*, and Polly Schaafsma, *Indian Rock Art of the Southwest*. For further information, contact Hueco Tanks State Historical Park at 915-857-1135.

禾 *Lobo Valley*

The Lobo Valley Petroglyph Site is located in the mouth of an unnamed canyon that drains east from the Van Horn Mountains, south of Van Horn, Texas. It is owned and managed by the Culberson County Historical Commission, which conducts tours to educate the public about the site and preserves it from further vandalism. Here only about a dozen boulders have petroglyphs, but the rock art is significant and the site is on the National Register of Historic Places (see description in Chapter 4). The rock art consists of pecked designs of human and animal forms, curvilinear abstract forms, circles, diamonds, and meandering lines. Although a continuum of styles seems to be present, much of the rock art is evidently a Middle/Late Archaic Representational Style, although presumably the abstract motifs are from Early Archaic times. Some of the panels may illustrate a transition from the earlier abstract motifs to later ones in which anthropomorphs and other representational elements are incorporated (Figure 271). There are a few depictions of spear points similar to the Archaic Schumla Type seen at Alamo Canyon, which reinforce the Archaic assignment. Distinct Jornada Style elements, such as Tlalocs, are

Figure 271. Petroglyphs, Lobo Valley, Culberson County, Texas.

Figure 272.
Petroglyphs, Lobo Valley, Culberson County, Texas.

missing. Although the pointed caps worn by the anthropomorphs in Figure 272 may be Jornada-related, there is not much else to suggest a Jornada presence here.[13]

There is no public land in the area so camping opportunities are limited. For more information, contact the Culberson County Historical Commission at P.O. Box 68, Van Horn, TX 79855, or call 915-283-2124 or 915-283-2436.

NOTES

Front Matter and Chapter 1

1. Peggy Pond Church, "Morning on Tshirege," in *Birds of Daybreak* (San Francisco: Greenwood Press, 1946).

2. Paul Horgan, *Great River: The Rio Grande in North American History*, vol. 1 (New York: Rinehart and Company, 1954), 56.

3. Tony Hillerman and Robert Reynolds, *Rio Grande* (Portland, Oreg.: C. H. Belding Graphic Arts Center Publishing Company, 1975), 19.

4. Horgan, *Great River*, vol. 1, 32.

5. J. A. Ware writes the following: "When large areas of the Colorado Plateau were abandoned by prehistoric farmers during the first centuries of the present millennium, many of those who were displaced migrated to the rich bottomlands of the Rio Grande and its tributaries, where there was perennial stream flow and longer growing seasons. The rift almost certainly influenced the seasonal movements of early hunters and gatherers in northern New Mexico. The region's first PaleoIndian inhabitants were undoubtedly drawn to the water source, as were the herds of Pleistocene animals they hunted. As water became increasingly scarce during the millennia-long droughts that followed the close of the Pleistocene, the river exerted an important influence on settlement patterns and seasonal population movements." (J. A. Ware, "Man on the Rio Grande: Introduction and Overview," in *New Mexico Geological Society Guidebook* (Albuquerque: University of New Mexico Press, 1984), 271–73. 35th Field Conference, Rio Grande Rift: Northern New Mexico.

6. Horgan, *Great River*, vol. 1, 19.

7. Basins are watersheds or drainage areas, and in this case refer to closed basins, which are enclosed topographic depressions with interior drainage; no runoff reaches the sea; it infiltrates or evaporates. The area covered in this book includes portions of the Central Closed Basin in the south-central part of New Mexico and the Southwestern Closed Basin in the extreme southwestern (boot heel) part of New Mexico. The Central Closed Basin covers an area of 15,000 square miles and lies east of the Rio Grande and west of the divide for the Pecos River. It includes four subbasins: the Estancia, Tularosa, Jornada del Muerto, and Salt Basins. The names indicate how arid some of these places are; there is very limited surface water present. The Southwestern Closed Basins consist of three drainage areas totaling 6,000 square miles: the Mimbres, Playas, and Wamel Basins. The Continental Divide forms the western edge of these areas, while the north and east limits are defined by the Rio Grande drainage. Arid desert and steppe climates prevail here also, although there is some perennial water in the headwaters area of the Mimbres Basin.

8. The notable exception is the great concentration of Archaic, shamanistic pictographs found in the area around the confluence of the Rio Grande and the Pecos River. These complex Pecos River Style paintings, dated at several thousand years

B.C., are beyond the scope of this book. Other scattered rock art sites occur along the lower Rio Grande, for example, at Big Bend National Park in Texas.

9. Ware, "Man on the Rio Grande": 271–73.

10. Cynthia Irwin-Williams, "Picosa: The Elementary Southwestern Culture," *American Antiquity* 32 (1967): 441–57.

11. Polly Schaafsma, *Indian Rock Art of the Southwest* (Santa Fe and Albuquerque, N.M.: School of American Research and University of New Mexico Press, 1980), 184.

12. Ibid., 235–36, and Stephen Trimble, *The People: Indians of the American Southwest* (Santa Fe, N.M.: School of American Research, 1993), 11. Mogollon sites show early adoption from Mesoamerica of pottery, ball courts, religious platform mounds, and so forth.

13. Schaafsma, *Indian Rock Art of the Southwest*, 186.

14. Ibid., 187.

15. J.J. Brody, *The Anasazi* (New York: Rizzoli, 1990), 182.

16. Carroll L. Riley, "Pueblo Indians in Meso-America: The Early Historic Period," in *Collected Papers in Honor of Florence Hawley Ellis*, ed. Theodore Frisbie, Papers of the Archaeological Society of New Mexico 2 (Norman, Okla.: Hooper Publishing Co., 1975), 452–62. Trade items from Mesoamerica included macaws, seashells, and copper bells; from the Plains Indians, buffalo hides and other items; and from the Salinas Pueblo area east of the Manzano Mountains, salt was a trade commodity.

17. Ramon A. Gutierrez, *When Jesus Came the Corn Mothers Went Away: Marriage, Sexuality, and Power in New Mexico, 1500–1846* (Stanford, Calif.: Stanford University Press, 1991), 139.

18. Horgan, *Great River*, vol. 1, 56, 63, 67.

19. James J. Hester, "Early Navajo Migrations and Acculturation in the Southwest," *Museum of New Mexico Papers in Anthropology* 6 (1962): 21–24.

20. Schaafsma, *Indian Rock Art of the Southwest*, 147.

21. Mark R. Guthrie et al., *Colorado Mountains Prehistoric Context* (Denver: Colorado Historical Society, 1984), 48.

22. Trimble, *The People*, 300.

Chapter 2

1. Anonymous, *Signs of Life: The Five Universal Shapes and How to Use Them* (Sonoma, Calif.: Arcus Publishing Company, 1992), 84.; Jamake Highwater, *The Primal Mind: Vision and Reality in Indian America* (New York: New American Library, 1982), 32; Henri Matisse, *Signs of Life: The Five Universal Shapes and How to Use Them* (Sonoma, Calif.: Arcus Publishing Company, 1992), 57.

2. Some notable exceptions are the Archaic pictograph styles of the Pecos River in Texas and Barrier Canyon in Utah, which are dated as old as 4,000 years. Certain pictographs in Australia are believed to be up to 20,000 years old, and some of the Paleolithic cave paintings in Europe are dated at 35,000 years.

3. David Muench and Polly Schaafsma, *Images in Stone* (San Francisco, Calif.: Brown Trout Publishers, 1995), 16.

4. David Lewis-Williams and Thomas Dowson, *Images of Power: Understanding Bushman Rock Art* (Cape Town, South Africa: National Book Printers, 1989), 202.

5. Jack Steinbring and Maurice Lanteigne, "Archeopsychological Process in Rock Art: Entoptic Phenomena or Relative Recurrence of Elemental Forms?" *Rock Art Papers* 8 (1991): 141–53. San Diego Museum Papers No. 27.

6. Muench and Schaafsma, *Images in Stone*, 17; Bill Weahkee, "Petroglyph Area Is Sacred Place for New Mexico Pueblos," *La Pintura* 23, no. 2 (1996): 1–3.

7. Arlene Benson and Floyd Buckskin, "Magnetic Anomalies at Petroglyph Lake," *Rock Art Papers* 8 (1991): 53. San Diego Museum Papers No. 27.

8. Jack Steinbring, "Phenomenal Attributes: Site Selection Factors in Rock Art," *American Indian Rock Art* 17, Proceedings of the Seventeenth Annual Meeting of the American Rock Art Research Association, 1992.

9. Patricia McCreery, "Another Look at Hunting Magic," *La Pintura* 23, no. 2 (1996): 6–8. American Rock Art Association.

10. Clay Johnson, "Methodology for Identifying, Observing, Recording, and Reporting Solar Interactive Rock Art Panels," *Utah Rock Art* 10:46. From Proceedings of the 10th Annual Symposium of the Utah Rock Art Research Association, Salt Lake City, 1992; Stephen A. Stoney, "Sun, Sandstone, and Shadow: Rock Art in Southern Nevada Takes on New Meaning," *Rock Art Papers* 8 (1991): 108. San Diego Museum Papers No. 27.

11. A. Sofaer, "A Unique Solar Marking Construct," *Science* 206, no. 44 (1979): 283–91. Spiral petroglyphs were placed on a rock face behind three vertically oriented stone slabs such that a "dagger of light" was cast by the sun onto the spirals at solstice times.

12. Polly Schaafsma, *Indian Rock Art of the Southwest* (Santa Fe, N.Mex. and Albuquerque: School of American Research and University of New Mexico Press, 1980), 6.

13. Ibid., 19.

14. Frank Bock, "PIT Crews Uncover Archaic Rock Art," *La Pintura* 20, no. 2 (1993): 5. American Rock Art Research Association.

15. Brent Abel, Santa Fe, N.M. National Forest archaeologist, personal communication, 1995.

16. Schaafsma, *Indian Rock Art of the Southwest*, 43.

17. R. F. Heizer and M. A. Baumhoff, *Prehistoric Rock Art of Nevada and Eastern California* (Berkeley: University of California Press, 1962), 9–11.

18. Schaafsma, *Indian Rock Art of the Southwest*, 56.

19. Ibid., 56.

20. Ibid., 187.

21. Ibid., 196.

22. Polly Schaafsma, *Rock Art in New Mexico* (Santa Fe, N.Mex.: Museum of New Mexico Press, 1992), 72.

23. Schaafsma, *Indian Rock Art of the Southwest*, 236; Elsie Clews Parsons, "Some Aztec and Pueblo Parallels," *American Anthropologist* 35 (1933): 611–31.

24. Schaafsma, *Indian Rock Art of the Southwest*, 21.

25. Ibid., 122.

26. Ibid., 160.

27. Schaafsma, *Rock Art in New Mexico*, 87–136.

28. Dennis Slifer and James Duffield, *Kokopelli: Flute Player Images in Rock Art* (Santa Fe, N.M.: Ancient City Press, 1994). This is the most current and thorough discussion of the nature and distribution of flute player images in the Southwest.

29. Schaafsma, *Indian Rock Art of the Southwest*, 305.

30. Ibid., 310.

31. Ibid., 323.

32. Ibid., 335.

33. Ibid., 339–41.

34. Sally J. Cole, *Legacy on Stone: Rock Art of the Colorado Plateau and Four Corners Region* (Boulder, Colo.: Johnson Books, 1990), 223.

35. Robert Nykamp, "Distribution of Known Ute Sites in Colorado," in *Archaeology of the Eastern Ute: A Symposium* (Denver: Colorado Council of Professional Archaeologists, 1988), 151.

36. Heizer and Baumhoff, *Prehistoric Rock Art*, 222.

37. William G. Buckles, "The Uncompahgre Complex: Historic Ute Archaeology and Prehistoric Archaeology on the Uncompahgre Plateau in West Central Colorado," Ph.D. diss., University of Colorado, 1971.

38. Cole, *Legacy on Stone*, 224.

39. Ibid., 226.

40. Ibid., 235.

Chapter 3

1. Cited in Campbell Grant, James W. Baird, and J. Kenneth Pringle, *Rock Drawings of the Coso Range*. (Ridgecrest, Calif.: Maturango Museum, 1987), v.

2. Mark R. Guthrie et al., Colorado Mountains Prehistoric Context (Denver, Colo.: Colorado Historical Society, 1984), 39.

3. Below Cochiti Dam, irrigation ditches of all sizes withdraw water from the Rio Grande. In the vicinity of El Paso, Texas, the river is often depleted in the growing season, until the Rio Conchos enters the dry bed of the Rio Grande with new water from Mexico. During the drought year of 1996, the Rio Grande was dried up by irrigation diversion at San Acacia Dam near Socorro, New Mexico, threatening the existence of an endangered species—the Rio Grande silvery minnow.

4. Ken Frye, Rio Grande National Forest, personal communication, 1997.

5. Ibid.

6. Ibid.

7. Dennis Slifer and James Duffield, *Kokopelli: Flute Player Images in Rock Art* (Santa Fe, N.M.: Ancient City Press, 1994), 100.

8. Ken Frye and Vince Spero, Rio Grande National Forest archaeologists. These

interpretations, and other information about San Luis Valley rock art, are presented in an exhibit made by Frye and Spero, which is on display at the Rio Grande County Museum and Cultural Center in Del Norte, Colorado.

9. Ken Frye, Rio Grande National Forest, personal communication, 1997.

10. Ibid. The Hopi informant, Merlin Kay, was escorted to the site by archaeologists with the Rio Grande National Forest. He claims ancestral Hopi people passed through this area during their migrations in prehistoric times.

11. Ibid.

12. Ibid.

13. Ibid.

14. Patricia McCreery and Ekkehart Malotki, *Tapamveni: The Rock Art Galleries of Petrified Forest and Beyond* (Petrified Forest, Ariz.: Petrified Forest Museum Association, 1994), 139–40. The Mother of Game is a Pueblo deity who "owns" the animals and is responsible for their increase. She allows hunters who follow the correct ritual to hunt her children. In eastern Arizona, she is depicted in rock art in rigidly stylized postures, often surrounded by images of animals and fertility scenes, and frequently accompanied by two disk-shaped objects at her side. Although apparently less common in rock art in the upper Rio Grande region, she is reported to be related conceptually to the Deer Mother of Taos Pueblo, which is not far from this site.

15. Gar and Maggy Packard, *Suns and Serpents: The Symbolism of Indian Rock Art* (Santa Fe, N.M.: Packard Publications, 1974), 54.

16. Matilda Coxe Stevenson, "The Zuni Indians: Their Mythology, Esoteric Fraternities and Ceremonies, *Twenty-Third Annual Report of the Bureau of American Ethnology for the Years 1901–1902* (Washington, D.C.: Smithsonian Institution, 1904), 294–295.

17. Polly Schaafsma, *Indian Rock Art of the Southwest* (Santa Fe and Albuquerque, N.M.: School of American Research and University of New Mexico Press, 1975), 192–95; and Packard, *Suns and Serpents*, 29.

18. McCreery and Malotki, *Tapamveni*, 139–40.

19. Paul Williams, BLM archaeologist, personal communication, 1996. Near this rock art site an Archaic Bajada Type projectile point as well as sherds of micaceous Pueblo pottery were found.

20. Ibid.

21. E. B. Renaud, "Petroglyphs of North Central New Mexico," in *Archaeological Survey Series*, 11th Report (Denver, Colo.: University of Denver, 1938).

22. Paul Williams, BLM archaeologist, personal communication, 1996.

23. Polly Schaafsma, "Anasazi Rock Art in Tsegi Canyon and Canyon de Chelly: A View Behind the Images," in *Tse Yaa Kin: Houses Beneath the Rocks*, ed. David Grant Noble (Santa Fe, N.M.: School of American Research, 1986), 27–28.

24. Packard, *Suns and Serpents*, 40–43.

25. Slifer and Duffield, *Kokopelli*, 52–54.

26. Sally Crum, *People of the Red Earth: American Indians of Colorado* (Santa Fe, N.M.: Ancient City Press, 1996), 129.

27. Frank Hibben, *Excavation of the Riana Ruin and Chama Valley Survey*, University of New Mexico Bulletin: Anthropological Series 2, No. 1 (1937), 48–49.

28. G. Benito Córdova, *Missionization and Hispanicization of Santo Tomas Apostel de Abiquiu, New Mexico: 1750-1770*. Ph.D. Dissertation, Albuquerque: University of New Mexico, 1979.

29. E. B. Renaud, "Pictographs and Petroglyphs of the High Western Plains," *Archaeological Survey Series*, 8th Report (Denver, Colo.: University of Denver, 1936), 18.

30. *New Mexico* Magazine, August 1933.

31. Renaud, *Pictographs and Petroglyphs*, 19.

32. Betty Lilienthal and Dorothy Hoard, *Sentinels on Stone: The Petroglyphs of Los Alamos* (Los Alamos, N.M.: Los Alamos Historical Society, 1995); and Lisa and Arthur H. Rohn and William Ferguson, *Rock Art of Bandelier National Monument* (Albuquerque: University of New Mexico Press, 1989).

33. K. M. Chapman, "The Cave Pictographs of the Rito de los Frijoles, New Mexico," *Papers of the School of American Archaeology* 37 (1917): 139–48.

34. Bill Weahkee, "Petroglyph Area Is Sacred Place for New Mexico Pueblos," *La Pintura* 23, no. 2 (1996): 2. This article first appeared in the *Albuquerque Journal*, October 16, 1996.

35. Polly Schaafsma, personal communication, 1994.

36. John Pfahl, "Elegy for the Drowned," in *Marks in Place: Contemporary Responses to Rock Art* (Albuquerque: University of New Mexico Press, 1988), 85–95. These photographs document the sites of rock art destroyed by not only Cochiti Reservoir but also by the Abiquiú and San Juan Reservoirs in New Mexico.

37. Polly Schaafsma, *Rock Art in the Cochiti Reservoir District* (Santa Fe, N.M.: Museum of New Mexico Press, 1975), 25–31.

38. *Santa Fe New Mexican*, May 27, 1997.

39. Ibid.

40. Bureau of Land Management, *La Cienega Area of Critical Environmental Concern Coordinated Resource Management Plan* (Albuquerque, N.M.: Albuquerque District Office, Taos Resource Area, 1995).

41. The La Bajada uranium mine was an abandoned, unreclaimed site on Santa Fe National Forest lands. Although posted with warning signs, it represented an environmental hazard for four decades until a joint reclamation project between the Forest Service and the New Mexico Environment Department restored the area in 1996–1997; this is yet another example of how short-term private exploitation of public resources costs the taxpayers in the end.

42. Bureau of Land Management, *La Cienega ACEC*, 3. The riparian areas are non-functional because of upstream water use, water quality violations, and a history of grazing abuse. The agency further states that the Santa Fe River Canyon and La Cienega areas have the potential to attract a greater variety of species if actions are taken to reestablish riparian vegetation and wetland habitats.

43. Schaafsma, *Indian Rock Art of the Southwest*, 315–16.

44. Elsie Clews Parsons, *Pueblo Religion* (Chicago: University of Chicago Press,

1939), 39; and Carol Patterson-Rudolph, *Petroglyphs and Pueblo Myths of the Rio Grande* (Albuquerque, N.M.: Avanyu Publishing, 1990), 79–82.

45. Slifer and Duffield, *Kokopelli*, 39–42, 170–71.

46. Pueblo Blanco is the only major ruin in the Galisteo Basin that is not privately owned. It is fortuitously located on a section of state land. In the early 1990s, the State Land Office, along with volunteers, attempted to mitigate the erosional damage to the ruins by constructing gabions and other erosion-control features there. In addition, the grazing permittee voluntarily suspended grazing in the vicinity. Long-term success of these measures is not yet certain.

47. Christina Singleton Mednick, *San Cristobal: Voices and Visions of the Galisteo Basin* (Santa Fe, N.M.: Museum of New Mexico Press, 1996), 16.

48. Ibid., 52.

49. Polly Schaafsma, "War Imagery and Magic: Petroglyphs at Comanche Gap, Galisteo Basin, New Mexico," in *Social Implications of Symbolic Expression in the Prehistoric American Southwest*, 55th Annual Meeting of the Society for American Archaeology (Las Vegas, Nev.: Society for American Archaeology, 1990), 21.

50. Ibid., 20.

51. Ibid., 9.

52. Packard, *Suns and Serpents*, 30.

53. Ibid., 29.

54. Bart Durham, personal communication, 1997.

55. Frank Bock, "PIT Crews Uncover Archaic Rock Art," *La Pintura* 20, no. 2 (1993): 5.

56. Robert Lentz and Eugene Varela, "The Pecos Petroglyph Survey," unpublished report for Pecos National Monument, Pecos, New Mexico, 1971, 6.

57. Lentz and Varela, "Pecos Petroglyph Survey" and personal communication with Judy Reed, Pecos National Monument archaeologist, 1997.

58. Lance Trask, *Ancient Billboards: The Rock Art of the Lower Jemez Mountains* (Santa Fe and Albuquerque, N.M.: Santa Fe, New Mexico National Forest and University of New Mexico Press, 1992), 17.

59. Slifer and Duffield, *Kokopelli*, 127–30.

60. Isaac Eastvold, "Ethnographic Background for the Rock Art of the West Mesa Escarpment," in *Las Imagines: The Archaeology of Albuquerque's West Mesa Escarpment* (Albuquerque, N.M.: Department of Parks and Recreation, 1986), 123.

61. Weahkee, "Petroglyph Area Is Sacred Place": 1–3; and Tony Davis, "Horses and Bikes Push into Petroglyph Park," *High Country News* 29, no. 1 (1997): 4.

62. Weahkee, "Petroglyph Area Is Sacred Place": 1–3.

63. Davis, "Horses and Bikes Push into Petroglyph Park."

64. Dianne Souder, National Park Service, personal communication, 1997.

65. Dorothy Durham, "Petroglyphs at Mesa de los Padillas," *El Palacio* 62, no. 1 (1955): 3–17.

66. Jesse W. Fewkes, "Tusayan Katcinas," *Fifteenth Annual Report of the Bureau of*

American Ethnology for the Years 1893–1894 (Washington, D.C.: Smithsonian Institution, 1897), 272.

67. The Salinas Pueblos were important in regional salt trade, as they gathered salt from evaporative deposits in nearby lakes. Spanish missions were built at Gran Quivira, Abo, and Quarai Pueblos in the seventeenth century. These areas are now part of Salinas National Monument.

68. Sherry Robinson, *El Malpais, Mt. Taylor, and the Zuni Mountains: A Hiking Guide and History* (Albuquerque: University of New Mexico Press, 1994), 152.

69. Polly Schaafsma, *Rock Art in New Mexico* (Santa Fe, N.M.: Museum of New Mexico Press, 1992), 157. Schaafsma was citing an unpublished manuscript by Joe Winters, which was published in the Impact Magazine of the *Albuquerque Journal*, June 12, 1984.

70. Robinson, *El Malpais, Mt. Taylor, and the Zuni Mountains*, 109.

71. Tony Latonski, Bureau of Land Management, personal communication, 1996.

72. Robinson, *El Malpais, Mt. Taylor, and the Zuni Mountains*, 4.

73. Ibid., 16.

74. Packard, *Suns and Serpents*, 23.

75. M. Jane Young, *Signs from the Ancestors* (Albuquerque: University of New Mexico Press, 1988), 122.

76. Packard, *Suns and Serpents*, 20.

77. Michael P. Marshall and Henry J. Walt, *Rio Abajo: Prehistory and History of a Rio Grande Province* (Santa Fe, N.M.: New Mexico Historic Preservation Division, 1984), 135.

Chapter 4

1. Cited in Jo Anne Van Tillburg, *Ancient Images on Stone* (Los Angeles: University of California, 1983), 18.

2. The stretch of the Rio Grande between Caballo Dam and the Texas border often is dry in winter months when dam storage is implemented. The stretch above the two reservoirs was dry during the growing season of 1996 (a severe drought year) when the Middle Rio Grande Conservancy District diverted the entire flow into irrigation canals at San Acacia above Socorro. This part of the Rio Grande was home to about 70 percent of the remaining Rio Grande silvery minnows, an endangered species. The imperiled fish currently inhabits only 5 percent of its historic range. Although some were saved by the rescue efforts of state and federal wildlife agencies, thousands perished—conditions I observed myself during a hike up the dry, sandy riverbed near San Marcial during the summer of 1996.

3. Lance Chilton et al., *New Mexico: A New Guide to the Colorful State* (Albuquerque: University of New Mexico Press, 1984), 267.

4. H. W. Yeo, unpublished notes at the New Mexico Laboratory of Anthropology 3, 36.

5. Bureau of Land Management, Mimbres Resource Area, Resource Management Plan, 1997, 5–45.

6. Kay Sutherland, *Rock Paintings at Hueco Tanks State Historical Park* (Austin: Texas Parks and Wildlife Press, 1995), 15.

7. Ibid., 8.

8. Ibid., 12.

9. Ibid., 14.

10. Polly Schaafsma, *Indian Rock Art of the Southwest* (Santa Fe and Albuquerque, N.M.: School of American Research and University of New Mexico Press, 1980), 55.

11. Ibid., 56.

12. Sutherland, *Rock Paintings at Hueco Tanks State Historical Park*, 9–10.

13. U.S. Department of the Interior, Nomination Form for National Register of Historic Places, September 19, 1988, prepared by Glenna Dean and Richard Hubbard.

14. Vivian Grubb and H. O. Haines, personal communication, March 1997. Culberson County, Texas, has at least nineteen known rock art sites.

15. Polly Schaafsma, *Rock Art in New Mexico* (Santa Fe, N.M.: Museum of New Mexico Press, 1992), 61.

16. Ibid., 78.

17. Ibid., 78.

18. Dennis Slifer and James Duffield, *Kokopelli: Flute Player Images in Rock Art* (Santa Fe, N.M.: Ancient City Press, 1994), 103.

19. Schaafsma, *Rock Art in New Mexico*, 80.

20. Michael Bilbo, "The Apache Wind God at Alamo Mountain," *Artifact* 26 no. 2 (1988): 89–112.

21. Ibid., 103.

22. Schaafsma, *Rock Art in New Mexico*, 48.

23. Schaafsma, *Indian Rock Art of the Southwest*, 232.

24. Ibid., 233.

25. Schaafsma, *Rock Art in New Mexico*, 77.

26. Slifer and Duffield, *Kokopelli*, 103–05.

27. Garrick Mallery, "Picture Writing of the American Indians," *Fourth Annual Report of the Bureau of American Ethnology* (Washington, D.C.: Smithsonian Institution, 1893), 704–5, 725–26.

28. Gar and Mary Packard, *Suns and Serpents: The Symbolism of Indian Rock Art* (Santa Fe, N.M.: Packard Publications, 1974), 22.

29. Packard, *Suns and Serpents*, 59.

Chapter 5

1. Octavio Paz and Lysander Kemp, *Collected Poems 1957–1987* (New York: New Directions Publishing Corporation, 1987).

2. Sherry Robinson, *El Malpais, Mt. Taylor, and the Zuni Mountains: A Hiking Guide and History* (Albuquerque: University of New Mexico Press, 1994), 239.

3. Ibid., 236.

4. Dennis Slifer and James Duffield, *Kokopelli: Flute Player Images in Rock Art* (Santa Fe, N.M.: Ancient City Press, 1994), 126.

5. Elsie Clews Parsons, *Pueblo Religion* (Chicago: University of Chicago Press, 1939), 170; and Gar and Maggy Packard, *Suns and Serpents: The Symbolism of Indian Rock Art* (Santa Fe, N.M.: Packard Publications, 1974), 29.

6. Patricia McCreery and Ekkehart Malotki, *Tapamveni: The Rock Art Galleries of Petrified Forest and Beyond* (Petrified Forest, Ariz.: Petrified Forest Museum Association, 1994), 179–80; and Packard, *Suns and Serpents*, 40.

7. Slifer and Duffield, *Kokopelli*, 58.

8. John V. Davis, "A Prehistoric Water Control System at Hueco Tanks State Park," *American Indian Rock Art*, ed. Shari T. Grove (Farmington, N.M.: San Juan County Museum Association, 1974), 92.

9. Forrest Kirkland and W. W. Newcomb, *Rock Art of Texas Indians* (Austin: University of Texas Press, 1967).

10. Kay Sutherland, *Rock Paintings at Hueco Tanks State Historical Park* (Austin: Texas Parks and Wildlife Press, 1995), 22.

11. Kirkland and Newcomb, *Rock Art of Texas Indians*, 194.

12. Sutherland, *Rock Paintings at Hueco Tanks State Historical Park*, 6.

13. Polly Schaafsma, *Rock Art in New Mexico* (Santa Fe, N.M.: Museum of New Mexico Press, 1992), 62. The Jornada Style extends along the Rio Grande to Sierra Blanca, Texas, approximately thirty miles east of the Lobo Valley petroglyphs.

BIBLIOGRAPHY

Abel, Brent. "Proposed Investigations at Two Western Archaic Petroglyph Sites Near Pecos, New Mexico." *American Indian Rock Art* 20 (1994).

Arrien, Angeles. *Signs of Life: The Five Universal Shapes and How to Use Them.* Sonoma, Calif.: Arcus Publishing Company, 1992.

Benson, Arlene, and Floyd Buckskin. "Magnetic Anomalies at Petroglyph Lake." *Rock Art Papers* 8 (1991): 53–64. San Diego Museum Papers No. 27.

Bilbo, Michael. "The Apache Wind God at Alamo Mountain." *Artifact*, 26 no. 2 (1988): 89–112.

Bock, Frank. "PIT Crews Uncover Archaic Rock Art." *La Pintura* 20, no. 2 (1993). American Rock Art Research Association.

Boyd, Douglas K., and Bobbie Ferguson. *Tewa Rock Art in the Black Mesa Region.* Amarillo, Tex.: U.S. Department of the Interior, Bureau of Reclamation, Southwest Region, 1988.

Brody, J. J. *The Anasazi.* New York: Rizzoli, 1990.

Buckles, William G. "The Uncompahgre Complex: Historic Ute Archaeology and Prehistoric Archaeology on the Uncompahgre Plateau in West Central Colorado." Ph.D. diss., University of Colorado, 1971.

Bureau of Land Management. *La Cienega Area of Critical Environmental Concern, Coordinated Resource Management Plan.* Albuquerque, N.M.: Albuquerque District Office, Taos Resource Area, 1995.

Chapman, K. M. "The Cave Pictographs of the Rito de los Frijoles, New Mexico." *Papers of the School of American Archaeology* 37 (1917): 139–48.

Chilton, Lance, K. Chilton, P. Arango, J. Dudley, N. Neary, and P. Stelzner. *New Mexico: A New Guide to the Colorful State.* Albuquerque: University of New Mexico Press, 1984.

Cole, Sally J. "Iconography and Symbolism in Basketmaker Rock Art." In *Rock Art of the Western Canyons*, eds. Jane S. Day, Paul D. Friedman, and Marcia J. Tate. *Colorado Archaeological Society Memoir* 3 (1989): 59–85.

____. "Katsina Iconography in Homol'ovi Rock Art." Kiva 54, no. 3 (1989): 313–29.

____. *Legacy on Stone: Rock Art of the Colorado Plateau and Four Corners Region.* Boulder, Colo.: Johnson Books, 1990.

Connor, Linda, and Rick Dingus, Steve Fitch, John Pfahl, and Charles Roitz, with essays by Polly Schaafsma and Keith Davis, and Foreword by Lucy R. Lippard. *Marks in Place: Contemporary Responses to Rock Art.* Albuquerque: University of New Mexico Press, 1988.

Cosgrove, C. B. "Caves of the Upper Gila and Hueco Areas in New Mexico and Texas." *Papers of the Peabody Museum of Archaeology and Ethnography* 24, no. 2.

Crum, Sally. *People of the Red Earth: American Indians of Colorado.* Santa Fe, N.M.: Ancient City Press, 1996.

Davis, Tony. "Horses and Bikes Push into Petroglyph Park." *High Country News* 29, no. 1 (1997): 4.

Davis, John V. "A Prehistoric Water Control System at Hueco Tanks State Park." In *American Indian Rock Art*, ed. Shari T. Grove. Farmington, N.M.: San Juan County Museum Association, 1974.

Di Peso, Charles C. Casas Grandes: *A Fallen Trading Center of the Gran Chichimeca*. Vols 1–3. Dragoon, Ariz.: Amerind Foundation, 1974.

Durham, Dorothy. "Petroglyphs at Mesa de los Padillas." *El Palacio* 62, no. 1 (1955): 3–17.

Eastvold, Isaac. "Ethnographic Background for the Rock Art of the West Mesa Escarpment." In *Las Imagines: The Archaeology of Albuquerque's West Mesa Escarpment*. Albuquerque, N.M.: Department of Parks and Recreation, 1986.

Fewkes, Jesse W. "Tusayan Katcinas." *Fifteenth Annual Report of the Bureau of American Ethnology for the Years 1893–1894*. Washington, D.C.: Smithsonian Institution, 1897.

Furst, Peter T. "Ethnographic Analogy in the Interpretation of West Mexican Art." In *The Archaeology of West Mexico*, ed. Betty Bell. Ajijic, Jalisco: West Mexican Society for Advanced Study, 1974.

Grant, Campbell. *Rock Art of the American Indian*. New York: Promontory Press, 1967.

_____. *Canyon de Chelly: Its People and Rock Art*. Tucson: University of Arizona Press, 1978.

Grant, Campbell, James W. Baird, and J. Kenneth Pringle. "Rock Drawings of the Coso Range." Ridgecrest, Calif.: Maturango Museum, 1987.

Guthrie, Mark R., Powys Gadd, Renee Johnson, and Joseph Lischka. *Colorado Mountains Prehistoric Context*. Denver: Colorado Historical Society, 1984.

Gutierrez, Ramon A. *When Jesus Came the Corn Mothers Went Away: Marriage, Sexuality, and Power in New Mexico, 1500–1846*. Stanford, Calif.: Stanford University Press, 1991.

Hadlock, Harry L. "Ganaskidi: The Navajo Humpback Deity of the Largo." *Papers of the Archaeological Society of New Mexico* 5 (1980): 179–210.

Hester, James J. "Early Navajo Migrations and Acculturation in the Southwest." *Museum of New Mexico Papers in Anthropology* 6 (1962): 21–24.

Heizer, R. F., and M. A. Baumhoff. *Prehistoric Rock Art of Nevada and Eastern California*. Berkeley: University of California Press, 1962.

Hibben, Frank. *Excavation of the Riana Ruin and Chama Valley Survey*. University of New Mexico Bulletin: Anthropological Series 2, No. 1 (1937).

Highwater, Jamake. *The Primal Mind: Vision and Reality in Indian America*. New York: New American Library, 1982.

Hillerman, Tony, and Robert Reynolds. *Rio Grande*. Portland, Oreg.: C. H. Belding Graphic Arts Center Publishing Company, 1975.

Horgan, Paul. Great River: *The Rio Grande in North American History*. Vols. 1, 2. New York : Rinehart and Company, 1954.

Irwin-Williams, Cynthia. "Picosa: The Elementary Southwestern Culture." *American Antiquity* 32 (1967): 441–57.

Johnson, Clay. "Methodology for Identifying, Observing, Recording, and Reporting Solar Interactive Rock Art Panels." *Utah Rock Art* 10. From proceedings of 10th Annual Symposium of the Utah Rock Art Research Association, 1992.

Kelley, Jane H. *The Archaeology of the Sierra Blanca Region of Southeast New Mexico.* Anthropology Papers No. 74. Ann Arbor, Mich.: University of Michigan, 1984.

Kirkland, Forrest, and W. W. Newcomb. *Rock Art of Texas Indians.* Austin: University of Texas Press, 1967.

Lambert, Marjorie F. "Paa-ko, Archaeological Chronicle of an Indian Village in North Central New Mexico." *School of American Research Monograph* 19. Santa Fe, N.M.: School of American Research, 1954.

Lentz, Robert, and Eugene Varela. "The Pecos Petroglyph Survey." Pecos, N.M.: Unpublished report for Pecos National Monument, 1971.

Lewis-Williams, David, and Thomas Dowson. *Images of Power: Understanding Bushman Rock Art.* Cape Town, South Africa: National Book Printers, 1989.

Lilienthal, Betty, and Dorothy Hoard. *Sentinels on Stone: The Petroglyphs of Los Alamos.* Los Alamos, N.M.: Los Alamos Historical Society, 1995.

Mallery, Garrick. "Picture Writing of the American Indians." *Fourth Annual Report of the Bureau of American Ethnology.* Washington, D.C.: Smithsonian Institution, 1893.

Marshall, Michael P., and Henry J. Walt. *Rio Abajo: Prehistory and History of a Rio Grande Province.* Santa Fe: New Mexico Historic Preservation Division, 1984.

McCreery, Patricia. "Another Look at Hunting Magic." *La Pintura* 23, no. 2 (1996). American Rock Art Research Association.

McCreery, Patricia, and Ekkehart Malotki. *Tapamveni: The Rock Art Galleries of Petrified Forest and Beyond.* Petrified Forest, Ariz.: Petrified Forest Museum Association, 1994.

Mednick, Christina Singleton. *San Cristobal: Voices and Visions of the Galisteo Basin.* Santa Fe: Museum of New Mexico Press, 1996.

Muench, David, and Polly Schaafsma. *Images in Stone.* San Francisco, Calif.: Brown Trout Publishers, 1995.

Nykamp, Robert. "Distribution of Known Ute Sites in Colorado." In *Archaeology of the Eastern Ute: A Symposium.* Denver: Colorado Council of Professional Archaeologists, 1988.

Opler, Morris E. *An Apache Life-Way: The Economic, Social, and Religious Institutions of the Chiricahua Indians.* Chicago, Ill.: University of Chicago Press, 1941.

Packard, Gar and Maggy. *Suns and Serpents: The Symbolism of Indian Rock Art.* Santa Fe, N.M.: Packard Publications, 1974.

Parsons, Elsie Clews. *Pueblo Religion.* Chicago: University of Chicago Press, 1939.

_____. "Some Aztec and Pueblo Parallels." *American Anthropologist* 35 (1933): 611–31.

Patterson, Alex. *A Field Guide to Rock Art Symbols of the Greater Southwest.* Boulder, Colo.: Johnson Books, 1992.

Patterson-Rudolph, Carol. *Petroglyphs and Pueblo Myths of the Rio Grande.* Albuquerque, N.M.: Avanyu Publishing, 1990.

Paz, Octavio, and Lysander Kemp. *Collected Poems 1957–1987.* New York: New Directions Publishing Corporation, 1987.

Pfahl, John. "Elegy for the Drowned." In *Marks in Place: Contemporary Responses to Rock Art*. Albuquerque: University of New Mexico Press, 1988.

Reichard, Gladys A. *Navajo Religion: A Study of Symbolism*. Vols. 1, 2. New York: Stratford Press, 1950.

Renaud, E. B. "Pictographs and Petroglyphs of the High Western Plains." *Archaeological Survey Series* 8th Report 4 (1936): 25–39. Denver, Colo.: University of Denver.

_____. "Petroglyphs of North Central New Mexico." *Archaeological Survey Series* 11th Report. Denver, Colo.: University of Denver, 1938.

Riley, Carroll L. *The Frontier People: The Greater Southwest in the Protohistoric Period*. Albuquerque: University of New Mexico Press, 1987.

_____. "Pueblo Indians in Meso-America: The Early Historic Period." In *Collected Papers in Honor of Florence Hawley Ellis*, ed. Theodore Frisbie. Norman, Okla.: Hooper Publishing Co., 1975. Papers of the Archaeological Society of New Mexico 2.

Riley, Robert A. "Rock Art at La Bajada Mesa, New Mexico." Unpublished manuscript. Santa Fe, N.M.: Laboratory of Anthropology, 1973.

Roberts, Frank H. H., Jr. *The Village of the Great Kivas on the Zuni Reservation*. Bureau of American Ethnology Bulletin 111. Washington, D.C.: Smithsonian Institution, 1932.

Robinson, Sherry. *El Malpais, Mt. Taylor, and the Zuni Mountains: A Hiking Guide and History*. Albuquerque: University of New Mexico Press, 1994.

Rohn, Arthur H. and Lisa, and William Ferguson. *Rock Art of Bandelier National Monument*. Albuquerque: University of New Mexico Press, 1989.

Schaafsma, Polly. *Rock Art in the Navajo Reservoir District*. Museum of New Mexico Papers in Anthropology No. 7. Santa Fe, N.M.: Museum of New Mexico Press, 1963.

_____. "Los Lunas Petroglyphs." *El Palacio* 75, no. 2 (1968): 13–24.

_____. *Rock Art in the Cochiti Reservoir District*. Santa Fe, N.M.: Museum of New Mexico Press, 1975. Museum of New Mexico Papers in Anthropology No. 16.

_____. *Indian Rock Art of the Southwest*. Santa Fe and Albuquerque, N.M.: School of American Research and University of New Mexico Press, 1980.

_____. "Kachinas in Rock Art." *Journal of New World Archaeology* 4, no. 2 (1981): 25–32.

_____. "Anasazi Rock Art in Tsegi Canyon and Canyon de Chelly: A View Behind the Images." In *Tse Yaq Kin: Houses Beneath the Rocks*, ed. David Grant Noble. Santa Fe, N.M.: School of American Research, 1986.

_____. "War Imagery and Magic: Petroglyphs at Comanche Gap, Galisteo Basin, New Mexico." In *Social Implications of Symbolic Expression in the Prehistoric American Southwest*. Las Vegas, Nev.: Society for American Archaeology, 1990. 55th Annual Meeting of the Society for American Archaeology.

_____. *Rock Art in New Mexico*. Santa Fe, N.M.: Museum of New Mexico Press, 1992.

Schaafsma, Polly, and Curtis F. Schaafsma. "Evidence for the Origins of the Pueblo Katchina Cult as Suggested by Southwestern Rock Art." *American Antiquity* 39, no. 4 (1974): 535–45.

Schmader, Mathew F., and John D. Hays. *Las Imagines: The Archaeology of Albuquerque's West Mesa Escarpment*. Albuquerque, N.M.: City of Albuquerque, Department of Parks and Recreation, 1986.

Sims, Agnes C. *San Cristobal Petroglyphs*. Santa Fe, N.M.: Southwestern Editions, 1950.

Slifer, Dennis. *Red River Groundwater Investigation*. Santa Fe: New Mexico Environment Department, 1996.

Slifer, Dennis, and James Duffield. *Kokopelli: Flute Player Images in Rock Art*. Santa Fe, N.M.: Ancient City Press, 1994.

Smith, Howard N., Jr. "A Survey and Stylistic Analysis of Rock Art in the San Juan Basin." Master's thesis, Eastern New Mexico University, 1974.

Sofaer, A. "A Unique Solar Marking Construct." *Science* 206, no. 44 (1979): 283–91.

Steinbring, Jack. "Phenomenal Attributes: Site Selection Factors in Rock Art." *American Indian Rock Art* 17. Proceedings of the Seventeenth Annual Meeting of the American Rock Art Research Association, 1992.

Steinbring, Jack, and Maurice Lanteigne. "Archeopsychological Process in Rock Art: Entoptic Phenomena or Relative Recurrence of Elemental Forms?" *Rock Art Papers* 8 (1991: 141–53). San Diego Museum Papers No. 27.

Stevenson, Matilda Coxe. "The Zuni Indians: Their Mythology, Esoteric Fraternities and Ceremonies." *Twenty-Third Annual Report of the Bureau of American Ethnology for the Years 1901–1902*. Washington, D.C.: Smithsonian Institution, 1904.

Stoney, Stephen A. "Sun, Sandstone, and Shadow: Rock Art in Southern Nevada Takes on New Meaning." *Rock Art Papers* 8 (1991). San Diego Museum Papers No. 27.

Sutherland, Kay. *Rock Paintings at Hueco Tanks State Historical Park*. Austin: Texas Parks and Wildlife Press, 1995.

Trask, Lance. *Ancient Billboards: The Rock Art of the Lower Jemez Mountains*. Santa Fe and Albuquerque, N.M.: Santa Fe National Forest and University of New Mexico Maxwell Museum, 1992.

Trimble, Stephen. *The People: Indians of the American Southwest*. Santa Fe, N.M.: School of American Research Press, 1993.

Van Tillburg, Jo Anne. *Ancient Images on Stone*. Los Angeles: University of California, 1983.

Ware, J. A. "Man on the Rio Grande: Introduction and Overview." In *New Mexico Geological Society Guidebook*. Albuquerque: University of New Mexico Press, 1984. 35th Field Conference, Rio Grande Rift: Northern New Mexico.

Warren, A. H., and Robert H. Weber. "Indian and Spanish Mining in the Galisteo and Hagan Basins." *New Mexico Geological Society Special Publication No. 8*. Albuquerque: New Mexico Geological Society, 1979.

Weahkee, Bill. "Petroglyph Area Is Sacred Place for New Mexico Pueblos." *La Pintura* 23, no. 2 (1996): 1–3. American Rock Art Research Association. Originally published in the *Albuquerque Journal*, October 16, 1996.

Young, M. Jane. *Signs from the Ancestors*. Albuquerque: University of New Mexico Press, 1988.

INDEX

Note: Italic numbers indicate pages with figures.

"Abiqui Pictures," 84, 85
Abo Arroyo, 138–142
Acoma (Sky City), 150
Acoma-Zuni Trail, 152
acoustical properties of rock
    art locations, 30–31, 162
agua es vida (water is life), 2
Alamo Canyon, *187*, 189, *190–192*, *199–200*
Alamo Mountain, *19*, *198–200*
Aldridge petroglyph panel, *154*, 155
altered consciousness and entoptic ("within the
    eye") phenomena, 26–27
Anasazi culture, 13–15, 37, 40
    Basketmaker Periods, 14, 41, 148–149
    map of area, *12*
    Pueblo Periods, 14, 15–18, 43–46
        language groups, 44, *45*
        map of Provinces, *45*
        Pueblo II, 153
        Pueblo III, 123, 153
        Pueblo IV, 89–90, 93, 123, 153
Anasazi Styles, 67, *68*, 72, *115*, *146–147*
    Basketmaker, *59*, *148*
    on bedrock, *127*
    on boulders, 67, *68*
    Early, 40–41, *42*
    Pueblo, 63, 67–68, 71, *74*, 75, 77, *78–79*,
        149 (See also Rio Grande *Style)*
"Ancient Ones," 14
Ancient People ("Hisatsinom"), 15
Angostura de San Acacia, 159
animal-shaped boulder, *218*
Ant People, 63
anthropomorphs, 39, *43*, 69, 83, 93, *118*, *124*,
    140, *154*, *160*, *174*, *191*, Plate 3, Plate
    6, Plate 10. *See also* flute players
    with antennae, *63*
    under a blanket, *88*, 89
    with bow and arrows, *112*
    and ceremonial activities, *61*, *79*, *95*, *137*,
        141, *161*, *164*, *206*, *227*, *236*,
        236–237
    with circle motifs, *135*
    as corn guardians, *114*
    distorted, *43*
    and elk, *73*
    with hats, *150*
    with headdresses, *95*, *145*, *201*
    holding children or puppets, *134*
    holding horned mask, *118*
    holding war club, *133*
    with horns, 70, *71*, *81*, *176*
    humpbacked, *158*, *196*
    humpbacked and phallic, *154*, *192*, *209*
    like spear points, *187*, *190*
    narrow-waisted, *198*
    pattern-bodied, *156*
    with plants, *182*
    in a row, *135*
    running, *142*
    sharing the same head, *94*
    square-bodied, *156*
    upside-down, *81*
    with wide shoulders, *148*
Apache Mountain spirit dancers, *195*
Apache rock art, *19*, *49*, *168–169*, *176*, *181*,
    182, *195*, *198*
    Mescalero, *188*, *199–200*, 202, 246, *247*
Apache Well, *197*
Apaches, 18
    Chiricahua, 198–199, 247
    Mescalero, 246, *247*
archaeoastronomy and rock art, 60–61, 63, 179
Archaic Period, 10–11
    Western Archaic, 33
Archaic Styles, *4*, 11, 33–37, *74–75*, *174–175*,
    184, *186*
    Chihuahuan Polychrome, 33, 36
    Desert Abstract, 33, *34*, *35*, 41, *117*, 131,
        179, 202, *225*, Plate 2
    Diablo Dam, 33, *36*, 37, *187*, 189, *190*
    Early, 186
    Middle and Late, 186
arms, 28
arrows, 97, *141*
Arroyo Aguaje de la Petaca, 75
Arroyo del Macho, *208–213*
Arroyo Hondo, *19*, 69, *70*
Arroyo Seco, 73
Ash Spring, *176*
Athabascan people, 47
Athabascan rock art, 18–19, 78
atlatls, 61, *62*, *149*, *184*
Austin, Mary, on El Malpais, 152
Awanyu, water deity, 16, *17*, 40, *80*, *84*, *108*,
    136, Plate 4
    compared to Tlaloc, 39

axis mundi (axle of the world), 30

badgers, *110–111*
Bandelier, Adolph, on Cochiti rock art, 92
Bandelier National Monument, 89–90, 91,
    218–219, *220*
basins, defined, 251 n7
Basketmaker Periods, 14, 41, 148–149
Basketmaker Styles, 59, *148*
bear paws, *69, 110*
bear shamen, *228–229*
bears, *108, 141*
    symbolism of, 67–69
    tracks, *164*, Plate 11
"Big Bird," *59*, 60
"Big Elk Panel," 66, *67*
bighorn sheep, *31, 120, 180, 184, 191*
"Bird Rock," 240, *241*
bird tracks, *37, 72, 78, 79, 119*
birds, *59, 78, 100, 110, 124, 135, 155, 174,*
    229–230, 235, Plate 9, Plate 13.
    See also macaws, parrots, turkeys
    ceremonial, *230, 231*
    eating, *154, 180*
    with rain imagery, *4, 213*
birth imagery, *221*
Biscuit Ware Pueblos, 83
bison, *61*
Black Mesa (Bernalillo County), 133,
    134–135
Black Mesa (Rio Arriba County), *4, 28, 78–83*
Black Mesa (Socorro County), *49,* 165,
    166–169
Black Range, 174–175, 195
bow and arrows, *112,* 113
Bowling Green Pueblo, *163–164*
breath, *168*
Broad Canyon, *180–181*
bull roarers and rock art, *199*
bullet holes in rock art, 52, 193
burden baskets, *148,* 149
butterflies, *153*
    symbolism of, 154

Cabezon, 126, 145–146
Candelaria Peaks (Chihuahua, Mexico), 37
Canyon de Chelly (AZ), 48
Carnero Creek, 215–216
Carnero Creek (CO), *58,* 59
carnivores, *192, 205, 212*
Carrizozo (NM), 33, *34*
Casas Grandes (Chihuahua, Mexico), 15, 38
Catholic eradication of rock art, 85–86
Catholic exorcism of rock art, 86
Cave Kiva, 89, *90–91, 245, 246*

caves
    as entrances to underworld, 76
    as sacred, 208
Cebolla Canyon, *155–156*
Cebollita Mesa, 153–155
ceramics and rock art, 210
ceremonial creatures, *78, 110, 230, 231,*
    235, 240
ceremonial figures, *61, 79, 95, 137, 141, 161,*
    164, 206, 227, 236–237. See also
    anthropomorphs
ceremonial staffs, *4, 61, 149, 180*
Cerro Indio (Black Butte), 159, *160–161*
Cerro Pedernal, 83
Chaco Canyon, 31
    outliers, 153
Chaco Culture National Historic Park, 220,
    221–222
chalk, misuse of, 51–52
Chapman, Kenneth, 219
Chihuahuan Desert, 36, 37, 38
Chihuahuan Polychrome Style, 33, 36
Chiricahua, 198–199, 247
Chloride Creek, *37*
Christian crosses
    added to rock art, 85
Church, Peggy Pond, viii
circles, *119*
cisterns, 185
Citadel Pueblo, 155
claws, *110*
"Cloud People," 16, *151*
cloud terraces, *4, 16, 124, 126, 136, 154,*
    155, 160, 223
    as headdresses, *161*
cloud-blowers, 101
Clumsy Foot and Pueblo culture, 68
Cochiti Dam and destroyed rock art, 91, 92
Colorado Plateau, 14, 41
Comanche Cave, *188, 246, 247*
Comanche Gap, *104, 106, 107, 109*, Plate 6,
    Plate 8
Comanche rock art, 87
Configurations, 214
conservation of rock art, 51–53
Continental Divide at North Plains Basin,
    156–157, 158
Cooke's Peak, *4,* 195, *196*
copulation scenes, *98, 121, 124, 222*
corn, *4, 16, 114, 120*
Cornudas Mountains, *200–201*
cosmology and rock art, 30
Cougar Man, 109
cougars, 109
coyotes, 211, *212*

cracks in rocks
    as entrances to underworld, *28, 29*
    as fertility symbols, 29–30
cranes, *59*
creation stories, 152
Cuchillo Negro Creek, *174–175*
Culberson County Historical Commission, 193
culture areas, map of, 12
curling lines, *153*

dancers
    with masks, *187, 244*
    victory, *188*
Davis, W. W. H., on Inscription Rock, 224
deer, *156, 174, 191, 242*
    tracks, *136, 180, 183*
Deer Dancer, *82*
Deer Mother, 66, 71
definition of rock art, 23–26
Desert Abstract Style, 33, *34, 35,* 41, *117,* 131, 179, 202, *225,* Plate 2
designs, geometric, *155, 174, 180, 191,* Plate 15
destruction of rock art
    by Catholics, 85–86
    by construction, 84–85, 87, 92, 129, 133–134, 198
    by dynamite, 178
    by mining, 95, 119
destruction of rock art by construction
    Renaud quote, 87
destruction protested, 92, 129–130
Diablo Dam Style, 33, *36,* 37, *187,* 189, *190*
Dinetah area, 18–19, 47
Dog Mountain (CO), *59*
Dominguez, Francisco, Rio Puerco description, 142–143
Doña Ana Mountains, 182–183
dragonflies, *4,* 75, *209–210, 213*
drums, *168*
Dry Creek (CO), 61, 216, *217*

eagles, *142*
    symbolism of, 141–142
El Camino Real (The Royal Road), 95
El Cerro de los Lunas, *135–136*
El Malpais
    Lummis quote, 152
El Malpais National Conservation Area, 151, *153–156, 222, 223*
El Malpais National Monument, 151, 222–223
El Morro National Monument, 223–224
elk, *73, 115*

Embudo, 78
endangered, 62, 77
entoptic ("within the eye") phenomena and altered consciousness, 26–27
entrances to the underworld
    in cracks in rocks, *28,* 29
    in springs, 16
entrances to underworld
    in caves, 76
Española Valley, 78–84
exorcism of rock art by Catholics, 86

Fajada Butte, 31
fantastic beasts, *124, 140, 204, 235*
Feather Cave, *208*
feathers, *211*
female symbols, *100, 116, 210*
fertility shrine, "Mother Rock," 65, *66*
fertility symbols, 29–30, *116*
fertility themes, 115, 125, *188,* 209, *210, 247.*
    See also copulation scenes
    and flute players, *89,* 100, 227
    at "Mother Rock," 65, *66*
    and rain, *4,* 101, *154*
Fewkes, Jesse, on winter solstice myth, 136
fish, *4,* 18, *180, 205*
"Flute Player Rock," 240
flute players, *4, 59, 82,* 99, *119, 124,* 161, *164.*
    See also Kokopelli; phallic figures
    and fertility themes, *89,* 100, 227
    humpbacked and phallic, *100, 101, 124, 238, 240,* Plate 9
    phallic, *221,* 227
food processing at rock art sites, 133, 177
footprints, *111, 127,* 128, *141, 142, 180, 183, 212*
Fort Hancock (TX), *36*
fossils incorporated in rock art, *137*
Franklin Mountains, *184*
Frijoles Canyon, 90, 219, *220*
frogs, Plate 5

Galisteo Basin, *43,* 102–103, *104, 105, 106–116,* 117–118, Plates 5–7
    erosion, *103*
game animals, *99,* 146–147, *182, 187*
Geronimo Springs, 174
Glorieta Mesa, 34, *35, 117, 225*
Gobernador Phase, 47–48
Gobernador Representational Style, 47, *48, 149*
Good Sight Mountains, 197–198
Grandfather Bear and Pueblo culture, 67–68
Grant, Gordon, 54
Great River, xvi

"great river," 6
Great Sand Dunes, 63
Guadalupe Pueblo, 146

hand kachina, *167*
hands, *16, 28, 62, 91, 112, 180, 183,* Plate 7
    six-fingered, *206*
    symbolism of, 112–113
Hands, 170
"The Healer," *62*
heart lines, *110,* 111, *141*
Hero Twins story, 146
Hidden Mountain, 143, 144, *145*
Highwater, Jamake, 22
"Hisatsinom" (Ancient People), 15
Hispanic elements, in rock art, 58, 216
Historic, petroglyphs, *97, 135*
hoaxes in rock art, 144
Holiday Mesa, *124–125*
Hopi Crane Clan, 60
Horgan, Paul, xvi
horned images, *167, 168, 198*
horned serpents, *4,* 16, *17, 39, 80, 84, 91, 108,*
    124, 136
horses, 18, *19,* 48
horses and riders, *48, 51, 63, 70, 78, 135, 176,*
    202
hourglass shapes, 97
"The Houses of the Holy," 76
Hueco Tanks State Historical Park (TX), *38,*
    39, 185, *186–188,* 242, *243–246,* 247,
    Plate 14
hunters, *120, 176, 182,* 189–190
hunting, *31,* 126, *186*
Hupovi Pueblo, 82, *84*

idolatry and rock art, 86
Inscription Rock, 223
    Lummis quote, 223–224
    W. W. H. Davis quote, 224
insects, *155, 205*

Jan Juan Mesa, 123
Jeffers, Robinson, 170
Jemez Mountains, 88–93, 123, *124–126*
Jemez River, 118, *119–122,* 126–128
jewelry and rock art, 210
Jornada Style. *See* Mogollon Styles: Jornada
    Style

kachina cult, 16, 39, 40
kachina imagery, 44, 46, 81, *91, 100, 119,*
    167–168, 240, Plate 9. *See also* masks
Keresan Pueblos, 88, 93
    mythology, 97

petroglyphs, *92, 94, 98–99, 119–122*
Kirkland, Forrest, 244
knives, *78*
Kokopelli, 46, 99–100, 209. *See also* flute play-
    ers; phallic figures
    Hopi story illustrated, *125*
Kolowis, water deity, 16–17
koshare (clown figure), *91*

La Bajada (The Descent), *94–95*
La Cienega Area of Critical Environmental
    Concern, 94, 225–226
La Cienega Creek, 95
La Mesita, 78–79
Largo Canyon, *48, 52*
Las Aguajes, *100*
legal protection for rock art, 53
legs, *29*
lightning, *4, 126, 213*
lightning arrows, *4*
lizard-man, *157*
lizards, *156,* Plate 5, Plate 15
    symbolism of, 29, 158
Lobo Canyon, *153*
Lobo Valley Petroglyph Site, 193, *194,*
    248–249
Los Alamos National Laboratory, 90
Lower Taos Canyon, 72
Lucero Arroyo (formerly Pictograph
    Canyon), *182,* 183
Lummis, Charles
    on El Malpais, 152
    on Inscription Rock, 223–224

macaws, *230*
"man who fell from the sky," *81*
Manzano Mountains, 137
maps
    of culture areas, *12*
    of Pueblo Provinces, *45*
    of pueblos and kivas in rock art, *135*
    of rock art sites, *5*
    of rock art styles, Plate 1
Masau, god of fire and death, 127–128, 141
    footprints, *142*
    and Seismosaurus fossil, 128
masks, *117, 136, 140, 164,* 185, *187,* 188, *209,*
    244, Plate 10, Plates 12–14
    with animal head, *179*
    bird, *161*
    with fish, *244*
    with frontal and profile views, 101, *102*
    horned, *118, 160, 179*
    kachina, *91, 100*
    outline, *245*

solid, *245*
  Sutherland quote, 187
Matia (hand) Kachina, *167*
Matisse, Henri, quoted, 22
Mesa Encantada, 150, *151*
Mescal Spring, *176–177*
Mescalero rock art, *188, 199–200, 202*, 246, *247*
Mesilla Valley, 184
Mesoamerican influences, 38, 40
Middle Rio Grande, sites, 118–137
migration, *111*, 112
Mimbres Basin, 194
mission churches, rock art images, 73
Mogollon culture, 13, 37, 187
  Desert Mogollon, 13, 38
  map of area, *12*
  Mimbres, 195
  Mountain Mogollon, 13, 37
Mogollon Styles, 37–40
  Jornada Style, 13, *29, 31*, 37, *38–39*, 40, 177, *178–184*, 187, 190, 195, *196–197*, 198, *200–201*, 203, *204–206, 208–213, 235–237, 243–244*
    elements in, 39
    influence of, 40, 44, 46
    and kachina cult, 39
    symbols, *4*
  Mogollon Red Style, *37*
    elements in, 37
Morning on Tshirege, viii
mortar holes, 177
"Mother of Game," 66, 71, 72, *80*, 255 n14
"Mother Rock," fertility shrine, *66*
moths, *205*
Mount Chalchihuitl, 15
Mount Taylor, 144–145
  other names for, 144–145
mountain lions, *102*, 109, *110, 157, 235, 237*
  tracks, *141, 164*, Plate 11
Mountain Mogollon, 13, 37
Muskrat House, 93
"Mystery Rock," 143–144

National Register of Historic Places, listed sites, 58, 88, 129, 193, 215, 238, 239, 248
Navajo rock art, 18–19, 19, 47, *48*, 52, *149*
North Plains Basin, 151–158
Northern Tewa, 78–79, 88, 232
Northern Tewa Province, *28*
Northern Tewa Pueblos, 88

observatories, 31, 217, *218*

Ojito Wilderness Study Area, 126
Oñate, Juan de, 223
  inscription, *224*
Orilla Verde Recreation Area (*formerly* Rio Grande Gorge State Park), 73, Plate 2
Otowi, 89

Painted Cave, *91*, 219, *220*
Painted Grotto, 36
Pajarito Plateau, 88–93, *90–91*
Paleo-Indians, 9–10, 131, 186
Palmer Park, *178*
parrots, *230*
patina, 23
Paz, Octavio, 214
pecked surfaces and rituals, 30
Pecos Classification, 40
Pecos National Historical Park, 115–116, 117–118
Petaca Canyon, *76*
Petroglyph National Monument, 128–133, *227–231*
  and storytelling, 131
"Petroglyph Rock," *207*, 233
petroglyphs
  defined, 23
  pecked, 117
  scratched, *49, 168–169*
phallic figures, *94, 116, 168. See also* flute players, Kokopelli
Pictograph Canyon, (now Lucero Arroyo), 182–183, 195
pictographs
  in black, *202*
  defined, 24
  polychrome, 139, 162, Plate 3, Plate 10
  stenciled, *112*, 113, Plate 4
  in white, *192, 244*
Picture Cave, 36
Piedras Marcada ("Marked Rock") Pueblo, 133
Piedras Negras Pueblo, 162, *163*
Pilar (NM), 77
Piro District, *16*, 144, 159–169, Plate 12
Piro Pueblo, *158*
pits (cupules), 30, 34
plants, *100*, 174
Pleistocene epoch, 9
pottery designs and rock art, 195
The Primal Mind, 22
proposed development and rock art, 130
public access to sites, 53
  in Colorado, 215–218
  in New Mexico, 218–241
  in Texas, 242–249
Pueblo Blanco, 107, *108*

Pueblo Colorado, 107
Pueblo Periods. *See* Anasazi culture: Pueblo
   Periods
Pueblo Revolt of 1680, 17, 47, 105
Pueblo Styles, 63, 67–68, 71, 74, 75, 77, 78–79,
   149. See also Rio Grande Styles
Puyé Cliff Dwellings, 89, 231–323

quadruped with cloven feet, 121
Querencia Arroyo, 127
Quetzalcoatl, 40

rabbits, *183*, 211, *212*
rain, *4, 99, 100–101, 154, 157, 199, 213*
   symbolism of, 16
rain deities, *151*
rainbows, *4, 213*
rattlesnakes, *196*
Red River, confluence with Rio Grande, 66–67
Renaud, E. B., on destruction of rock art
   by construction, 87
Riana Pueblo, 84–85
Rincon (NM), *178*
Rinconada (NM), 77, *78*
Rio Bonito, *207*, 208
Rio Bonito Petroglyph National Recreation
   Trail, 233
Rio Chama, 82–84, 85
   confluence with Rio Grande, 82
   confluence with Rio Ojo Caliente, 82
Rio Grande
   compared to Ganges, 6
   confluence with Arroyo Hondo, 70
   confluence with Jemez River, 119
   confluence with Red River, 66–67
   confluence with Rio Chama, 82
   confluence with Rio Pueblo de Taos, 71
   confluence with Rio Salado, 159
   other names for, 6
   power and importance, 2–3, 6
   source, 3, 6
Rio Grande County Museum and Cultural
   Center, 216
Rio Grande Gorge, *4, 64–78*
Rio Grande Gorge State Park (*now* Orilla
   Verde Recreation Area), 73
Rio Grande headwaters, sites, 56–64
Rio Grande Rift Valley, 8
Rio Grande Style, *4, 43, 79–81,* 88, 90, *95–96,*
   99, 106–107, 114–115, 131–133,
   160–161, 163–164, 166–169, 219, *226,*
   227–231, 238, 240, Plates 3–12
   elements in, 44
   evolution of, 40–42
   Keresan, *92, 94, 98–99, 119–122*

locations, 46
   Northern Tewa, 78–79, 88, 232
   regional variation, 44, *45,* 46
   Southern Tewa, 105, 132
Rio Grande Valley, 3, 43
Rio Grande watershed, 3
Rio Ojo Caliente (Hot Spring River), 75, *84*
   confluence with Rio Chama, 82
Rio Piedra Pintada (Painted Rock River),
   61–63
Rio Pueblo de Taos, *73*
   confluence with Rio Grande, 71
Rio Puerco, 142–145, *146–149,* 150–158
   confluence with Rio San Jose, 144, 150
   description, 142–143
Rio Salado, 158
   confluence with Rio Grande, 159
Rio San Jose, *150,* 151
rivers and rituals, 17–18
rock art as "art," 25, 101
rock varnish, 23
rubbings, misuse of, 52

sacred web of life, 9
Salinas National Monument, 233–234
Salt Basin, 198–201
San Diego Mountain, *179–180*
San Juan Anthropomorphic Style, 148–149
San Luis Valley, 49–51, 57, *58,* 59–64
San Marcial (NM), *16*
San Pasqualito, 162, 165
Sandia Cave, petroglyphs, *24*
sandpainting and rock art, 48
Santa Fe River Canyon, *42,* 93–94, *95–102*
Schaafsma, Polly
   on Apache rock art, 49
   classification of styles, 32
   defining rock art, 25–26
   on imagery, 106, 203
   on Rio Grande Style variations, 44
Schumla Type points, *187, 190*
Seismosaurus fossil and Masau myth, 128
serpents. *See* snakes
The Shaman at Ending, 54
shamanic imagery, *62,* 70, *71, 168, 176, 181,*
   189–190, 228, 244, Plate 4
   with sunburst head, *49*
shamanic practices and rock art, 27
shield bearers, *136–137, 166, 191*
shields, *71, 74, 78, 81, 104,* 106, *125,* 211, *223,*
   241–242
Shivano Valley (CO), *51*
Sierra Blanca, 203
Sierra Caballos, *176–178*
Sierra de las Uvas, 179–181, *182*

271

significance of locations, 27–31
sipapu (earth navel), 63
sites
    map of, *5*
    northern, 55–169 (*See also* specific locations)
    with public access, 53, 215–249 (*See also* specific locations)
    southern, 171–213 (*See also* specific locations)
    typical locations near water, 3
smoke damage to rock art, 53
snakes, *74*, *124*, *155*, *156*, *210*, Plate 7, Plate 9
    coiled, *139*
    crested, *190*
    feathered, *137–138*, 139
    horned, *180*
    one-eyed, *241*
    with shamen, *181*
    symbolism of, 29, 140
    two-headed, *157*
Sonoran life zone, 172
Southern Tewa, 102, 105, 132
    imagery, 132
Southern Tiwa, 137
Spanish imagery, *73*
spear points, *187*
spears, *97*
spirals, *91*, *94*, 253 n11
spiritual qualities of rock art, 213
springs
    associated with rock art, 65, 70, 75, 77, 82, 90
    as entrances to underworld, 16
staffs, *4*, *61*, *149*, *180*
star paintings (planetaria), 47–48
star-beings, *107*, *120*, *132*, 133, *139*
stars, *107*
stencil method pictographs, 112, 113
stick figures, *37*
"Storyteller Panel," 190, *191*
"Strong Lion," 86
styles, 31–33. *See also* specific styles
    components of, 31
    composites of, *74*, 223
    continuity between, 35, 40, 46, 153, 202, 248
    design similarities, 198
    evolution of, 189
    influences on, 38, 50
    map of, Plate 1
    superimposed, 34, 85, 147, 149, 202, *224*
Summerford Mountain, *183*
sun symbols, *154*, *157*, *247*

supernatural beings, *150*, *161*, *206*, *212*, Plate 4, Plate 6
Sutherland, Kay, on masks, 187
symbolic nature of rock art, 25–26
symbols related to water, 3, *4*, 39–40

tadpoles, *4*
Tajique Canyon, *137*
Tano, 102
    war cults, 105–106
    war symbols, *104*
Tapia Canyon, *146–149*
Tawa (sun), 136
Tenabo, 134, 139–141
Tetilla Peak, 98
Tewa origin myth, 63
theft of rock art, 52, 53
"Thirsty Mask," *243*
Three Rivers Petroglyph National Recreation Area, *4*, 29, *31*, 203, *204–206*, 207, 234, *235–237*, Plate 15
three-dimensional designs, 101, *102*
thunderbirds, *134*
time, perceived as cyclic, 9
Tlaloc
    compared to Awanyu, 39
    water deity, *4*, *38*, 39, 40, 177, *178*, *184*, *200*, *207–208*
Tomé Hill, 237, *238*, *239*
Tompiro, rock art, *137–142*, Plates 10–11
Tonque Arroyo, *119*
Tonuco Mountains, 149, Plate 13
triangles, *155*
Trinchera Creek (CO), *63*
Truth of Consequences (NM), 173–174
Tsankawi, 89–90
Tsipinguinge (House of the Flaking Stone Mountain), 83–84
Tsirige, 89
Tularosa Basin, 201–202
turkeys, *78–79*, 80–81
turtles, *4*
twins, *204*
Tyuonyi, 218

upper Rio Grande watershed, 6–8
    defined, xii
    map of, *5*
Upper Sonoran Zone, 8
"Ute Battle Scene," *62*
Ute rock art, *20*, 49, *51*, *58*, *63*, 216
    Early Historic, 50
    elements in, 50
    Late Historic, 50–51

Utes, 19–20
Mouache Band, 20, 49
in San Luis Valley, 57–58
warrior burial, 62

Vado (NM), *184*
vandalism of rock art, *52*, 53, 184, 185, 246
Vargas, Diego de, 93
Rio Grande ford, 63–64
Virgin Mesa, *126*
combining petroglyphs and pictographs, 126

warriors, *106*, *177*, Plate 8
on shields, *211*
with shields, *198*
with weapons, *74*, *104*
water as sacred, 16–18
water deities. See Awanyu; Kolowis; Tlaloc
water jars, *113*

water themes, 212–213, 243
West Mesa (Albuquerque, NM), 128, *132–133*, *227–231*
White Rock (NM), 219
White Rock Archeological District, 89
White Rock Canyon, 42, 88, 239, *240–242*, Plate 3
sites, 88–93
Wild Boy Spring, *202*
wind, *199*
Wind God, *199–200*
winter solstice, 134, *136*
Women's Dance, 87
wood rats, 97, *98*

Yei's (Navajo deities), 47
Young, Jane, on lizard stories, 158

Zuni-Cibola Trail, 150